HUMOR STRAIGHT
Jiggers of drollery and whimsy

Hugh McClintock

Copyright © 2014 Hugh McClintock

Disclaimer
Any resemblance to actual locales or to persons living or dead is entirely coincidental.

All rights reserved
No part of this book may be used or reproduced in any manner whatsoever without written permission of the author except for brief quotations embodied in critical articles and reviews.

ISBN 10: 0615997163
ISBN 13: 978-0615997162

Printed in the United States of America.

Humor Straight is a gathering of Hugh McClintock's previously published humorous newspaper columns that were printed in the *Meadville Tribune,* plus a dozen wholly fictional burlesques that are included under the title "The Dawning of the Age of Invention."

The management of the Meadville Tribune newspaper has graciously assented to the inclusion of the columns previously published in that newspaper.

About this book

Humor Straight has two parts. Part I consists of the author's published, 1,000-word newspaper columns. Part II consists of brief reports addressing the little-known facts of the discovery of a number of prehistoric man's esteemed inventions, not to mention his cool social achievements.

While commuting, waiting around, lazing about, fighting the urge to doze, or leisurely moving one's bowels, read *Humor Straight,* or parts thereof, to nudge boredom into a grave of lonesome misfits.

LIST OF ARTICLES

ENGLISH UP WITH WHICH NO ONE SHOULD PUT

Not all proverbs age gracefully 11

Beyond buzz, cookoo and splat 17

When a long noisy sigh just doesn't work 23

Turn off the bubble machine 29

Potholes on the road to wisdom 35

Lost in translation 41

Even the Greeks don't have a word for it 45

If all else fails, pun 51

A good joke is a good joke is a good joke 57

Some epigrams just do not compute 63

Looming dictionary crisis easily averted 69

Headline Writing 101 77

In any case, that certainly is not what I meant 83

Trolling for figgy pudding 89

GAMES PEOPLE PLAY AT

She rode off with a knight on a white horse 95

Besides – it should be called rolling 101

Feet! Grip! Spot! etc. 107

I bowl because I am 113

Hooked on high-school football 119

Catting about on Pymatuning Lake 125

Under B – isn't for me 131

Jim Thorpe shrugged, too 137

NOT IN THE TRIBUNE, YOU PHILISTINE

Cheerless in Pottstown, PA 143

Sometimes saying only "Nuts!" just doesn't cut it 149

Getting to the bottom of things 155

Head of PIA sits on press release of new spy gadget 161

De-tweaking the culture 167

THE FAR SIDE OF SCIENCE

Big Bang and then what? Big Pfft? And what about obtuse cats? 171

Yes, but Dr. Einstein never came to grips with relative pronouns 177

Elementary, my dear Watson – and Crick 183

Better Extant I than Sextant I 189

It's about Time 195

Moose on the loose 199

AS THE TWIG IS BENT

Chances are, Lizzie Borden's mother was Irish 207

Second only to Drano 213

Baggage that comes with the name Hugh 219

Food for thought 225

Could be my father was Custer's nephew 231

On cooking breakfast and kindred adventures 237

More on coming to terms with household appliances ... 243

Please, Santa Claus, not even gold. And especially no frankincense or myrrh 249

EITHER HIS PULSE QUIT OR MY WATCH STOPPED

On the wrong road again 255

And how is, ah . . . your lovely wife? 261

Fancy that 267

Knights of the road, errant 273

A get-well card for Aaron 279

Caught on tape 285

I'm half-deaf, fella, not half-witted. 291

The skinny about human organs 295

The skinny about human organs 299

Sweating the small stuff 305

THE BONE YARD

The turkey has landed 309

More precious than gold 315

"Everybody wants ta get inta da act!" 321

By any other name, it's still blather 327

A few short hops to peace on earth 333

Me? A Baron? Awesome! 339

Antlers and horns and tusks? Really, Sir. 345

Ten? Only ten, Moses? Are you sure? 351

Maybe the name Hugh isn't so dorky after all 357

More a favor than a Christmas gift 363

In broad daylight, too 369

Hardly a shaggy dog story 373

Your Lordship? Hmm. I've been called much worse.... 379

Where goes Peter Cottontail? 385

In bad taste 389

Sometimes it was the best of times...............395

THE DAWNING OF THE AGE OF INVENTION

Introduction 403

And President Washington thought wooden teeth were a bummer......................407

The first hand-propelled wheelbarrow...........413

Homer was a good poet, but he was not the first ever...419

Fishing for cardinal numbers..................423

The first bisexual tunic..................427

A dining room for nobles..................433

The perilous pastime of bowling..................439

Standing up to the challenge of ensuring fertility..........445

Premier democracy..................451

A titanic raft..................455

Plucking for rain..................459

The making of a visionary..................463

The postman always rings once..................467

ENGLISH UP WITH WHICH NO ONE SHOULD PUT

Not all proverbs age gracefully

Proverbs, like sturdy trees with deep tap roots, live forever. Some are as old and bewildering as antiquity itself. Many, unfortunately, are puzzling and a few are just flat wrong.

I remember the first proverb I ever heard – even before I knew what the word proverb meant. I was feeling a bit down-in-the-mouth, and my mother, a pragmatic soul if ever there was one, said to me, "Hugh, my son, you must never forget that beauty is only skin deep." My spirit took wing, but a minute later augured-in when I realize she had me in mind, not the pretty girl who had stiffed me at a sixth-grade roller-skating party.

The original version, "Beauty is only skin deep, but ugly goes all the way to the bone," has, of course, been browbeaten into only five words, "Beauty is only skin deep," and given the cold shoulder by the minions of political correctness. In any case, the invention of BOTOX has all but rendered the saying meaningless. In fact, a shot of BOTOX is about the only thing that could save the proverb itself.

Who, at sometime or other, hasn't exclaimed, "Better late than never!" More a quip than a proverb, and seldom true at that. Chance muttering those words to your wife while returning home after arriving fifteen minutes late to pick her up after church. During the car ride home you can expect to experience first-hand the funereal quiet of an anechoic chamber.

Then there's the one, "Any port in a storm." Bad advice, period. Port (sometimes simply called Vinho do Porto, Porto) is absolutely the worst of all libations for riding out heavy seas. Brandy is more soothing, and bottles with screw-on caps cost only a little more than cheap California port.

Mull over the saying, "All cats are gray in the dark." Plainly that just isn't so. As it turns out, the word "gray" is a typo. The proverb should read, "All cats are gay in the dark." It alludes, I found out, to the festive noises alley cats make from dark until six a.m.

"A bad workman blames his tools." – as he should if he's working with cheap imports from China. Trade agreements between Washington and Beijing have made this saying as useless as a dull tool itself.

"The best of men are but men at best." Not only ambiguous but likely no more than the musing of a spinster in her cups. Better this thoughtless aphorism had been stillborn.

"A bird in the hand is worth two in the bush." Maybe. Birds, remember, have a very short gastrointestinal tract. Whether you want a robin, for example, perched on your hand depends on both its state of anxiety and how long it's been since the little beggar gobbled a worm. Real proverbs should not be time-dependent, as this one obviously is.

"The best things in life are free." Yes, but so are the hiccups, bunions, and the inevitable unsolicited advice on playing a bad golf lie. Little more than a half truth, the saying should have been set out years ago along with other rubbish on trash pick-up day.

"Don't change horses in midstream." Of course not. Would you change a baby in midstream? Personally, I wouldn't change a horse in the warmth and comfort of a draft-free stall. That aspect of equine husbandry isn't a fit subject for glorification as a proverb in the first place.

"An ape's an ape, a varlet's a varlet, though they be clad in silk or scarlet." Dying if not already dead, but well worth reviving, the saying fell out of use once King Arthur stopped mumbling it to Sir Galahad while he, Sir Lancelot, and other Knights of the Round Table, were working at codifying the ground rules of chivalry. Maybe updating "varlet" to "scoundrel" would fix it.

"Toast never falls but on its buttered side." This remark isn't even a proverb, though some academics dress it in the finery of one. Wholly consonant with the Milky Way's gravitational influence and Sir Isaac Newton's law of interplanetary gravity, it is no more than a statement of the obvious. Promoting it as a proverb makes as much sense as trying to ring a milk pail with a length of clothes line knotted at the end.

"Boys will be boys." Not only sexist, but also the silliest tautology of all time. Include a line in our final list of proverbs that is both discriminatory on the basis of sex and needlessly repetitious of the obvious? Hardly. "Boys will be boys; girls will be girls" merely compounds the offense. Besides, that saying would be only half true.

"Ask a silly question and you get a silly answer." Not every time, however. Occasionally you get a poke in the nose. Sometimes one man's silly is another man's pride.

"The darkest hour is just before dawn." Nope. The darkest hour is the twenty minutes during an electrical power outage when you can't find your only kerosene lamp, which wasn't put away after the last power failure. Already four hundred years old, the proverb should have been allowed to decompose totally once the state of Mississippi was fully electrified.

"Don't teach your grandmother to suck eggs." An early 18th-century proverb, at best it's a mere redundancy, at worst a hollow admonition. Ever try instructing a grandparent about anything? The saying itself sucks.

"Eat to live, not live to eat." This proverb was first uttered by the Greek philosopher Socrates several hundred years before the birth of Christ. Charged with corrupting the youth of Athens, Socrates, whose first name, incidentally, was Wilbur, is alleged to have died bravely by his own hand. Believe that if you want, but isn't it plain he died ingloriously of malnutrition? "Eat to live, not live to eat"? Indeed! The saying should have been buried along with the tendentious old Greek himself.

Good proverbs, like the well-nourished perennials of a flower garden, are vigorous and hardy. Like any garden, however, weeds creep in. The few proverbs I've mentioned in this column are dandelions, not orchids, and it's high time an eminent philosopher stopped and smelled the dandelions, so to speak, and cranked up the old language cultivator.

Beyond buzz, cookoo and splat

Plovers are shore birds – feathered friends that can't sing a lick. Nevertheless, they compensate for this curious inability by prattling endlessly while they wander back and forth on beaches. Granted, many a wife is no less annoying, but this piece is about the etymology of oddball words, not about the proclivities of our mates.

The German word for plover is kiebitz, and from kiebitz comes the word kibitzer. A kibitzer is a human plover, a person more aggravating than starched long-johns. As a matter of fact, it is both legal and socially acceptable for a card player to spring from his chair and boot a kibitzer in the caboose.

Another name for a plover is pewit, which is pronounced pyoo'it. Pewit, however, is sometimes spelled with two ee's, i.e., as peewit and pronounced pea wit.

I would bet a fiver that peewit is Birdish for pea brain. Of course, I can't prove it. I have observed, however, that both peahens and peacocks look down on pewits. In any event, if I were a plover and another bird called me a peewit, I'd give him a fierce peck on the rump; maybe disenfranchise him of a tail feather or two.

Enough, however, of pondering the unknowable, this column is about the provable origin of words, not insightful conjecturing about ornithological issues.

Many words just naturally make sense, seem to define themselves. Most, however, are no more meaningful than the oddly-spelled brand names of prescription medicines.

I remember seeing the word "hunch" for the first time in a word list chalked on a blackboard by our sixth-grade teacher at elementary school. Our assignment was to use each of the three words in a sentence. After finishing the assignment – and after Miss Vernon teased us a little about the meaning of each word – she ordered several of us to read aloud our compositions. My recitation, "At noon, we will stop and hunch lunch," propelled Miss Vernon's hand to her mouth, palm outwards. My classmates, seeing her poorly thwarted amusement, turned into a mob of obstreperous hooligans.

Of course, I now know that a hunch is a premonition. Its origin as a word can be traced to the time long ago when persons with spinal malformations were thought to possess psychic powers.

The term for the back part of the human foot, the little four-letter word "heel," has far outgrown its britches. Besides "heel" (a cad), "heeled" (armed), and "well-heeled" (rich), it's the seedling of endless drab metaphors: "Down at the heels," "On the heels of," "Kick up (one's) heels," and so on.

"Well-heeled" is a throwback to the days when the spurs of fighting cocks were doubled in length with metal gaffs, making the birds "heeled" (armed). As the gaffs affixed to the birds of wealthy owners were often made of precious metal, the practice gave rise to the expression "well-heeled."

Plainly, a common everyday hat is hardly something that's fit to be eaten. One could think of a gent's straw boater as edible roughage, I suppose, but that's about it. Wolf down a grimy, sweat-stained gimme cap? No way! On the other hand, "hatte," many years ago, was the name of a stew. Evidently a bowl of "hatte" was less than tasty chowder since agreeing to down a bowl of hatte became the cost of losing a wager. (At least the loser didn't have to wear the bowl of "hatte.") Over the years, "hatte" metamorphosed into hat, and these days, consenting at the time of a bet to "eat one's hat," as the penalty for losing, is offered only in fun.

Until the middle of the nineteenth century hats were made by hand, popularly of felt, and over time the mercuric nitrate used in the process gave hat-makers the "vapors," that is, caused hat makers to act batty as cats cranked on catnip. The Mad Hatter of Lewis Carroll's Alice's Adventures in Wonderland wasn't merely a figment of the author's imagination; he was a stereotypical English hat-maker of the day. "Mad as a pickle-maker" might make sense today.

"Blond" and "blonde" are from the French: blond is the masculine form and blonde the feminine form. I wasn't able to run down the etymology, but in trying, a novelist friend warned me that some female editors go ballistic every time they spot a passage in a manuscript where the word "blonde" is used to mean a woman. The appended letter e, in their view, amounts to a subtle put down. He said it was okay, however, if a writer's fictional blondes were so plain they couldn't attract men without wearing rib-eye steaks for earrings. (Ordinarily not given to clichés, I suspect my friend was suffering the pain of an unhealed wound inflicted by a sharp-tongued female editor. I knew one who could lick the barnacles off a rusty Chinese oil tanker.)

Some linguists argue that "buckaroo" comes from vaquero, the Spanish word for cowboy – traceably, apparently, to the fact that vaquero is pronounced as if the first letter is a "b" instead of a "v.'

Nonsense. The word "buckaroo" is a corruption of the slightly off-color indigenous Australian word "bangaroo, an all-purpose, mild epithet used incessantly by the aborigines inhabiting that country's vast Outback. The evolution of "buckaroo," that is, bang-aroo, beng-aroo, bong-aroo, and finally buck-aroo, is as certain as animal droppings at a rodeo.

By the way, the wranglers of political correctness slap holsters at mere mention of the word "cowpoke," "cowpuncher," or "broncobuster." As yet, they haven't shot down "cowhand" but are likely taking a bead. And "range rider" is bullet proof for the time being.

W. A. Spooner, an English clergyman and Oxford don, is fondly remembered for his tendency to accidentally transpose the initial sounds of adjacent words. Called spoonerisms, almost everyone sometime or other says "a naughty horseman," for example, when he or she meant to say "a haughty Norseman."

While Dr. Spooner was teaching at Oxford, Mr. K. G. B. Fokker (nee, K. G. B. Forcher) was gaining fame building airplanes for Germany. Just as Dr. Spooner was inclined to transpose the initial sounds of consecutive words, so, too, was Herr Fokker inclined to transpose the endings of adjacent words. Called fokkerisms, few do it – that is, say, "naughtman horsey" when he or she means "haughty Norseman."

Nevertheless, reverse metathesis, as that kind of verbal slip is called, has been well-studied by language specialists, most notably by the eminent German linguist Perpendiken Pfeifel (whose name, incidentally, inspired western singer-songwriter Roger Miller's rendering of "A pendulum swings like a pendulum do." (Or however it goes.).

Herr Fokker never said why it was that he decided to change his name.

When a long noisy sigh just doesn't work

Logorrhea is a high-brow word for verbally rattling on and on – for uncontrollable talkativeness. Like the common cold, there is no cure, and some strains may be infectious, so it is a good idea to give a wide-berth to persons who never stop talking.

Golfers froth invincibly after a bad round of play. Duffers, especially, prattle on and on, blame an errant drive on everything from golf-cart motion sickness, to the beady glare of an angry buck rabbit, to slippery footing caused by a diarrheic goose. The nineteenth hole of a golf course is to logorrhea as warm, still water is to mosquito larvae.

Some bowlers become all but incoherent after rolling a bad game. And some fishermen can take longer describing their struggle to reel-in an eight-inch perch than it took to net the crafty whopper itself.

Naturally, some women are similarly afflicted, have this unyielding tendency to crochet scarves of words so long that they would dangle all the way to the floor gracing the necks of NBA basketball centers. Symbolic of that sisterhood is a chapter in my wife's heftiest cook book (edited by a female TV personality) esoterically titled "Mastering the Art of Boiling Potatoes." It begins: "First, purchase a bag of recently harvested potatoes." How she missed opening with something along the lines of, "First, get plenty of sleep the night before," is beyond me. Anyway, her written piece on the culinary preparation of spuds was a mere thousand words long.

The mental distress of enduring the persistent, mundane yakkety-yak of a person of lackluster interests easily equals the physical pain of a turn on a medieval torture rack. (No moaning. I could have written, "...the physical pain of a stretch on a medieval torture rack.") In fact, spending an hour on a torture rack is not nearly as agonizing as enduring a half-hour in a comfortable recliner listening to your brother-in-law explain how he dexterously constructed a model of the Golden Gate Bridge from discarded Popsicle sticks.

Remember how Shakespeare has Hamlet, in his play of the same name, mumbling to himself about "suffering the slings and arrows of outrageous fortune?" Perhaps you already know the circumstance of Shakespeare's inspiration for that deft metaphor of mental grief. Anyway, if you don't this was it: he had to share a carriage on his way from Bristol, England, to London, England, with a chatty couple returning home from vacationing in the resort city of Bath. If you have ever motored from, say, Meadville, Pa. toPittsburgh or Cleveland, Ohio with a couple who had recently vacationed in Cancun, Mexico, you undoubtedly appreciate the torment suffered by Shakespeare.

Short of feigning a heart attack, how does one avoid listening to Barf Shaughnessy endlessly explain how to roll-paint the children's bedroom in your home. You can't simply throttle the guy. In fact, that approach has been used and was subsequently ruled unjustifiable homicide in a 5-4 decision passed down in the sixties by the liberal Earl Warren Supreme Court. Broadly hinting, as in, "Zipper your pie hole, you frothing idiot!" works but sometimes has unintended physical consequences.

So, what's the answer? My bright but penniless friend Clifford Yorick claims the only proven solution to stifling a non-stop yakker is a deft put-down, a verbal interruption that leaves your windy assailant reeling in speechless confusion. Two examples, which Yorick insists are fail-proof, follow. The settings, that is, the context of their applications, are exactly as related to me by Cliff:

1) You're descending in an elevator with five co-workers, and between stops one of the nine-to-fiver goes on and on about how he's swamped with work, is barely able to keep up, takes unfinished business home every night, etc., etc. As the elevator is slowing for the ground floor you thoughtfully remark, your manner grave, your head angled downward: "I imagine George

Armstrong Custer would have been a hero if the Indians had attacked one at a time."

2) Your wife's friend Sophie is visiting, and you're obliged to help entertain her. Sophie, a voracious reader, and fancying herself an expert on American authors, maintains that John Updike is our greatest living writer. Bored numb after ten minutes of politely nodding each time she pauses briefly to refuel with a gulp of air, and in spite of a warning glance from your beloved, you interrupt her: "Actually, Sophie" – you slightly shake your head, clearly uncomfortable with what you're about to say – "I'm inclined to agree with Herm Pebble (made up name of course) the Pulitzer Prize winning senior fiction editor of The Atlantic. Remember, a few years back, when he opined that Updike's prose is better than it reads?" Sophie, according to Cliff, will take a moment to digest your words, a second of rumination that will temporarily caramelize her tongue, and then she will distractedly sip a little of whatever beverage you're serving. At that instant you make your move, change the subject to hunting moose in Canada. Never mind that the pop of a child's cork gun jangles your nerves. What matters is that she won't know squat about hunting. Moreover, absorbed in deciding on how low to devalue your intelligence, she won't be listening any way.

Cliff explained to me that he cribbed both formulas, the first from a Texas writer he'd lost track of and the second from Mark Twain. Twain, a master of the put-down, wrote that "Wagner's music is better than it sounds." (Richard Wagner, if you're not an opera buff, was a nineteenth century, heralded composer of operatic music.) The beauty of Twain's concise but efficient one-liner (okay, his squelch), as Cliff pointed out, is that, with only a little tinkering, it can be used in almost any situation, even in sports: "Penn State's heralded freshman fullback Brick Kapowsky is a far better runner than he looks to be."

There are half a dozen verbal devices available for deflating long-winded self-important experts. Ever effective are, "Lowbrowmanship," "Utter Indifference," and "The Naked Rebuff." True, all three are situation-dependent, but they are unfailingly productive when correctly used. I'll pass the application details of all six along in another column. In the meantime, you may want to work up adaptations of Twain's put-down of Wagner's music – someday spare your ears of a cauliflowering no less painful than that of the pummeling by a prizefighter.

Turn off the bubble machine

Winston Churchill, the prime minister of Britain during World War II, once said in a speech that dogs look up to us and cats look down on us. Besides being a distinguished statesman, Churchill was also a philosopher of sorts. Philosophy is the study of what is left after hard facts are accounted for, and philosophers solve puzzles in the same slapdash way rats stumble onto the target bait in a maze. I do not know how long it took Churchill to understand that plain-to-see predisposition of cats and dogs – years I suppose – but in any event I address that common failing, the inability to hastily generalize, in a positive way in this column.

In the same speech, Churchill averred that pigs treat us as equals, which behavior he gave as the reason he was fond of them. I doubt, however, if he let one of the porkers sleep with him, the place where my beloved and I allow our resident mutt to spend his nights. British natives, as I am sure you know, are persnickety to the bone.

Anyway, when I came across Churchill's words I was reminded of a point of view I read years ago in a popular magazine, possibly Holiday, a single line that was cast, more or less, as: "A man's home should include both a cat and a dog, a cat to utterly ignore him and a dog to constantly toady up." Short and witty, the remark struck me as sensible advice, and it still resides in my mind.

The idea of pet behavior framing a man's perspective sounds a bit like one of Mark Twain's wry advisements. But if it is, I couldn't run it down. Oh well, the word "perspective" allows me to easily transition to another topic.

Artists and draftsmen use the word perspective to mean the representation of an object in three dimensions, that is, the depiction of objects more or less as they appear to the eye. On the other hand, philosophers think of the word perspective as meaning a point of view for understanding ideas. This difference explains why philosophers scrawl endlessly on and on, why their minds take forever to converge on a specific point. (If their game was football they'd be flagged every play for piling on.)

Consider the saying, "There is nothing new under the sun." To a philosopher worth his weight in soy beans, the sheer conciseness of that observation is not only downright reprehensible but also smacks of the linear thinking of a simple rustic. Seventeenth-century French philosopher Rene Descartes used roughly three times as many words to say the same thing: "One cannot conceive anything so strange and so implausible that it has not already been said by one philosopher or another." Frankly, that's as brief as philosophers get.

Remember the quip of a few years back that went something like this: "Ask Jake (or whoever) what time it is, and he'll explain how his watch works"? It was first uttered by a student of the Greek philosopher Aristotle who whispered to a fellow student during one of the great man's lectures: "Ask 'Sledge' (Aristotle's nickname) what time it is and he explains how a sun dial works." Aristotle lived four hundred years before Christ was born, raising the question of whether there isn't a strain of human long-windedness traceable to our distant ancestors, a genetic influence so powerful that some smart men and smart women can't help but rattle on endlessly – persons who just can't seem to close once they've made the sale.

Famous American author Louisa May Alcott (1832-1888) defined a philosopher as a man up in a balloon tethered to earth with ropes held by family and friends who were trying to haul him down. A metaphor on the "love of wisdom" (her personal definition of philosophy) centered on the lifting efficacy of hot air? Darn, she was good! (Okay, that may not have been exactly what she intended, but she certainly left the door open.)

Never mind what Alcott may or may not have meant; Roman politician Cicero unerringly got it right.

A reformer and hallowed man of letters, this is how he sized up philosophers: "There is nothing so ridiculous but some philosopher has said it." Obviously wise and clear-headed, it is easy to see why historians consider Cicero's speeches to be models of eloquent Latin.

Hollywood film buffs will remember the name Cicero as a footnote to Silver-Screen history: Actor Leslie Nielsen's retort, "And stop calling me Shirley!" (supposedly because he misinterpreted a fellow actor's line that began with the word Surely,) was merely an edited version of Cicero's angry rebuke: "And stop calling me Cissy!" which he once bellowed at a political opponent who was heckling him from across the pool of Rome's exclusive Seven Hills Spa.)

Alfred North Whitehead, an English mathematician-philosopher who packed all and moved to America in the 1920s, wrote that a "philosopher of imposing stature doesn't think in a vacuum." Of imposing stature? Good grief! Until reading that line, I hadn't realized that philosophers could be rated like contestants in a Miss America pageant – that some are stately and awe-inspiring while others are only journeyman deep-thinkers.

A philosopher, according to Dr. Laurence J. Peter, is "a person who never feels badly after he has made an ass of himself." Dr. Peter is best known for his Peter Principal, the proposition that corporate employees are promoted once too many times, that is, that they are boosted up the managerial ladder until becoming perched on a rung that is above their ability to cope. Philosophers are eligible for canonization and promotion to sainthood by the Church of Endless Talk once they have stuffed five pounds of words into a one-pound bag, a miracle of bloviating well beyond the talent of ordinary persons.

In proofreading my draft of this column, I sensed a slight tinge of negativity in my characterization of philosophers. If I'm right – and I certainly hope I'm incorrect – maybe it's because I'm suffering the hangover of a recent unproductive meeting with Dr. Mykos Spirale, an ensconced professor of philosophy who is not only incurably logorrheic (an autoimmune disease suffered by persons who convince themselves that they are Aristotle reincarnated) but also massively unable to handle disapproval. In any event, I offer a cleaned-up account – the man can't handle even restrained criticism – of our meeting in the piece I titled Potholes on the road to wisdom.

Actually, Dr. Spirale isn't even a genuine philosopher. According to the New York Public Library Desk Reference, only three of seventy-four bona fide philosophers are alive. And he's not one of them. Sir Winston Churchill didn't make the cut either.

Potholes on the road to wisdom

Last January I resolved to become a philosopher, figured that I'd begin at an entry-level position and work my way up. Being retired, I knew I'd have hours – maybe days – free for the long periods of idle sitting and deep, profound meditation demanded of that occupation.

Certain that a little quality time with a professor of philosophy would jump-start my program, I dialed the main telephone number of a nearby college and was told that a Dr. Spirale chaired the Philosophy and Religious Studies Department.

Dr. Spirale agreed to see me the next morning. When I arrived at his spacious office at nine o'clock sharp, he was pondering a stretch of books on the middle shelf of a four-section, floor-to-ceiling bookcase behind his desk, affixed there, evidently, to reinforced masonry.

I rapped lightly on the door jamb. After a moment he turned and invited me in. "Hugh McClintock, Doctor," I offered smiling humbly.

He waved me to a chair facing his desk. "Remind me," he said pleasantly, "of the reason for your visit."

Jacketless, bald, mid-fortyish, Dr. Spirale was barely my height, five-foot six-inches. Like most bald men, his beard, the color and density of steel wool, was robust. Metal-rimmed spectacles hung from his neck by a thick, cloth lace. His belly was spherical, more or less.

I nodded. "I'd like to become a philosopher, Sir."

"I see," he said. Pulling Kleenex from a box on a shelf of the bookcase, he swiped at the seat and arms of the high-backed, tufted-leather chair sitting behind his desk. Kicking off his sandals, he slipped into his freshly dusted chair. "And why is that?" he asked understandingly.

Wanting to be certain that he saw how my mind was seriously occupied in reflecting on his question, I very slowly eased into a metal folding-chair facing his desk.

"The meaning of life," I answered finally. "I want to know why I exist. Why, exactly, Sir, am I here."

He seemed to be confused. "Oh, I thought we had an appointment and you wanted–"

"No, no," I interrupted. "I didn't mean literally why . . . I meant, why did God – or whoever . . . or whatever – put me in this world. Why, exactly, am I . . . ." I allowed the sentence to dangle unfinished.

"I was kidding," he said. "Do you have a favorite philosopher? Socrates? Confucius? Hegel?"

I could play that game, too: "Cosell," I answered grinning.

He leaned back and his eyes narrowed. "Who?"

"Howard Cosell," I said, forcing a more generous grin to my lips.

He shook his head ambivalently. "Athenian? Zoroastrian? Taoism?"

The man obviously had never heard of sportscaster Howard Cosell. "*Professors!*" I said to myself. His dignity was at stake, however, so I improvised: "Cosell was a Frenchman. Seventeenth century, if memory serves. Descartes was his protégé."

"Ah," he mused. "Rene Descartes. The Age of Rationalism. `I think, therefore I am'."

"Yep, Descartes was Cosell's star pupil," I said firmly, on sure footing again. "Only, I believe, Professor, his signature remark was, 'I am, therefore I think.'" I smiled understandingly. "I, uh, believe you transposed his, ah, thought. Accidentally, I'm sure."

Dr. Spirale, inexplicitly troubled by my gentle rebuke, didn't speak for several seconds. I silently respected his moment of uncertainty.

His initial friendliness disappeared. "I don't think so," he replied finally.

I smiled tolerantly. "You see , it would make sense if he had written 'I am therefore I think,' or, for example, 'I eat, therefore I am,' but, ah, 'I think, therefore I am,' really . . . just doesn't compute."

"That's ... not ..." Dr. Spirale began haltingly. After stopping in mid-sentence, he tried tacking even tighter into the gale of my logic: "Descartes was searching for an indisputable sense of truth, a proposition that he could prove was mathematically unassailable."

I nodded politely. "With all due respect, Sir, I seriously doubt that. You know, it's even possible that the saying – as, uh, you read it – was little more than a typo, two clauses that somehow merely got flip-flopped."

Dr. Spirale slightly trembled; his replies became snappish. "A typo? In the seventeenth century?"

"Well ... not literally Professor. Of course not. But, you know what I mean."

Dr. Spirale turned and stared a long second at the book shelf that was engaging his attention when I arrived. He slowly shook his head. Plainly, I had backed him into a corner. He sighed and turned back.

"Mr. McClintock," he said, "I recommend you begin your quest by immersing yourself in the collected works of Sancho Panza."

Now I was confused. "Sancho Panza? Wasn't he–"

"Indeed he was – Don Quixote's right-hand man."

"I didn't know–"

"That Panza was a renowned philosopher? Not many people do. He was a lot more, Mr. McClintock, than the squatty little coward Cervantes made him out to be."

Dr. Spirale glanced past me: someone had stopped in the doorway. "Mr. McClintock here wants to be a philosopher," he said to his visitor.

A tall, gawky brunette also wearing sandals clopped into the room. Eye glasses with huge, circular lenses dangled by a white shoelace from her neck. She offered her hand: "Lindsay Knorr."

Dr. Spirale explained that Lindsay was pursuing a doctorate in American Indian cultures. He tactfully implied that she worked for him.

I released her hand, returned to my chair, and rested one knee, stork-like, on its seat. Dr. Spirale rose to his feet while Ms. Knorr and I were shaking hands.

"Her special study is ..." His voice tailed off. He probably said "Confucianism," but to tell you the truth it sounded more like he had said "Convolutionism."

"Interesting, very interesting," I said, glancing back at Ms. Knorr.

Dr. Spirale, in full voice again, said we'd have to meet later, that he had to review the Fall class schedule with Lindsay.

"I understand," I said graciously. I bid goodbye to Ms. Knorr and glided past her.

A step into the hall, I spun back and stuck my head in the doorway. Dr. Spirale was staring gloomily at his protégé.

"I'll be eating a big lunch," I said brightly. "I eat, therefore I am. Ha ha!"

Preoccupied, Dr. Spirale barely nodded. Knorr's visage was one of puzzlement.

I was unable to arrange another meeting with Dr. Spirale, which was just as well since he didn't inspire me anyway. Moreover, the bowling season was just around the corner, and I feared that studying to become a philosopher would cut into my practice time.

Lost in translation

Recently I read where two juxtaposed vowels sometimes end up as a diphthong. The writer, it seemed to me, was suggesting an inappropriate union, perhaps a dalliance of sorts. On reflection, however, I decided: So what? If his raffish allusion rests comfortably with hard-shell Baptists, his target audience, why should I get worked up over his indiscretion?

Do you see my problem? I thought the sentence had something to do with – I'll fudge it a little here – shower footwear. Favored with barely average intelligence, beeline comprehension isn't something I can boast of – otherwise, I would have bragged about it long ago.

Most of the time I read a sentence laced with strange words as nimbly as a professor waxing on and on at a faculty meeting. Reality sets in when I reflect on what I had just finished reading and realize that I haven't a clue.

Consider Dr. Einstein's famous equation, E=M(c2). Pronounced, "E equals M C squared," the expression tumbles out of my mouth as easily as the fragments of a hard taco shell. Only, what in the world does it mean?

Sure, I know E stands for energy, M stands for mass, and the letter c represents the speed of light. So? I'm expected to infer from that dinky little three-element equation that mass and energy are different forms of the same thing? As scientists are wont to claim? Ha! Were that true I'd be a marvel of perpetual motion, the mass of blubber around my middle constantly re-forming as kinetic energy.

Economists throw around the word "elasticity" as if they were lightheartedly sailing Frisbee saucers. Do they use it in reference to, say, the expandable waistband of their Jockey shorts? Hardly. They write weird stuff like, "Where demand is elastic, sales revenue moves in the opposite direction to price." Is that their fancy way of saying that if enough people buy a particular brand of, say, red snuggies, the price will come down? Or if they don't squander oodles on zebra-striped snuggies the price won't come down? Personally, I'm thankful that the up-and-down nature of selling that economists call elasticity is not just another one of their dismal ruminations, not just another nutty warning that the planet earth is about to sail off into space.

No sensible person should pay attention to the musings of economists anyway. One, an eighteenth century Scotsman, portrayed as enormously influential by those who are supposed to know, believed in invisible body parts! In particular, he conjured up an image of an invisible hand that somehow mysteriously guides the collective decision-making of free-market participants. Honest!

Foreign words also throw me. Here's about as simple a sentence as you'll ever run across: "If an act is legal, is it "*ipso facto*" moral?"

That's lawyer talk for asking if legal behavior is inherently moral behavior.

I had to look up the meaning of ipso facto, which imposition on a neophyte's time is itself immoral and ought to be illegal. Is it any wonder polls show the public holds trial defense lawyers in lower regard than Taliban weasel ranchers?

Shake any high-brow literary magazine, say, *The Atlantic*, by the binding and inevitably the expression "*de rigueur*" will slither out – maybe two of them. De rigueur is French, of course. The English equivalent is "fashionable." Evidently self-esteeming American authors think the word "fashionable" is lowbrow—or unhip. (Or, is the adjective "uncool"? I can't keep up.)

Also hopelessly beyond the understanding of a person of ordinary intelligence is what today passes for poetry. Throw a ball of shellac-wetted words against a wall and call whatever sticks a poem? Free verse? Indeed! By any other name, prose is prose is prose – disjointed or otherwise.

Give me poems like James Whitcomb Riley's, *When the Frost Is on the Punkin*. True, Riley couldn't spell worth a lick (Besides misspelling "Pumpkin," as he did in the title of his poem, try finding his "kyoucking" and "hallylooyering" in your Funk & Wagnall desk set. But his poetic compositions have regular rhyme and meter, however, as any real poetry must.

Speaking of fowl, that is, of Riley's chickens clucking and cock-a-doodle-dooing, I feel obliged to mention that the meaning of "flipping someone a bird" isn't exactly self-defining – at least, not to me it isn't. Initially mistaking the associated gesture as a smart, insider's greeting, it cost me the goodwill of my pastor (among others). As I am very democratic in my choice of friends, I eventually learned that flipping someone a bird amounts to exclaiming, approximately, "Up your bucket, fella!"

And so it goes. If I've learned anything in my three-score years of adulthood it's this: unless a man is pretty bright to begin with, all the studying in the world won't turn his sow's ear of gray matter into a silk purse of powerful intellect. It's best to learn early who you really are, persevere, and surprise everyone with your small accomplishments – except your mother, of course, who always knew you were an undiscovered genius.

Even the Greeks don't have a word for it

There are zillions of English words and yet none have been coined for many common everyday events and activities.

There is no word for the anger a person feels when he's interrupted by a self-important blockhead? "Urgetoreachoutandthrottle" is a long but apposite expression for that sentiment, even if a little awkward. Hyphenation helps with the pronunciation: Urge-to-reach-out-and-throttle is at least a marginal improvement.

Barbara Wallraff, a senior editor for *The Atlantic Monthly*, calls these voids in our language "word fugitives," and every other month, in a column of that name, she asks readers to coin a word for a language gap defined by a reader, that is, to invent a well-suited word for a thing, a feeling, or a situation that is nowhere aptly described by one English word.

A reader of *the Atlantic*, as reported by Ms. Wallraff in the October, 2006, issue, needed a word describing how a beam of moonlight on a lake seems to follow a person walking along the shoreline. The reason a word doesn't exist seems pretty obvious: the English language just isn't up to the job. Even my own crackerjack inventions: lunedalusion and moonshinealong are pitifully inadequate.

I suggested, in an e-mail to Ms. Wallraff, that German was a perfect alternative language for creating new words, that is, for creating neologisms. Germans, when they need a new word, simply string existing words together – endlessly if need be. (I explained this native habit of Germans in a previous column, using the example "water moccasin," which translates in German to "mokassinwasserschlange," i.e., to slipper / water / snake.)

Anyway, nondstrahlbleich translates to folgenimmerwandererufer, an apt, self-defining German-language neologism that perfectly defines the phenomenon of moonlight following a person walking along a shoreline. It immediately popped into my head. True, it is a tad long. But as I pointed out in my correspondence to Ms. Wallraff, the Teutonic eloquence easily makes up for its length.

Evidently Ms. Wallraff agreed that German was ideally suited to define the phenomenon of meandering moonbeams because she judged my offering worthy of a prize.

Ms. Wallraff has gathered several hundred reader-submitted word coinages into a book, *Word Fugitives,* subtitled In Pursuit of Wanted Words that was recently published.

A few of her entries are not terribly practical – not compared to my own neologism for a meandering moonbeam – but all are either witty, wacky, or both, and the book is a fun read. I have included below some of the submissions that tickled my fancy. (Incidentally, until *Word Fugitives* arrived, my fancy hadn't been tickled for months.)

A self-assured chef is "cooksure," which certainly characterizes every chef bobbing ceaselessly about on TV. I would call myself cooksure except there still are few breakfast cereals that I haven't mastered – porridge, for example. My savory, puffed-wheat casserole, however, is a comer.

An "errorist" is a member of a radical Islamic cult who blows himself up in a mannequin factory. No reader sent in Isblamanut, which I herewith propose is a better coinage, notwithstanding that the humor is in the dumbness of the act itself.

A man who can turn the bathtub faucet off and on with his toes is "aquadexterous." Not bad. Drizzeldexterous works, too.

An *Atlantic* reader who lives in Albuquerque, New Mexico, wanted a word to describe the people one sees in cars, airports, and shopping centers that have cell phones glued to their ears. "Phoneglommer" and "cell mates" were submitted, but far and away the best offering was "yakasses." (One who can't help but express himself burrobombastically?)

A "perversifier" is a man – has to be a man – who thinks that making a popular song vulgar by changing a few words is outrageously funny. "Songwronger" and "leericist" were also suggested by fans of Ms. Wallraff's column. I guess no one submitted a word for the men who actually sing the vulgarized lyrics, but "croonatics" works for me.

Another fan wanted to know why there's no English word for the sound produced when a camel snorts – or whatever it is camels do. Is it any wonder? Arabs themselves can't agree on whether it should be a one- or two-syllable expression.

A woman from Texas wrote Ms. Wallraff to say that she had a "desperate need" for a word that conveys the essential meaning of the phrase "trailer trash" without maligning innocent residents of those abodes. Whew! That gal likely neuters male cattle for recreation. Never mind. Inventing a word to mock a thing or situation is word-coinage heavy lifting. According to Ms. Wallraff, the word the reader desperately needs, one that doesn't inadvertently malign mobile-home residents, has yet to be rounded up.

Dreaming up neologisms isn't all that easy. Here's three more examples where Ms. Wallraff says no latter-day Shakespeare has come up with a defining term: (1) a word that describes a wife's sudden, unpredictable urge to rearrange furniture; (2) a word for when you can't purge a catchy but silly jingle from your mind; and (3) a word that means the polar opposite of procrastinator, i.e., a word describing a person who can't wait to begin a task. Unfortunately, finding a unprocrastinator, especially a male hop-to-it kind of guy, is like trying to find a four-leaf clover in a field of mustard weeds.

I mentioned above that I don't know of a good word for the annoyance a person feels when he's interrupted by an egotistical dumbbell. An *Atlantic* reader also wanted to know what to call such a person: "what to call an individual who is not competent to provide advice but insists on doing so anyway." Ms. Wallraff said that such a word is still at large. Although Ms. Wallraff is a renowned linguist (or lexicographer or whatever), I must humbly disagree. In fact, a word already exists for that particular species of dope: it is "brother-in-law."

If all else fails, pun

Confusing headlines often clutter the pages of the sports sections of newspapers, and the appallingly misguided editors of those sections will one day surely have to atone for their journalistic sins, i.e. they will eventually have to settle accounts with the Great Publisher in the Sky or one of his deputies – Ben Franklin, Ida Tarbell, Joseph Pulitzer, maybe. (No. William Randolph Hearst did not make the cut).

The Meadville, Pa., *Tribune* newspaper headline, "Wood decks cards," makes no sense whatsoever – unless you're a fan of high-school sports. If you're a sports fan, however, and live within forty miles of Meadville, you know that that cryptic headline means Maplewood High School drubbed the Cardinals of Cochranton High School in an athletic contest.

Although the particular flaw in "Wood decks cards" – a common failing defined in the stylebook of rules and good-enough usage published by the Associated Press as "blatant fuzziness" – is itself worthy of a serious essay. This piece, however, isn't a critique of the way newspapers deficiently trumpet sports news. Rather, it's a long-overdue reminder to newspaper editors of the utter disdain with which literate people hold the lowly pun. "Wood decks cards." Indeed!

A pun – I am paraphrasing someone, but I can't remember who – is a play on words, often as not a vain attempt at humor. The whimsy is achieved, if at all, by twisting the words of a common phrase (The bathroom, where is?), by misusing a homonym (write for right), or attempting to season the batter of a tired old saying with spicy new words (amped, savvy) . If you didn't noticed, the title of this piece is a pun, a simple corruption of the weary football cliché, "If all else fails, punt." (I loathed using it, but my ego body-slammed my id thereby totaling my natural instinct for good taste.)

In any event, a pun has no more business heading a newspaper story than a skinny woman has singing a Wagnerian aria. Journalism, of all places, should be the last refuge for the nincompoops of literature.

"He who would pun would pick a pocket," is how all-but-sainted English poet Alexander Pope expressed his distaste for puns. John Dennis, another eminent eighteenth-century English versifier, neatly tucked Pope in his hip pocket with this modest embellishment: "A man who could make . . . a pun would not scruple to pick a pocket." Still another consequential British writer of that era, Charles Lamb, compared a pun to "a pistol let off at the ear, [not] a feather to tickle the intellect."

William Shakespeare was a pretty good playwright, good enough that he could get away with one of his characters, a dying man, say, "Ask for me tomorrow and you shall find me a grave man." Tackiness of that sort kept him from being a truly renowned dramatist.

U.S. Supreme Court Justice Oliver Wendell Holmes, remembered not only for the shades of his opinions but also for the eloquence of their rendering on paper, likened punsters to "wanton boys who put coppers on the railroad tracks."

First, please understand that jurist Holmes, in using the word "coppers," was referring to coins not policemen. Second, only a city-raised mama's boy would describe the behavior of such lads as "wanton." No fellow stripling of my youth ever twice passed up the chance to watch from the bushes as a slow-moving freight train utterly flattened a penny. In those simpler times, the paper-thin likeness of a penny dangling from a fancy silvery-plated watch chain (or a simulation thereof, in the form of a length of metal links cut from a dog leash) was exactly the ticket to impress female classmates. Naturally, a nickel squashed to the diameter of a poker chip was five times more awesome. Flattened nails, washers, and screws, incidentally, didn't even impress one's kid brother.

Are sports editors simply unaware that puns are just plain schlocky, were dismissed by pioneering

lexicographer Noah Webster, among others, as a "low species of wit?" (Puns, not editors – I think he meant.)
Maybe they should spend more time in the press box and less time in the locker room. Lucky for us, Mr. Webster's unyielding contempt for punning didn't leave him wordless.

Calling MIT professor Steven Pinker's book Words and Rules a "Peven Stinker" reeks of the envy of a lesser philologist; describing vice-president Al Gore's children as "Agoreable" is just flatly deplorable. And characterizing former Secretary of State Alexander Haig's leap-frog mutterings as "Haigravations," as syndicated newspaper columnist William Safire once did, doesn't sparkle at all.

A shaggy dog story that ends in a pun is worse than the mangiest of doggerel and should be hounded right out of the English language. An acquaintance once entertained me with a long story about the murder of a woman bootlegger, relating the exact location of her still (Ryeville, Kentucky), the nickname given her by fellow revenuers (Mama Moonshine), her legendary skill with a gun (Bullseye Bettz, and so on – and on. We were riding in my car to a Pittsburgh Pirates baseball game. I shrugged impatiently when he asked me to guess where the authorities found the body. And the next thing I heard was him crooning the words, "In the still of the night," the first line of the song of the same title.

Worse, he sang most of the rest of the first stanza: "As I gaze from my window / At the moon in its flight." Besides being mercilessly addicted to punning, Jack thought of himself as some kind of blue-collar "basso profundo." (Italian for deep voice). A huge man, he made a respectable living shuttling iron ingots around in a foundry. He was convinced that incessant heavy grunting imbued a person's voice with timber.

Spoken unblushingly, most puns would cause a starving hog to vomit. One of the few that wouldn't goes something like this: An Indian brave, suffering from chronic irritable bowel syndrome, was told by the tribe's medicine man to chew off an inch of a thin strip of bear leather each morning, which the medicine man provided. When the medicine man asked the brave two weeks later how the cure was working, his patient answered, "I'm barely alive. The thong is ended but the melody lingers on." I came across it in a Reader's Digest book, titled "Success with Words," which title, I can personally attest to, is highly misleading.

On the other hand, a New York Times writer punned horribly in characterizing tax shelters, deductible yachts, and stock options as "artifacts to succor the rich and sucker the poor."

Puns have been attacked virulently by every person of letters of any consequence. The sample I've included here, will, I hope, nail the lid on the coffin of punning in our hometown newspaper and save subscribers from wasting precious time trying to decipher the likes of "Wood decks cards."

A good joke is a good joke is a good joke

I still remember the first dirty joke I ever heard. It was told by, of all people, my mother to her friends. I just happened to be hanging around.

Some klutz, who stumbled upon a man and woman amorously engaged on a roadside slope, stupidly asked an indecorous, mis-construable question along the lines of "How far to the 'Old Log Inn'," and was forthwith popped in the nose by the romantically involved male.

Doesn't sound all that funny, does it? It wasn't.

One night Mother and three of her girlfriends were sitting around our kitchen table swapping gossip, spinning yarns, and in general yakking it up. I was standing off to the side, leaning against the kitchen sink. Ten or eleven years old at the time, I expected Mother to shoo me off to bed at any moment, but she didn't.

Looking back, I realize much of the hilarity that night was fueled by the oxygen of nervous energy: World War II was grinding on, engaging the husbands of Mother's friends in dangerous, offensive attack campaigns overseas. My father was categorized by the draft board as 4F, that is, he was physically challenged (as his condition would be described these days).

Mother's joke was so bad, so utterly forgettable, that it should have been deployed to the most dangerous front-line of World War II right then and there. I guess I remember it because it was the very first dirty joke I ever heard. The truth is I all but keeled over laughing.

Some jokes are so funny they should be recycled every generation and never allowed to vanish without a trace. Others are no more suited for posterity than verse scribbled on the walls of gas station restrooms.

Below, I repeat a few jokes that tickle my funny bone, humor in the form of a gag or one-liner that I judge to be a keeper and therefore worthy of archiving.

During the winter I bowl on Wednesday nights in a men's league. By and large, a bowler is either a "stroker" or a "cranker," depending on how he or she delivers the ball. Strokers – I and most other seniors – ease the ball onto the lane with a relatively smooth pendulum motion; crankers muscle the ball, launch it smartly with a snap and brisk follow through.

A week ago our team of five seniors bowled a team of younger men. Our opponent's anchor man, explaining a nuance of delivery to one of his teammates, used the word "stroke."

Indifferently scanning the pin action at the far ends of the lanes, his teammate casually offered, "Never ever use the word 'stroke' around old people." My teammates and our adversaries exploded in laughter.

Here's my point. That's an old joke – actually a stand-up comic's throw-away line – but if you hadn't heard it before, it's pretty funny. True, the line can't be interjected uninvited into a typical bull session, but on the other hand the quality of being extemporaneous works its usual charm. For the record it was a crack uttered by one of Johnny Carson's Tonight Show guests, an entertainer playing the part of an old man. Or maybe Jack Parr was still the host of that show. I've forgotten.

In any case, the events that night at Lake Side Lanes set me to recalling jokes I hadn't heard for years: some could respectfully enliven church sermons and some would bring the cheeks of a veteran Pittsburgh traffic cop to full blush. Quite a few, irrespective of protocol, were timelessly funny and, to my way of thinking, worth resurrecting once every generation.

So why not make that a reality? That is, why not establish a national repository for quality jokes? There are untold volumes of empty cyberspace free for the asking and no good reason a bill shouldn't be working its way through Congress even as you read this column. Publicly accessible, the joke libraries stacks would taxonomically shelve everything from rambling anecdotes, to endless shaggy dog stories, to witty puns, to snappy one-liners, and so on. Of course, only the really funny stuff would make the cut. A web site address, say, "greatjokes.com," would be easy to remember, not to mention much easier to spell right the first time than, say, EncyclopediaBritannica/esteemedjokes.

Naturally, a Congressional selection committee would have to be formed – The House Select Committee on Selection of Keeper Jokes? – and rules hammered out. For example, do we save really funny dumb-blonde jokes? (In theory, "blonde" is gender neutral; in practice it's about as neutral as "girlish.")

Remember the story that circulated some thirty years ago about the goofball who had to be coaxed from a shower after reading the words "Wash, rinse, repeat" on his bottle of shampoo? Surely that's a keeper. And immortal – or it should be – is a line from comedian Red Button's routine that has Eve asking Adam if the leaf she was wearing made her look fat.

Most puns, wormy from the keel up, capsize at launching – and deservedly so. Not so the pun versed by English poet Anita Owen, which sailed a following sea across the Atlantic Ocean to America over a hundred years ago:

O dreamy eyes,
They tell sweet lies of Paradise;
And in those eyes the love light lies.
And lies – and lies – and lies!

In other words, we couldn't rule out all puns.

I could go on, offer more samples of wit and humor that should never be allowed to molder away in unmarked graves but should be passed on religiously from generation to generation as if they were precious heirlooms – even include a long, drawn-out shaggy dog story or two.

Alas, a thousand words, the length of my draft of this article, are all the humorless opinion-page editor allots to one of my columns. He's a real nice guy, though. So is the lovely lady he works for.

Some epigrams just do not compute

An epigram is a short, pithy statement – sometimes the concise formulation of a common truth. Many, either for poignancy or humor, depend on a twist of thought.

In their brevity, some are not all that clear, however. Or, they hit the target but badly miss the bulls-eye. In this column – only to prove my argument – I amend or otherwise tidy up several epigrams that are near misses plus the wording of a few epigrammatic arrows so badly aimed that they appear to have been shot from an ordinary barebow. In the rest of this piece, the epigrams I have selected to illustrate my point, are italicized.

Men come of age at sixty, women at fifteen. That thoughtless nonsense, which first appeared in 1944 in a popular British newspaper, was advanced by Irish novelist James Stephens. Men never come of age. Who was he trying to kid? Himself?

Controversial film and stage star Mae West claimed that *a man in the house is worth two in the* street. Worth two what in the street, Mae? Pistol-packing boy friends? We can't read your mind, Mae. And, which room of the house, Mae? The kitchen?

Gloria Steinem, still in pain from when she pumped a man's bicycle up a steep hill and her foot slipped off a pedal, quipped in her Ms Magazine that a woman without a man is like a fish without a bicycle. Physical hurt dramatically colors a person's thinking, and a Ms.Magazine editor should have footnoted Steinem's remark with a mention of her cycling mishap.

According to Anton Chekhov, a famous Russian man of letters, women deprived of the company of men pine; men deprived of the company of women become stupid. But that's not what he wrote. What happened is that the female translator couldn't find an English word equivalent in meaning to the Russian word "torpid" and she figured "stupid" was close enough.

Women would rather be right than reasonable, or so Ogden Nash, a tireless writer of light verse, declared. As any married man can tell you, women are picky in every way imaginable. So, proclaiming reasonableness to be the one worthy of an epigrammatic rendering is foolish. That's the kind of sound thinking one expects to find in an epigram, not some vague generalization about one of the plethora of shortcomings of women. Nash also wrote that a door is what a dog is perpetually on the wrong side of.

Nash could have learned a thing or two about specificity from author Jean Kerr who wrote: This nonsense about beauty being only skin-deep. That's deep enough. What do you want – an adorable pancreas? No, but a gall bladder with a toothy, pearl-white smile would be nice.

Brilliant but irreverent American physicist Richard Feynman, quoted in the *Independent*, said, only one thing is wrong with our noses. They are too far off the ground to be of much use. Some noses are also pointed too high in the air to be of much use – maybe suitable for telling the aroma of Ivory soap from the fragrance of eau de Cologne, but that's about it.

Francois de Malherbe, sixteenth century French poet, critic, and translator, slyly reminded us that God repented of having created man but never of having created woman – proving that God was either fallible or a man himself. I have to go with scripture on this one, but I'd like to hear from a feminist – preferably by Pony Express.

Joseph L. Mankiewicz, Hollywood screenwriter, director, and producer, said in a speech "the best friend of a boy is his mother, of a man, his horse; only it's not clear when the transition takes place." Of course it's not clear. The transition never occurs. See my correction above in the matter of James Stephen's flawed observation about the inevitable maturation of men.

One of England's prodigious literary figures, Dr. Samuel Johnson, remarked, according to his biographer

James Boswell, that when a man knows he is to be hanged in a fortnight, it concentrates his mind wonderfully. No mention of what knowing that death is foredoomed does to the control of one's bowels. Surely an incomplete thought shouldn't qualify as an epigram.

Oscar Wilde, in his novel "The Picture of Dorian Gray," has a character say, "I should fancy that murder is always a mistake. One should never do anything that one cannot talk about after dinner." Obviously the writers of the TV hit The Sopranos never read Wilde's book. Never mind. Some ars, hopefully, is brevis. (Even I am smart enough to know what *ars brevis* translates to in English.)

Genuine literary critics, wrote Walter Benjamin, a notable German literary critic himself, approach a book, as lovingly as a cannibal spices a baby.

As an epigram, Benjamin's is not exactly faultless. I thought it too good, however, to leave out. In fact, here's another in the same vein, this one penned by British screenwriter Christopher Hampton, that is also faulty but still one I couldn't resist including: Asking a writer what he thinks about critics is like asking a lamp post how it feels about dogs.

A diplomat, according to Robert Frost, is a man who always remembers a woman's birthday but never remembers her age. Huh? What's so hard about remembering the number twenty-nine? Or even the number thirty-nine, for that matter?

Poet Anne Sexton, in All My Pretty Ones, wrote, "In a dream you are never eighty." True, but sometimes you're fat, bald, and more wrinkled than a Shar Pei puppy. What's your point, Anne?

Soap and education are not as sudden as a massacre, but they are more deadly in the long run. Smacks of something Mark Twain said, doesn't it? As it should because it's his line. Had Twain been better educated, he'd have written "Soap, education, broccoli, Brussels sprouts, and all green vegetables except lima beans are not as sudden as a massacre, but etc., etc."

Contrary to what most sports fans think, Dan Cook, a TV commentator, not baseball player Yogi Berra, was the first person to remark that: "The opera ain't over till the fat lady sings."

Most newspaper columns must end when the word-count reaches one thousand, which for this piece is right now. Incidentally, the moment I finish writing a column a sense of euphoria kicks in and I either break into Figaro's opening aria from the "Barber of Seville" or abandonedly cavort about the room to the tune of "Wooly Bully," as performed by Sam the Sham and the Pharaohs. There's little difference in the beat, you know.

Looming dictionary crisis easily averted

It is time to proscribe the coining of new words. In fact, it is long past that time. A dictionary comprised only of computer-derived words runs to hundreds of pages. How many words would a dictionary comprised only of quill-pen-driven words run to? (Never mind. Like political campaign speeches on the hustings of the downtrodden, facts don't matter.) The day is not far off when library dictionaries will be fitted with wheels and a pull strap and their spines embossed with a word such as Samsonite instead of, say, Prentice Hall.

Moreover, if the problem isn't addressed soon, before too many more years our aging population of university professors will begin massively suffering groin hernias from hefting mere office-size dictionaries. Already curmudgeons nonpareil, imagine if an English Literature professor had to endure the irritation of a worn leather truss while grading tests. One inadvertent play on words, one threadbare pun, one dangling participle, and the student's blue book would come back bloodier than the rare cut of a prime rib roast.

I broached the subject the last time a few of us who like to smithy a phrase now and then gathered for a brew at Turk's Bar and Grill on Market Street. I knew my fellow imbibers would share my concern.

Tyler, who makes a good living as an accountant, was first to offer a comprehensive strategy for keeping dictionaries light: "Easy. We make lexicography a zero-sum game. If we add a new word we take away an old word."

Erma, who designs internet web sites, excitedly agreed. "Exactly! We add "blog" and remove "blot!" Erma reads Wired magazine and even seems to understand the technical stuff. Anyway, she easily (and intentionally, I suspect) buffalos the rest of us.

Tyler shook his head firmly. "No, I meant we clean out the dead wood. You know, words like thou, thee, and thine. All that archaic crap. Who needs *"methinks"* anymore? Give me a break, Cybersally!"

Randy was aghast. A newspaper photographer, he pretends to retch. "Not a chance! If anything, we start by trash-canning technical words, toss out modem and dot-matrix and acronyms like RAM, that kind of drivel."

Lad, a finish carpenter was next to weigh in. When asked his occupation he inevitably assures the person who asked him that although he is a finish carpenter he is at least six intermediary persons removed from being related to Helsinkian Lars Per Deinen, inventor of beanbag furniture.

Lad also disagreed with Tyler's proposition. "Zero-sum will never work. A committee would have to select the obsolete words. Every institution in America holding either a private or public charter would want an input. Make the United Nations look like an exclusive downtown New York club for men. If I were Shah of America, I'd–"

Erma interrupted. "Oh pshaw, Lad! How about this. We chuck all foreign words, beginning with French imports. And we don't allow any new ones to cross the Atlantic Ocean."

Randy chuckled. Pretending to address the bartender, whose attention was on the TV show *Wheel of Fortune*, he said loudly, "What we're dealing with here is Meadville's only true female jingoist." He turned to Erma. "Same problem, Erma, as for Tyler's zero-sum approach. Even the city of Quebec, Canada, would want representation on the selection/removal committee."

"Well," Erma answered, "we can't just cherry-pick the words we don't like. We need," she added brightly after a moment of thought, "a word selection algorithm. Plug in a word and get a totally objective answer out, that is, to either discard or save the word. And no half-hearted half-measures either."

Tyler took a long pull of his drink. "Your algorithm itself would be subjective." He fell back into his chair. "Objectivity is a myth."

The rest of us, our outlook doomed by Tyler's axiomatic assertion, fell back into our chairs.

Randy straightened and set his beer stein heavily on the table. "Hey! This would work. We eliminate all words that begin with the letter H."

"Like hammer and hoe . . . and hankie?" I asked, making plain my skepticism.

"There are synonyms," Randy countered.

"The devil's in the details," Lad offered.

Randy brushed away our concern. "Think about it. Words that begin with the letter H not only sound ugly they look ugly. Most are so damned ineffectual they make politicians who use a lot of H words sound like abbey nuns on downers.

"Take the Latin writ habeas corpus. Why not simply, 'Hey Dude, deliver the body?' Or, the word 'huckster.' Is the speaker referring to a peddler or working up a big hawker of snot? And, 'stinky breath' isn't good enough? We have to call noticeably unpleasant odors exhaled in breathing 'halitosis'? The word halitosis itself stinks. In fact, the pronouncing of any H-word order itself causes bad breath."

Randy grinned. "Did you know that operatic tenors discolor the bunting on the side balconies of New York City's Met. Especially when the libretto calls for frequent sarcastic " Ha ha ha's?" The pit musicians keep clothes pins for their noses handy."

"Methinks," Erma said, her chin elevated piously, "thou doth protest too much."

"Very good, Erma," said Tyler.

"Who invited her?" asked Randy, feigning anger.

"At least," I broke in, "we purge first names that begin with the letter H."

Suddenly the focus of curious looks, I apologized. "Okay then, all proper nouns that begin with H. Throw 'em all out. Even the most dimwitted lad wouldn't pick Hugh for his first name. Might as well pack a kid off to school wearing British knickers. Then there's Homer and Hugo–"

Irma laughed. "Sounds to me as if someone's getting a tad biographical here."

"Yeah," I mumbled, "Mother made me wear short pants until the sixth grade.

"I've got to leave," Tyler said rising. "We've just averted a coming language tsunami then, agreed?"

"Right on!" Lad exclaimed, also pushing away from the table. I offered an "Amen, brothers" and Randy a "So be it."

Irma asked, "Do we go national right away or only Pennsylvania to begin?"

"I'll compose a letter for our vaunted national capitol," Randy answered. "We'll need federal legislation, commensurate funding ... and so on and so forth."

"Yeah," Lad said, "a national law with real bite."

"Break the law," Erma added, "and you have to wear a red H on your chest."

Tyler, a few steps from the door turned and waved. "Perfect, Irma!"

"To Noah," Randy said, thrusting his stein toward the center of the table and upward.

"And Daniel, too!" Lad exclaimed over the clinking of our mugs.

By now all of us had put away a couple steins of beer, and truthfully the clinking sound was more a clanking noise.

"You break one of my mugs," the bartender yelled past a customer sitting at the bar, "and it'll cost ya."

Irma's eyes found the ceiling. "Of all the gin joints in all the towns in all the world, we had to pick Turk's."

Headline Writing 101

The headline "States or Bust" all but jumped off the first page of the sports section of our perky little hometown newspaper. It brought back an old memory, reminded me of a trivial event of my boyhood that I'd all but forgotten.

The Sunday before my first day as a fifth-grade student at Neason Hill Elementary School, Paul, my cousin, neatly scratched the words "EIGHTH GRADE or BUST!" in one-inch block capital letters on my new black metal lunch box. Proud of his handiwork, he added cartoonish pictures of heavenly bodies, birds on the wing, exploding rockets, and lightning strokes. Self-decorated student lunch boxes were popular in the late 1930s.

Naturally, I wanted to know what the expression "Eighth Grade or Bust!" meant, and I asked Paul, a venerable eighteen years of age, to explain.

"That's easy," he answered high-handedly. "You're promising the world that you'll make it to the eighth grade or die trying."

I looked at Mother, who, ironing clothes, had kibitzed all the while Paul was turning my plain black lunch box into a tiny billboard advertising my own private excelsior. She nodded sternly, her visage suggesting that, furthermore, if I didn't die trying to make it to the eighth grade she herself would do me in "Soprano style," meaning "whacked" as performed in that Emmy-winning TV series.

The point is, for a long time I've known the meaning of the word "bust," as used in that newspaper headline of a few weeks ago. Moreover, I'm a fan of high-school sports. So, putting two and two together, in mere seconds (math comes easy to me) I had correctly deciphered the meaning of the headline "States or Bust."

As I was reading the opening line of the accompanying story, however, it crossed my mind that likely not many Tribune subscribers would be able to figure it out. I decided, then and there, to put my supposition to the test.

Pretending to be puzzled, I showed the headline to my sister. "What's it mean," I asked innocently.

Jennifer is one of those smart people who snub any conversation involving athletics and doesn't know the difference between "athlete's foot" and "footloose."

"It's a misprint," she answered without hesitation. "It should read, 'States of Bust,' not 'States or Bust.'"

"Yeah," I said, "but what does it mean?"

Shrugging as if to suggest my question answered itself, she said the story, which I had folded away under the big headline, obviously dwelled on women's figures.

I showed her the text.

"You know I hate sports," she snapped. A Rottweiler defending a bone couldn't have flashed me a meaner warning to get going.

I telephoned my brother. From the tinny sound of his voice I knew he was on the extension connected in his muskrat-skinning room.

Silas can shatter fifty of fifty well-flung clay pigeons from 40 yards with a full-choked, 12-gauge shotgun, but he can't hit a pitched baseball with a tennis racket. In other words, athletics just are not his cup of tea.

Even quicker than my sister, Silas explained what the headline meant, certain – as was Jenny in her way – that the topic of the story was pending game-land legislation. Besides being dead wrong, the adjectives he used in characterizing everyone even remotely connected to the upcoming legislation are not well-suited for a family newspaper, so I won't repeat our conversation here.

I telephoned a friend who writes magazine articles for a living. I had hardly finished reading the headline when he declared that "Bust" was a synonym for "Arrest" and that "States" was obviously shorthand for "the Slammer." He hung up when I explained that the subject of the article was volleyball. He does that to me a lot, and should he ever call me I'll return the favor.

I called another friend. Don has advanced degrees from a respected south-western university and may even be as smart as Jenny. He said the word "States" obviously referred to some aspect or other of quantum physics.

"Can't be," I said, and I explained why. He became snippy so I told him the doorbell was ringing, and that I'd call back.

An interview and three telephone calls and what had I learned? For starters, I discovered that four intelligent people didn't have a clue as to the subject matter implied by the headline "States or Bust."

I set out for the offices of the Tribune.

Take my word for it, don't ever visit the sports department of a newspaper while cold sober. Granted, the Tribune's sports editor and the scalawags (wags, get it?) he theoretically superintends are first-rate reporters. Still, the reality is that a Chinese fire drill is more focused, a riot more organized, a pop concert not so noisy. Furthermore, when reporters return from assignments there's more snarling, hissing, and outright wailing than goes on at a midnight gathering of neighborhood cats. And the only reporter who dressed better than a roustabout following the elephants in a parade was a journalism intern still in college.

I shortly convinced the department's managing editor that the headline "States or Bust" just didn't compute for most of his readers.

"Whatever," he said, once he realized I wasn't just another loony with nothing better to do. "The next time that headline crosses my desk," he continued, "I'll change it to read, `High School girls' volleyball team vows neither bad weather nor gloom of night will stay their journey to Harrisburg, Pennsylvania, where they will determinedly compete in the State Volleyball Class AA Championship finals.'"

Clearly droll wit does not become the man. Nevertheless, I departed his office feeling good from my sense of a budding mutual respect brought on by our folksy little talk.

In any case, that certainly is not what I meant

When used as a verb, the word "kid" means to tease or ridicule playfully. Most people enjoy being kidded, understand intuitively that more often than not to be joshed is to be liked.

It's okay to razz men about anything except their manliness and to kid women about anything except their age or weight.

(I had a cousin, a father of two, who once made the near fatal mistake of teasing a middle-aged woman about her ample . . . er, bottom. A nice guy, but sometimes as insensitive as a wingless insect, he keeps that painful memory alive, to inhibit any future inclinations of that nature, by contributing two bucks yearly to NOW, the National Organization for Women.)

I take pains never to make such an unfeeling mistake in one of my columns.

Still, I get negative feedback – like the scribbled letter from an intemperate resident of a nursing home declaring that my use of the mild expression, "Pulling one's leg," impacts like the "inept foot-in-mouth of a language-challenged Neanderthal." Apparently the old bitty doesn't comprehend the difference between a tongue-lashing and a deft, tongue-in-cheek observation.

Of course, it's minimally possible that I'm at fault in this matter, that on occasion my prose isn't the model of clarity and benign thoughtfulness that friends and relatives have led me to believe. In any event, I've looked into it, as I explain in this column.

Initially, I turned to "Whip" Whipple for guidance. Whip is smart but timid and indirect. I've known him for years.

"You lack perception, Noodlehead" he said, before I had finished explaining. "Not to mention that you're deficient in comprehension, insight, and ... you always were. You seem to think you're never wrong. Why don't you sign up for a class in sensitivity training at the university? Have you no values?"

He didn't stop there, but as the rest of his advice wasn't nearly as constructive, so I won't repeat it. Moreover, his language turned salty when I chidingly suggested that he wouldn't know an anal-retentive personality from a meat rump roast.

Unconvinced by the reasoning of my erstwhile friend, I determined to tackle my problem from a different perspective. Specifically, I decided to take the bull by the horns and in this column publicly answer my infrequent critics. This approach, I figured, would help me see where my scrupulously accurate phrasing could sometimes mislead and, eventually, would quench the inflow of mail sent by persons fixated on the word "crap" and its derivatives.

In the selections that follow, unsigned mail is indicated by the capital letter U; other correspondence is identified by the writer's first name. In a few cases, I felt that defense of my journalistic credentials demanded a reply commensurately harsh: sometimes, as the saying goes, you have to whack a mule between the eyes with a plank to get the beast's attention.

Dear Ralph: In my column "Hooked on high-school football," I certainly did not have you in mind when I "mocked" (as you put it) your play-by-play account of last year's high-school football game between Onion City and Conneaut Valley. I tactfully suggested that some FCVC League announcers, although personable, bright, and articulate, wouldn't know an incomplete forward pass from faulty predication. Big deal! What's more, I carefully excluded you from that group. Learn to read, Sorehead! My home address is none of your business.

Dear Daniel: How could you not think I was kidding when I wrote in "More precious than gold" that a bricklayer "would kill" for the chance to side a wall with bricks that had been trued up on a metal-shaping machine? The expression "would kill" bothers you? It's called hyperbole, fella! I've known a number of masons in my life, and none were homicidal. In fact, my mother claimed her father (my grandfather, naturally) was a thirty-second-degree mason, meaning, I suppose, he could brick a wall with the best of them. He passed from this life when I was a shade past seven years old and whether he was that good or not I'm unsure (Mother, you see, was genetically programmed with the Irish gift of exaggeration). I understand the old gent drank heavily and swore a blue streak, but that may also have been irrepressibly genetic as he too was full-blooded Irish. Anyway, your letter itself is a brick. Do you sometimes forget to wear your construction helmet?

Dear Milton: Had I known you were still alive, I wouldn't have described you in my column "A Christmas card for Aaron" as a blowhard. Actually, "blowhard" was my uncle Clyde's characterization. Clyde was your next-room neighbor, remember? So you see, I was only upholding a tradition, not initiating a Nursing Home hand-me-down as claimed in the silly letter I received from your lawyer. Had I referred to you as a blowfly, which I didn't, you might have a case. Also, Crabby, I can prove indisputably that I was not one of the men involved in hiding your brand new lounger chair in the Home's warehouse. Incidentally, if it wasn't well known that you take forever to eat lunch, your chair would have never vanished in the first place.

Dear Valerie: What ails you woman? "Valerie Crowe" is a splendid name. Pretending in a column that I wanted to use the eponymic pen name Val Crowe was merely a trick that I had once played on my pitiless editor, who is given to hacking up my deathless prose as if he's a fireman chopping into the roof of a house leaking smoke. No, since you asked, I definitely wouldn't change my name to V. Affpuddle Crowe, even though your great grandparents were raised in Affpuddle, England. (Naturally, I thought you made the name Affpuddle up, and, truthfully, I was surprised to learn otherwise.) Stick with Val Crowe.

Dear U: I positively did not write, Gutter Mouth, that being smart was a handicap to good bowling. I merely said that being smart could be a handicap. In your case, it obviously isn't – not if you're as good as you let on. Incidentally, "foolscap" doesn't mean the same thing as "fools cap," as you seem to think.

Dear Percival: Lighten up! In the early years of our great Republic, characterizing an American politician as monarchical in spirit, if not in fact, was truly the "whale dung of political insults," i.e., the lowestand meanest of political insults. Political foes called portly John Adams "His Redundancy," and John Tyler, who succeeded to the presidency upon the death of William Henry Harrison, was chidingly addressed as "His Accidency." Frankly, I'm surprised you even know what the adjective "scurrilous" means let alone that you were able to work it into a nearly coherent sentence finding fault with me calling a spade a spade—anyway, you know what I mean.

Darn, I'm just getting warmed up, and I've run out of space. I'll return to the issue in another column, I kid you not.

Trolling for figgy pudding

Musical talent runs in my family. My maternal great grandmother, Inghean Affleck, could play a wooden orange crate with metal serving spoons as deftly as legendary drummer Buddy Rich could sweet talk jazz from drums using ordinary drumsticks. And my paternal great great grandfather, Fergus McClintock, the first Scotsman to master two-part harmony on the Portuguese flugelhorn, blew the doors off Lisbon's Grand Ol' Oprey riffing in 4/4 time on the song, "It Wasn't God Who Made Honky Tonk Angels." Yes, Grandfather Fergus was ambidextrous.

Sadly, Grand*mother* Inghean, her musical career shaken by the encroachment of cardboard boxes and the subsequent routing of wooden orange crates, spent most of her elder years in a mental institution trying hard to drum hot licks out of a milk pail. The acoustics, however, had a noticeably sour ring, and she finally threw in the spoon. (Shameless punning is among the least of my faults.)

Unfortunately, Grandfather Fergus McClintock's knobby-kneed, blue-veined legs were so ugly that his fellow band members made him wear an ankle-length kilt. Consequently, he couldn't keep up in a parade without tripping on the hem. For a while his wife, Cullodena, would wheelchair him behind the bagpipers, but she grew tired of him barking orders, such as Column right! Parade rest! and Flight halt! So she rolled him off a cliff. Grandmother Cullodena was half-Irish. Dark complexioned, she may also have had a pint or so of Spanish blood. Lord knows, one could always find empty pint jars in the room where she spent afternoons darning socks.

Evidently my own uncommon appreciation of music is most strongly a trait passed down by my great grandmother Inghean. There's evidence, incidentally, that she invented the succession of light blows called a drum roll, as my innately favorite Christmas song is "The Little Drummer Boy."

Remember the lyrics? The poor little tyke had only his drumming to offer as a gift to baby Jesus: "I am a poor boy too, pa rum pum pum pum. I have no gift to bring, pa rum pum pum pum."

I love the song, but personally I can't get a feel for the rhythm. The ox and lamb could keep time with it, but not me. Also, sometimes, in singing it, I can't remember how many "pums" follow "rum."

Actually, there are few Christmas songs I don't like. One is the aforementioned, not-so-Christmassy "It wasn't God who made honky-tonk angels," which is a country radio staple in December. According to a verse of the lyrics, there's always a man to blame for every woman's heart that is broken. Indeed!

At least all the words to "It wasn't God who made honky-tonk angels" are in plain English. The words of some Christmas songs are all but meaningless – to me, anyway. Retired now, I decided a ground-level read of a few was in order.

The carol "Deck the halls with boughs of holly" includes a stanza that begins, "Don we now our gay apparel" (so far so good) and then, after a refrain line, "Troll the ancient Yule tide carol." Troll? The word troll means to trail a lure through water. Trailing a song through the water makes no sense whatsoever – except, maybe, in fishing for bass. (Shameless punning is among the least, etc., etc.) For the few of you who are as word-challenged as I am, "troll" also means to sing lustily.

What in the deuce is figgy pudding? Pudding with figs in it? I guess so. My dictionary didn't help. A verse of "We wish you a merry Christmas" goes like this, "Oh bring us a figgy pudding – and a cup of good cheer." The next time I dine out I'll end my order: "And for desert, I'd like a saucer of warm figgy pudding." Who knows, I might learn what goes in to making figgy pudding.

Frequently hearing a rendition of the song "We wish you a merry Christmas" on the radio these days reminds me of how, years ago, on the final morning of school before Christmas break, I led a class of fellow students in a rousing chorus of that song, giving the downbeat a second before the professor walked into the room. Of course we were mocking ourselves, pretending to curry his favor in hopes of improving our grades. Professor Lawrence laid his notes on the desk, looked up, and said with a chuckle, "I'm Jewish." A wit sitting in the back of the class quickly yelled, "Sung respectfully to the tune of "Happy Hanukkah," Sir!"

Remember the lines "I love Thee, Lord Jesus / Look down from the sky / And stay by my side / 'Til morning is nigh."? It's the fourth stanza of "Away in the Manger"? I was unsure of the meaning of the word "nigh" but guessed it meant, roughly, "until the dawn breaks," as it does, more or less. Anyway, it definitely does not mean "And stay by my side until almost noon," as a smart-alecky friend insisted when I asked him.

The carol "O Christmas Tree" opens: "O Christmas Tree! O Christmas Tree! / Thy leaves are so unchanging / O Christmas Tree! O Christmas Tree! / Thy leaves are so unchanging." It's not the words that are unclear, it's the, uh, breathtaking, untrammeled imagery that looses me. Oh well, the lyrics eventually warm up a tad, mention the adornment of candles that "shine so brightly" and vaguely attribute the tree's "rich" decking to God's hand – with His reluctant approval I suspect. (Perhaps He was distracted by the song "Jingle Bell Rock.")

As mentioned in a recent editorial in the Tribune, "The Twelve Days of Christmas" is a rollicking carol, fun to sing and listen to. Most people would agree with that. A point the editorial writer overlooked, however, was that, unlike many venerable yuletide songs, the lyrics make sense too. All twelve presents are expressed in clear English. The editorial fails, however, in covering the bizarre nature of each. Twelve drummers drumming – under one Christmas tree? I don't think so. Eleven pipers piping? Ten lords a-leaping? Nine ladies dancing? Yeah, and "Ho ho ho."

There's a solution of sorts, however. Politely refusing the choreography of the drummers, pipers, and lords, would free up a lot of space, maybe clear enough room to accommodate the nine dancing ladies. After all, nine female hula dancers gyrating under a Christmas tree on Christmas morning, to the tune of "Hawaiian War Chant," wouldn't take up all that much space.

Naturally, in my case refusing a gift of dancing ladies would flat cut against the grain of my love of good music.

GAMES PEOPLE PLAY AT

She rode off with a knight on a white horse

Yesterday our local newspaper reported on a three-day chess tournament underway at the historic Riverside Inn in the nearby borough of Cambridge Springs. The article reminded me of a week or so of my life that I had completely forgotten about.

Mother, early in her dotage, got it in her head that a friend and I often played chess together on wintry Sunday afternoons in the cozy oven room of our little family-owned bakery. At the time, Don and I were veterans attending college on the Korean G.I. Bill.

It was years before I came to understand Mother's obsession, why it was that she had fixated on the indefensible notion of her oldest child being something of a chess player.

I finally figured it out: Growing up I was singularly homely, a buck-toothed runt with the beginning of a

Lebanese nose passed on by my maternal grandfather. Rare were the days when I had the energy of a three-toed sloth with a full belly. Croquet gave me shin splints. In other words, Mother (being a mother) was strapped for something – anything – to brag on me about. Desperate, she settled on the implausible idea that I was one of those quiet but really smart kids you read about in a newspaper feature article, a youngster who knows gamma rays from gummy bears and can make up a relevant haiku faster than most of us ordinary humans can recite a simple limerick.

As the game of chess is clearly a cerebral activity, I'm sure you've connected the dots, have puzzled out the reason for Mother's strange confusion in the matter of my aptitude for that game.

Actually, when I was much younger I played, maybe, a total of thirty games of chess, though never, to the best of my recollection, in the presence of my Mother. I've even won several games, once whipping the snot out of my youngest sister, her pretense of bored indifference fooling no one.

Though miles from being a good player, I can promise you this about the game: it nurtures character, brings out the best in a man. And never mind that it utterly annihilates a woman's maternal instincts, which is another issue altogether.

A person can learn the value of resourcefulness, for example – or its first cousin, inventiveness – by playing chess. The following two brief accounts illustrate this point. Though in each case the setting is the battlefield of chess, the strategies work for almost any board game. (Rather than chance suffering the misplaced rage of feminists, in the scenes that follow the players are all males.)

For some wacky reason – the particulars of which are unimportant – you find yourself matched against a really hot-shot player from Brooklyn, a pallid, bespectacled, geeky looking guy who tosses around French chess words like en passant and knows exactly what they mean. Anyway, positive you'd have a better chance going mano-a-mano against Mike Tyson than outplaying this nerdy little sourpuss, you don't even try. Instead, you get inside his head, misdirect his attention with the verbal equivalent of a rabbit chop to the back of his neck.

Certain that he's read a ton of books on the game of chess and subscribes to a half-dozen chess magazines, right after his second move – no later than his after his third – you poke him in the nose with a straight left jab of pure bunkum.

"Wasn't that cool," you say softly, pretending you're working out a counter move with one of your knights, "how Vladimirovich Tupin kicked butt last year at the Dresden Invitational? What was the name of the young Spaniard he mugged in the championship match? Cantu, if memory serves. Tupin wasn't even breathing hard . . . only took him twelve moves. No idea why the English edition of *Schach Meister* didn't carry the blow-by-blow.

All this is blarney, naturally, but check the look on Chucky Checkmate's face: he's so fiercely trying to recall the alleged match that even determined, single-minded H. M. Stanley – he of "Doctor Livingston, I presume?" fame – couldn't steer his attention back on the game. And if the subject matter itself doesn't turn his mind, the pedestrian slang alone will do the trick. (All serious chess players think of themselves as highbrow intellectuals.)

I can't personally vouch for this next maneuver, but I understand it is highly effective in tournament settings. As an example of the power of chess to cultivate resourcefulness, however, it is unassailable.

Essentially, you let on you can't keep your eyes off a curvy, provocatively dressed blonde, a knockout who is watching the action from a vantage point behind your opponent. You've already aimed a low wolf whistle past his ear, the equivalent of one of those sly, male, get-a-load-of-that nudges to the ribs. Each time, after moving a piece, you instantly cut your eyes back to where this imaginary sex bomb is allegedly observing the match. When your opponent finally turns to see for himself, you gaze disappointedly at one of the doors leading from the room.

Clearly, as these two examples show, the game of chess can perfectly incubate many worthy traits of human conduct – all the virtues, in fact. Naturally it can't make you smart. But then you don't have to be very brainy to muddle your way through a game in which you slyly misdirect an opponent's attention, something my mother never came to grips with.

Mother, incidentally, went gently into that good night long ago. Etched permanently in her mind was the false picture of me courageously battling a Russian grand master for the world chess championship. Still, better that image than one of me clutching a shin and writhing in agony on the sideline of a croquet court.

Besides – it should be called rolling

Merely rolling a bowling ball is easy. The hard part is trying, to make the darn ball go where you want every time. Or in my case make it hit the target pin at least now and then.

To bowl well, you don't have to be a young, supple athlete able to run like a deer, throw a basketball *down* through the hoop, or bench press a weight equivalent to that of a Volkswagen beetle. It helps if you're marginally coordinated, say, able to ride a bicycle without training wheels. But even balance isn't critical. Eyesight? Some really good bowlers wear glasses fitted with lens that would stop a bullet fired from a varmint rifle.

Few bowlers are up to arguing the nuances of Einsteinium Relativity (although some can read lane conditions as if they had a PhD in surface physics), so being smart could even be a handicap. Most bowlers are physically average people, but men with pot-bellies and women with, er, "sturdy" hips are often able bowlers, too. Good bowlers – the pros, for example – range in build from chubby to skinny, from looking as if their daily three-squares consisted only of mounds of potatoes to looking as emaciated as men stumbling up a sand hill in the Sahara Desert.

When I turned seventy a few years ago, I began looking for a little more exercise than walking a couple miles daily and mowing the lawn once a week. And since I qualify both physically and mentally, I decided to try my hand at bowling.

Now, even though I'm not a bit good at it – makers of shotgun shells could learn plenty about the nuances of load scatter by watching me bowl – the dang game has become a monkey on my back.

Boys as young as twelve and men in their late eighties have bowled perfect games – toppled all ten pins each of their first twelve rolls. Some women bowlers wax the behinds of men bowlers with a regularity that would bring tears to the eyes of the toughest Hells Angels biker. Wheelchair bowlers have their own national organization. Lions Clubs raise funds to benefit blind bowlers.

Unlike golf, which is fundamentally as uncomplicated as bowling, weather isn't a factor. (Actually, golfers are congenitally unable to tell when it's raining.) On the other hand, bowling centers, which are windowless and seamless except at entrances, are corked so tight that beseeching the Almighty for help (in either a noble or lowborn way) is an exercise in futility – not that it stops bowlers from trying.

In a typical session of league bowling, a hacker like me will incrementally hoist close to a half ton of dead weight consisting typically of a wildly colored, perfectly spherical plastic mass, containing an oddly shaped clump of metal usually suspended near its center. The metal influences the ball's route to the pins – causes it to heed a curved path that even Dr. Einstein himself couldn't mathematically predict.

I can't explain my obsession, but I bowl in three leagues and practice on off days. I own five bowling balls: one is too light, two are too heavy, and two are about the right heft. I mentioned to a veteran bowler that I might try selling the two heavy balls. After a long, overblown chortle, he said, breaking off a muffled laugh, "Lots of luck." The market, I found out, is an indifferent grizzly bear of an outlet for used bowling balls.

Sometimes I wear my long wrist brace, sometimes my short wrist brace, and sometimes I don't wear a wrist brace at all. It depends on the score of my last game.

I've gone from a conventional grip, to a finger-tip grip, and back to a conventional grip. I've finally settled again on a finger-tip grip – I'm pretty sure.

Four-, five-, and six-step approaches? I've tried them all, everything but a no-step approach – a hunched-over-the-foul-line, two-hand delivery.

I talk to my ball, but the words go in the thumb hole and out the finger holes.

I advise it loudly on its way to the pins: "No, no! Take, take!" hoping it will respond to my mildly imparted spin on the ball and follow a curved trajectory into the target spot between the head and number-three pins. It never hears.

Many good bowlers, I've observed, let their shirttails hang out. I've tried that too. Nothing helps.

My friend Don, who is also my age, is no less hung-up on golf than I am on bowling. He is better at golf than I am at bowling, however. At least on paper. Since cheating in golf is irrefutably systemic, I appropriately discount his boasting – and commensurately raise his stroke count.

Anyway, Don is college-educated and a lot smarter than I am, so I asked him to explain why in the deuce I have this fever about bowling. He went on and on, as I knew he would (I prudently snacked before telephoning him) pressing me about the nature of my dreams and throwing in words like "ego" and "superego." He finally convinced me, his hundred shades of opinion notwithstanding, that he was as clueless as I was.

If he can't figure it out, likely no one can. So I've decided to leave it at that, stop brooding over why something as mindlessly simple as rolling a perfectly spherical, dent-free fourteen-pound ball at a triangle of ten paunchy wooden cylinders standing sixty feet away, with no other goal in mind than to knock down as many of the wooden cylinders as possible, has me in a hammerlock of misguided purpose.

Besides, at my age I can't help but wonder why I waste even a thimble of energy chasing an impossible dream when, with a little brushing up on the basics, I could be losing at cards and board games with equal ineptitude. Or, instead of bowling for physical exercise, take up croquet.

Feet! Grip! Spot! etc.

"Hugh!" Nellie yelled from the kitchen. "It's for you."

I picked up the extension line in the cellar. The caller was my friend Dormant. Dormant's real first name is Don, but his wife of fifty years swears he's long been Dormant to everybody that knows him.

"Busy?" he asked.

"Very," I answered. "I'm pumping iron."

The sound of guffawing and loud knee-slapping eventually faded. "I've seen you in your winter snuggies, Hugh." The chortling and knee-slapping resumed.

"So?" I said, when he eventually stopped, "what's your point?"

"My point?" he said. "Atlas you ain't, Hugh!"

He continued. "Did you read that article under Healthbeat in today's newspaper, the piece quantifying the way a person slows down with age?"

"Naw," I said. "I never read about stuff that doesn't apply to me."

'Uh-huh," Dormant said dismissively. "It explains why your bowling has fallen off worse than ever."

"I know exactly why my game has gone a little south," I replied. "I just–"

"A little south! Last week it found a safe port in Antarctica."

"I just need to practice more."

"Practice! No, that's not it, Hugh. Here's your problem." I could hear the rustle of a newspaper unfolding, and he began reading aloud: "The study found moderate decline in performance among athletes in their fifties and sixties, and then a steep decline starting at seventy-five."

He paused, evidently wanted me to mull over that last part of the line: "The study found moderate decline . . . ."

"You've reached the tipping point, Hugh. Age seventy-five is the tipping point for athletes. It says so in the study."

"What study," I snapped, ignoring his remark that added a good year to my true age.

"One by U-Pitt researchers."

"University of Pittsburgh? Big deal. As if it–"

"Oh, wait," he said. "The article is specifically about athletes, so technically you're not covered, Hugh."

Dormant, my age, played croquet well into his fifties, and he lords it over me. He's forgotten that I was a tournament knuckles-down marble champ in grade school. The two of us bowl on the same five-man team in a senior league at Plaza Lanes.

Bowling isn't the easy game it seems. Sure, any klutz can bowl a two-hundred game once in a while. I've proven that. But averaging a score of 200 over a season? That is a different matter altogether.

Concentration is the key. Senior bowlers, whose muscle memory is typically as flabby as their waist, have to concentrate with all their might. Dormant has told me he uses a five-word memory aide: FEET, GRIP, SPOT, SLOW, and ROLL. The word FEET reminds him to carefully position his feet, the word GRIP reminds him to firmly hold the ball, and so on. He said if he doesn't include the word SLOW, he "rushes the line" – meaning something or other about his getting out of rhythm. (Truthfully, the only thing Dormant rushes for anymore is the bathroom.)

One of our teammates, who is older than the rest of us, and proportionately more sluggish, takes forever after he steps onto the bowling approach lane.

Like Dormant, he uses a similar, five-word memory aide, often unintentionally mumbling it out loud. Say it is Torpid's (as he's furtively known at the lanes) turn to bowl. Glaring at the pins, he leaves his seat. "Feet!" we hear him say stepping onto the approach and exactly positioning his feet. Next, we hear the word "Grip!" and the ball, which he is holding at his waist, wobbles slightly.

He pauses, and we wait.

"Feet!" we hear again, and he briefly looks down at his feet. Then we again hear, "Grip!" and so on. Eventually he gets it together and rolls the ball.

Torpid's friend, our anchor bowler, likes to gig him: "If you didn't take so dang long to bowl you wouldn't forget your keys."

Torpid, a funny look on his face, reaches into his pocket. He shows us a ring of keys. "I did not forget," he assures our anchor bowler.

A very good bowler when he was younger, for the most part we're patient with Torpid. Besides, often his slower-than-cold-molasses play hacks off at least one player on the opposing team, bugs the poor guy to where his tears of rage obscure the pins: good bowlers won't abide delays when it's their turn to bowl.

Dormant may have seen me in a bathing suit years ago, but he's never seen me wearing what he called snuggies – by which I assumed he meant long-handled underwear.

"You know," I told him, "there's a word for old geezers who enjoy gazing at disrobed old men."

"What," he said, "is that supposed . . . to . . . ."

Obviously befuddled, he changed the subject. "I really called," he said, "because I need the name of a collection agency. And I figured your dentist nephew might use the services of one."

"You mean Cecil?" I said. "I guess he does. Want me to call him?"

"And then get back to me. Okay?"

That evening I called Dormant and told him that my nephew, Cecil the Diesel, gave me the name of his collection agency.

Dormant said to wait while he found a pen. A minute later he was back on the phone.

"It's a national outfit based in the Bronx," I said. "Are you ready?"

"Where?" he said.

"In New York city. They have branch offices across the country."

"I'm waiting," he said.

"They call themselves, 'Pay Up or Sleep with the Fishes.'"

He began repeating the name a word at a time, as if he was writing it down. He reached the word "with," and began sputtering.

"Talk about reaching the tipping age" I said, "you're not so quick– "

He hung up before I finished.

I bowl because I am

I bowl in a geezer league at Lake Side Lanes on Tuesdays. All the members are good-natured seniors, and the kidding goes on endlessly. When Mark rolls a solid strike, someone asks, "That one get away Mark?" Or, as Pat will likely hear if one of his deliveries barrels into a gutter short of reaching the pins, "Going with your straight ball today Pat?"

We begin bowling at eleven a.m. Most of us arrive by ten-thirty, however, and shortly everyone is involved in a discussion of current events. Last Tuesday was typical of one of our sessions.

Referring to a Health & Science article in the newspaper, Adam captured everyone's attention when he said loudly, to no one particular, "Did you see that story about how us seniors have an ongoing need for sex?"

"We, seniors," said Jerome, whom everyone likes, but I can't stand.

"Exactly," Adam said.

Adam suffers from macular degeneration. He has almost no central eyesight, and his peripheral vision is severely limited. A veteran kegler, he bowls instinctively. And he's good. A teammate tells him which pins, if any, are left standing after his first delivery.

Now and then an opponent will tell Adam that he's left standing the two widely separated back corner pins, the seven pin and the ten pin. Adam sees well enough to suspect otherwise and growls a two-word reply along the lines of, "Mind your own business, you dumb excretion of a male bovine."

Unlike Adam, most bowlers aren't too careful of their language. In fact, their bowling ability, as in golf, seems to depend not only on the quality of their muscle memory but also on the fullness of their vocabulary of ready cuss words. (In the case of male golfers, wearing ugly, gaudy slacks apparently also improves one's game.)

Lady bowlers, incidentally, internalize their anger, that is, they deceive, by forcing a smile through teeth clamped together tighter than vise jaws holding a heavy cantilevered work piece. I've also noticed that unlike many senior men, mature women bowlers don't wobble approaching the lane to deliver the ball. Likely, it's because they have a lower center of gravity.

"How's that again, Adam?" Fred asks, lacing on a bowling shoe. Normally laid-back, Fred's eyes, nevertheless, are narrowed skeptically.

"I said," Adam replies impatiently, "it turns out that we elders have a big need for sex."

Tim chuckles and says to Fred, "Think we should tell him?"

Fred, after a moment says, "Naw, let it play out."

Wes, the fellow in charge of the center on Tuesday mornings, pulls a Tribune from under the counter, finds the article that caught Adam's eye, and reads aloud the headline: "Sex-Ed for seniors a growing need. Sex ed," he adds forcibly, holding the paper for Adam to see. "Sex Education!"

Adam contemptuously waves at the paper, which he can hardly see anyway, and tells Wes to mind his own damn business.

Hollis saunters over to the counter and begins reading the article. "What," he asks, his brow furrowed, "is canoodling."

Ossie glances at me. "It's white-water rafting in a canoe," he says loudly. Hollis can't see his slight grin.

"Exactly," I say.

Wes scoffs and advises Hollis to ignore us.

Most of my fellow members are either pot-bellied, bald, or both. On the plus side of being aged, our ready stash of alibis for bowling poorly is virtually inexhaustible.

A few of us – wild scamps in our salad days – have "Mother" tattooed on our forearms. To a man, we're disdainful of the tendency of young bowlers (kids under fifty) to have large stretches of their limbs decorated with gaudy tattoos.

Sherm remarks on the condition of the lanes. "Boy are the back-ends ever dry this morning."

Bowling centers dress lanes with a protective coating of mineral-based oil before league play and before tournaments, and Sherm means that the tail ends of the lanes are especially void of the dressing, thereby causing his ball to hook more than he wants.

Earl, a teammate agrees. "Uh-huh. Speaking of back ends, did you know that it's not the year 2007 but the year 4705?"

Several of us, unsure of the connection between dry bowling lanes and the numbering of years, look at Earl expectantly.

"That's right," he says. "I read it in a column in the Tribune. By the Chinese calendar, it's the year four thousand seven hundred and five."

"Ah so," someone says, imitating the voice and manner of the late cloak-and-dagger film detective Charlie Chan.

"They give names to their years," Earl continues. "The Chinese. They call this one 'The Rear of the Dog.'"

After a second, we realize we've been set up, and we collectively groan.

By and large, serious bowlers may be characterized as either "crankers" or "strokers." Crankers are generally youngish bowlers. They whip the ball toward the pins with a lot of revs and a follow-through swing that ends with their launching hand alongside their ear. Kids twelve and younger can crank the ball. (If you're a beginning or a senior bowler, never ever bowl in a lane next to one of the little showoffs.)

Strokers, by and large, deliver the ball as if they were tossing a hoop for a carnival prize – and only a tad more energetically. Almost all seniors are strokers. (I made this point – uttered years ago by a TV Tonight Show guest – in a previous column, but it's too poignant not to repeat: "Never mention the word stroke around senior bowlers!")

Golfers like to say that it never rains on a golf course. Big deal. It truly never rains inside a bowling center. Besides, geese can't get in bowling centers, so you don't have to carefully meander everywhere as if you were heading for a green or a tee.

In fact, the only bad thing about bowling is that modern bowling centers display your score on an overhead TV screen – in real time, frame by miserable frame – to kibitzers, spouses, and other persons with a bent for disparaging sarcasm. Anymore, however, I barely hear the giggling and the sass from the peanut gallery of onlookers that begins when I step onto the lane approach area.

Sometimes a little aged deafness isn't a bad thing.

Hooked on high-school football

My wife and I retired to a quieter life in the little town of Conneautville, Pennsylvania, after thirty-plus years of living in a suburb of Dallas, Texas, where, among other missteps, we became avid fans of the Dallas Cowboys football team.

Conneautville, a borough of about one-thousand residents situated in the northwest corner of the State, is surrounded by gentle, rolling fields of farmland that is irregularly broken up by dense forests of mostly maple trees.

We're still lukewarm followers of the National Football League, Nellie and I, but if we had to choose between watching a Superbowl game on TV and seeing the Conneaut Valley High School Indians play football, we'd opt for the Valley game – every time, home or away, rain or snow.

Besides the excitement of the game itself, there's entertainment by splendidly attired marching bands and pretty, nimble cheerleaders. A hot-dog costs a dollar and a can of pop fifty cents. Now, I ask you: Is that a full plate for a Friday night or what?

Nellie and I attended our first Valley game the season of 1998. I don't recall who we played, but I remember that Valley kicked off, the other team made a first down, faltered the next series of plays, and punted the ball back to Valley.

I panicked when Valley lined up for its first offensive play from scrimmage. "Where's our quarterback!" I yelled, jumping up and pointing at the field. "We don't have a quarterback!"

Heads swiveled in my direction, scorn showing on every face. Nellie elbowed me hard in the thigh. "Yes we do!" she snapped.

"No we . . ." I began, before catching myself.

Suddenly a runt of a lad wearing number eight spun away from where he was crouching behind the team's large center and initiated a play that resulted in a nice gain by a Valley running back.

The fans around me stopped cheering long enough to glare briefly again at where I was now back in my seat unwaveringly watching the action on the field.

In my defense, please understand that the last football game I watched was an NFL contest on TV, where all the players were hulking six-footers with calf muscles big as small hams. At Valley, where quarterbacks are always height-challenged and skinny-legged – at least they have been since Nellie and I became game-attending fans – we don't have hidden-ball plays, we have hidden-quarterback plays!

Another thing I learned at that first game: everybody rooting for Valley – trust me, absolutely everybody – was related to one or more of the football players, to a cheerleader, or to a band member. In other words, to avoid a vicious pummeling at the hands of a gray-haired grandmother wielding a buttressed bleacher seat cushion, never ever utter even the mildest criticism of one of the home-town participants on the field. I've no doubt the peril is as great at Saegertown, Maplewood, Linesville, and all other French Creek Valley Conference schools.

Settling down after recklessly blurting out that our quarterback was missing, I kept my mouth shut, my eyes on the game, and my ears on the words blaring from the public address system. No matter the school, most of the PA talk at FCVC games is first-cousin to a nightclub comedy routine, which even Red Buttons would envy. (Remember comedian Red Buttons? For some reason I can't forget his line about Eve asking Adam if the leaf made her look fat. Never mind.)

After a few preliminary announcements, the playing of the school anthem and then the national anthem by the home school's marching band, the identification of starting players by their position and uniform numbers, and so on, the PA announcer gets into his play-by-play account of the game, which goes something like this:

"The Onion City Bears won the toss and have elected to receive the ball.

"We have a nice crowd tonight so you can bet the fifty-fifty pot will be a good one. Did you catch that, folks? Bet. Ha, ha.

"Half of the money, as you know, goes toward the Valley band's . . . oops, there's the kick off!

"And it's a beaut!

"All the way to the twenty yard . . . make that the thirty-yard line! That's number sixty-two who . . .

"Make that number forty-two. That's, uh, Frackle, who caught the ball, the Bear's hard-charging senior fullback –uh, junior fullback."

Watching from the top bleacher on the visitor's side of the field, a cluster of Onion City fans, undoubtedly blood kin of the player who returned the kick-off, yell out loudly, "Friechel! It's Friechel, not Frackle!"

The announcer, who's describing the action from across the field in the press box of course doesn't hear.

"Frackle," he goes on, "is gang-tackled by a Conneaut Valley Indian just short of the mid-field stripe.

"The owner of a red Ford F-one-fifty, license plate number (here the announcer evidently turns away briefly from the microphone) ____zero eight, your truck is blocking an emergency exit. It will be towed if not moved immediately. Thank you.

"The Bears run plays from what's called a winged-T formation, but they don't make much on their first play from scrimmage. I'll call it second down and seven yards to go. Make that second and two.

"While the Bears are in their huddle, let me remind all students that after the game a dance sponsored by the Conneaut Valley Sports Boosters will take place in the big teepee, the Conneaut Valley high-school gym – following the game. Admission is–

"Oh my! Look at that folks! He's going all the way! Thirty! Twenty! Ten! Touchdown, Onion City!"

I've set the above action at Conneaut Valley, where, in truth, the hometown PA announcer knows his stuff. In any event, who cares if most of the FCVC announcers are gabby English lit teachers who love the sound of their own voice and believe footballs truly are made of pig skins. They come across as nice persons. Besides, the overall effect is part of the charm of small-school Friday-night football.

If you're not a fan of high-school football, become one. Get hooked, as Nellie and I did. Buy your wife a foldable bleacher seat. Dress warm. On your way into the stadium, buy hotdogs and sodas at the concession stand. And for a good two hours, enjoy the circus, never letting your attention wander too far from the center ring where the kids are playing their hearts out.

Catting about on Pymatuning Lake

It's been all of fifty-five years since I was the proud owner of the first catamaran ever to sail the waters of Pennsylvania. (If I mention the launch date, just as sure as ants do picnics some landlubber who lives catty-cornered across the State in Philadelphia will claim that he had launched a catamaran on the Delaware River many months before, if not years before.)

A recent photograph in our hometown newspaper reminded me of that delightful time. The picture was of a catamaran "catching a breeze," as the caption read, on a nearby lake.

I was given the boat (true) by Kyle, a friend, who had acquired it from the original owner in trade for twenty peanut-vending machines and one dollar cash (also true).

Kyle's gift to me came wrapped in a condition: I had to make the twin-huller seaworthy by early summer so he and his fiancée could cruise nearby Pymatuning

Lake – the largest lake in Pennsylvania, incidentally – on weekends.

The day Kyle handed me the tiller, "Double Trouble" – so christened by the craft's first owner – was about as seaworthy as a rusted-out wash tub. One hull was totally submerged near a dock in Conneaut Lake, where Kyle had tried to launch it the summer before, and the other hull, more or less airborne, was indifferently unresponsive to the crests and troughs of that lake's small waves. The mast was angled at roughly seventy degrees to the horizon, its azimuth suitable for launching a mortar round in the general direction of Hartstown, a one-traffic-light village some five miles to the south.

Shipped as a kit to Erie, Pennsylvania, from San Diego, California, the hulls of the finished product had all the eye appeal of elongated plywood caskets – leaky elongated plywood caskets. As for appearance, the craft's one saving grace was its two sparkling, red-and-white striped nylon sails – a mainsail and a jib. If nothing else, the sails alone were worth the price of twenty peanut-vending machines.

"Fair enough," I jubilantly replied to Kyle's conditional offer. And with the help of three good buddies – all ex-GI's on summer break from college – sealed the outside of every seam of both hulls with a fiberglass mesh. At the time, fiberglass, in that form, was a quite novel, three-part product that wouldn't set up if the ambient air temperature was below 80-degrees Fahrenheit.

Amazingly, for the rest of "Double Trouble's" seagoing life, the inside of its hulls remained dryer than the sandy plains of West Texas.

That summer Kyle and his fiancée enjoyed the use of "Double Trouble" exclusively the first two weeks in July, and my friends and I – two, three, or four at a time – sailed her almost every other sunny day. Actually, describing our summer of skimming the meager waves of Pymatuning Lake as "sailing" is a bit misleading: making turns we rowed from one prow or the other.

Becalmed, rowing a small, motor-less sailboat is not only a practical means of locomotion it is virtually the only means of propulsion. It is also an embarrassing way to negotiate a course in what is ordinarily a wind-propelled vessel.

Suppose the skipper of a sailboat wants to sail a straight line from point A to point B smack against the wind. As even novice seadogs know, he or she would resort to a stratagem called tacking, that is, to zigzagging across the teeth of the wind at about forty-five degree angles until the craft eventually reached its destination.

Close-hauled tacking is the term used to describe sailing as tight against the oncoming wind as possible but not so close that the jib flutters doubtfully and the prow of the boat wavers uncertainly. In other words, it's a technique that produces the most efficient course in a wind-bucking situation.

In our case, however, we didn't zigzag so much as we zagzagged, as "Double Trouble" every time stubbornly refused to cut across the eye of the wind. Consequently, after we had zagzagged and zagzagged until coming dangerously close to going aground – always within easy eyeshot of a busy beach of gawky swimmers and sunbathers – one of us would stealthily make his way to the prow of one hull and paddle hard until we were headed in the other direction, that is, in the zig direction.

Never once did we manage to "come about," as changing paths from a zig line to a zag line (or vice versa) is called, except by side-rowing the prow. So, that winter I wrote to the company that made the boat: catamarans, I had decided, were unusual in the matter of sailing into the wind.

"It's easy," the firm's sales manager wrote back. "To come about, just back the jib and sail about."

Right. Just back the jib.

Exactly how the heck does one go about "backing a sail boat's jib"? (The jib on "Double Trouble," as on most other small sailboats, was a forward, boom-less sail attached to the mast's forestay.)

The following summer, we figured it out – and at that purely by accident. Backing the jib amounts to pulling the rope attached to the sail's bottom rear clew (eyelet) until the sail is flatter than a sheet of construction drywall. This allows the sail to fill with wind from the opposite direction, which pushes the prow of the boat past the sticking point.

The gratification of finally solving that problem was only a tad less rewarding than the pleasure I felt at no longer hearing one of my wise-cracking buddies yell out, toward the end of every long monotonous zag, "Make ready to back the jib and sail about, Skipper! (Chortle, chortle), a command later refined to, "Hard alee there, Skipper! (Chortle, chortle)."

At last a real sailor, and largely self-made at that, I added a seat, of sorts, to the boat's full beam-width cockpit, fastened a make-do yacht club pennant to the top of the mast, and began mockingly referring to my sailing friends as "hands."

Had I paid closer attention to the shouts and frantic gestures of one of my "hands," we'd never have rammed the submerged stump I couldn't see from my ersatz captain's chair. The collision not only irreparably damaged one of "Double Trouble's" twin plywood hulls, it also tarnished for all time my reputation as a doughty and crafty skipper of close-hauled sailing.

Under B – isn't for me

Feeling a tad uneasy, I barely glance at the name painted on the big window of the dumpy-looking storefront. Located between a pawn shop and a downtrodden retail business, the place is obviously a concern of doubtful purpose. Nevertheless, I purposely stroll on in.

From inside, the block lettering on the front window reads sdnoB liaB yrucreM, which I translate in my mind to read Mercury Bail Bonds. I take stock while waiting for a busty, sour-pussed woman to look up from her stool behind a counter where she's reading Astrology Monthly. Two shabbily dressed women, their faces lined and drawn, are sitting behind me in the middle seat of a row of wooden folding chairs. Their hands are resting in their laps. One hand of one woman is relentlessly kneading a gob of moist tissue.

I am visiting Mercury Bail Bonds because last night my wife and three of her girl friends, enraged that an "outsider" – and a man at that – had won the high-stakes cover-all game at the bingo hall where they play, had cornered the interloper in the bingo hall's parking lot, mercilessly beat him about the head and shoulders with their bingo-card daubers, and were arrested for their miscreant behavior.

A bingo dauber, which is only a little smaller than an ordinary two-cell flashlight, makes a handy, but ineffective truncheon.

A stocky, thick-featured man of about forty gives me the once-over from a desk situated behind the woman reading the astrology magazine. The man looks tough, like he could be an enforcer for the Mob. I return his nasty look in spades; he pretends not to notice.

I am completing a form, with help from the top-heavy woman, when suddenly I feel someone pawing my left arm. To my surprise, the tough-looking man has left his desk and is standing at my side. "Queenie wants out," he snarls. His voice is anomalously high-pitched.

"Queenie?" I repeat confusedly. I sense my voice trailing off.

"She's scratching the side of the bed," the man says morphing into my wife. "It's your turn to let her out."

After another long moment of bewilderment, I roll to where I can read the clock on the stand beside our bed: its twenty minutes past five a.m.

My wife loves bingo. I'd rather spend three hours – about the time it takes to complete a night of bingo – watching a candle burn. I suppose that's why I had the stupid nightmare about bonding her out of jail.

My wife plays eighteen bingo cards at a time, three strips of six cards each, which is the usual number for serious players. I accompanied her twice to sessions. The first time I tried helping, but I only got in the way and ended up spending most of the time watching the other players. The second time, I bought three bingo cards for myself.

A session typically begins after some preliminary banter between the players and the person who calls the numbers – a bearded, round-faced man the session I attended. He never once doffed his grungy, baseball-style gimme cap. (Likely he was bald.)

"Gimme Cap," signaling the end of the banter, holds up a hand. The first game, he says into his microphone, will be "single bingo," meaning a player wins as soon as he or she marks off a single straight line of numbers, horizontal, vertical, or diagonal.

Occasionally, I'm told, a player will bingo on the first four numbers called, completing the required string of five numbers by using the "Free" square that is in the middle of every card.

After the first game, the patterns are more complicated, ranging from a cross or an X, to concentric picture frames, to a representation of boiling storm clouds, to an outline of The Last Supper (as far as I could tell). Usually the final game is a cover-all in which every number of a given card must be called for a card holder to win.

Bingo players are a democratic lot, if anything bunched a tad left of the middle of the socioeconomic bell curve and slightly right of the middle of the seniority bell curve. At any given session, roughly four-fifths of the players are women, half of them secretly ticked-off over men being allowed in their bingo hall. (A bingo hall likely was the cradle of America's feminist movement.)

In the middle of the next game a leather-lunged male player prematurely shouts "Bingo," and immediately a woman player sitting across the room wonders aloud why he isn't home carving a new fishing lure, her attitude all but challenging his masculinity. My wife quietly tells me that this happens at many sessions; the culprit, so she claims, is always a man.

Widely mumbled approval of that sentiment follows, and then someone says to cut the chatter and quiet is restored, which leaves the human tuba red faced and either smiling guiltily or scowling stubbornly.

A session of bingo typically consists or fifteen or so games, all but the first game are considerably more complex than "single bingo."

With the first shout of bingo, the hall erupts in a collective moan, and the players sitting near the winner fix him or her with their best flinty looks. Inevitably, someone says disgustedly, "She always wins."

If it's a valid bingo, a "runner" pays the winner in cash and another game is quickly begun.

In and around Meadville, Pennsylvania – the city nearest to where I live – the prize for winning a feature game usually is a hundred dollars; the prize for a regular game is most often fifty dollars. Frequently the prize money must be shared, that is, split with another player who has simultaneously bingoed – or even split with two or three players who have simultaneously bingoed.

I didn't win a game the session I played, didn't even come close. I'd no sooner get two or three numbers in a line, start feeling good about my chances, and some frail-looking, shawl-wearing granny across the hall would shout bingo in a voice so powerful that it rattled the hall's windows. In the cover-all game, so help me half the numbers on my best card were still showing when two players simultaneously yelled bingo. Bingo mocks me.

By and large, bingo is a game of chance. True, sharp players will miss fewer opportunities to bingo, but all things being equal, each game is a seventy-five-number crap shoot, the prize going to the person with the luckiest set of cards.

If I were a bingo nut, I'm sure I'd be disappointed at losing. But considering that winning is so much "a roll of the dice," I would never have bad dreams about playing poorly.

I wish I could say that for my bowling. In fact, it's a wonder I don't have a nightmare after every session. Never mind.

Jim Thorpe shrugged, too

It's not true that my father had to install training wheels on my tricycle as an acquaintance once insisted loudly to our softball teammates. We were playing a game in the long-defunct Crawford County League (circa 1950), and our infielders were regrouping after I had tripped over my own feet trying to complete a double-play while playing second base; a well-made pivot would have resulted in the third out of the inning. Of course, I had about as much chance of performing a well-made pivot in softball as I did of dunking a medicine ball on a basketball court. The remark about my need for training wheels didn't strike me as particularly funny, but every player within earshot thought it funnier than anything Bob Hope ever uttered.

Luckily for me, we were so far behind in the score – as was usually the case for any team on which I was a member – that my goof didn't figure in the outcome.

As a boy, I loved sports. As a participant, I was horribly inept, maxing out athletically at croquet. I always looked for an angle, fiddled with my equipment, read "How To" books, tried anything that promised a remedy. I mentioned in an earlier column the many ways that I tried to elevate my bowling average, even to the point of talking to my ball (the words just went in the thumb hole and out the finger holes). Nothing helped.

The first ball glove I bought for myself was so big – which largeness I thought would improve my fielding – that it would have barely fit inside a galvanized wash tub; was so heavy I had to drag it to my position in the outfield. A wisenheimer on an opposing team once asked me if it was made in Africa from the ear of an elephant. Occasionally pressed into playing the infield, when I had to back-hand a ground ball I did it with all the aplomb of an infielder with his wrist strapped to an anvil. Slow rollers dribbled past me that the Venus de Milo statue could have kneeled down and fielded.

One evening in the spring of 1950 the late, great Meadville softball pitcher, Verda Stevens, was rounding into shape at the local YMCA for the coming season. "Steve," as his teammates often called him, pitched in the City League, which was faster company than the County League.

It was virtually impossible, batting against Steve, to tell if he was throwing his drop or his riser – his entire complement of pitches. I've watched from the stands as a batter, after twice futilely striking out (and in the process looking like a man suddenly beset with spastic paralysis), square around to bunt his next time up, anticipate one of Steve's drops, and stumble headlong into the infield taking a poke at Steve's riser. Steve pitched dozens of no-hitters, possibly more than fifty. (I left Pennsylvania for California while he was still pitching.)

I caught some of Steve's pitches that night at the Y. He always warned me ahead what pitch he was launching, and I still ended up with a stoved left thumb that stayed sore for a month. He didn't ask me to try out for the team on which he played.

Steve was also a good Ping Pong player. We both played on the Talon Corporation team. Talon at the time manufactured immensely more zippers than any other company in the world, employing almost two-thousand people in Meadville alone.

One Saturday late in the winter of 1949-50, led by Norman Babcock, our top seed, ten of us (as I recall) traveled south some forty miles to Sharon, Pennsylvania, to play a team of boys who were members of the Buhl Club of that city. Norm, a Talon executive, was also a first-rate athlete in several sports.

We collectively got the living spit kicked right out of us by the Buhl team, won only two of roughly thirty matches. The late Phil Saggio, brother of retired Meadville businessman Lou Saggio, prevailed in one of those two matches, and another low seed, whose name I've forgotten, won the other match. Nineteen, at the time, and greener than rye grass in winter, I was nevertheless struck by how modestly the Buhl team of youngsters accepted the rout, almost with oriental indifference.

Riding home – as a passenger in a car driven by the late Roy Stump, a teammate, bandleader, and resident Meadville nut (Roy would have been incensed had I described him as anything less than an escapee from a loony house) – I concluded that the Buhl players didn't lose very often.

When I was in the eighth grade, a boy from Massillon, Ohio, boarding temporarily with his grandparents in South Meadville, where we lived at the time, taught me how to correctly punt a football, that is, how to kick a spiral. A week later I was easily outpunting most of the aspiring football players around my age, except for one or two – and certainly not besting the late Paul Chess, who in few years later would be booting rain-makers for the University of Pittsburgh on a football scholarship that he earned while a star running back for Meadville High School.

We practiced football on a dirt side street of South Meadville. My only punt that I distinctly remember – a pretty good effort that went awry – broke a garage window. That dang ball bounced from the roof of one garage to the roof of another and then back through a window of the first garage. The garages were separated by a narrow walkway. Not in a thousand kicks would a football bounce that way again.

Ah, basketball! I was often the shortest player on the court, but I was also slow. Moreover, I was a lousy shot, making about fifty per cent of my uncontested lay-ups. If you've never played basketball, trust me, that portion is not good. Had he been around back then, I would have envied Shaquille O'Neal's mastery of foul shooting. (I'm being sarcastic, as all basketball fans know: in the matter of shooting free throws, "Shaq," one of the most dominant NBA centers ever, can't hit an ox in the butt with a bull fiddle – as the saying has it.)

For a couple of seasons I was a back-up setter for the Meadville YMCA volleyball team, being pressed into action only if our two regular setters couldn't play – say, if both were in the intensive care unit of our local hospital. In those days, teams were generally made up of four big men who could "spike" the ball down into the opponent's court, as well as block the other team's tall, hard-hitting spikers, and two short men who "set up" their own big guys and tried to help with defensive blocking.

My saving grace, as a volley ball player, was that no one, teammate or opponent, ever knew where in the deuce one of my set-up passes was likely to come down. That may not sound like a positive, but it kept our opponents tripping over each other clambering to block the spike of one of our big guys who knew beforehand that one of my "sets" might descend anywhere on our side of the court – not to mention occasionally fall on the opponent's side.

I got used to the nasty screaming of our own spikers who, in any game I played suffered wrenched backs (the likes of which bulldoggers in a rodeo never endured) twisting to adjust to my errant sets.

I was pretty good at knuckles-down marble shooting, croquet, and table-top shuffleboard, however. Alas, no one of stature ever knew.

NOT IN THE TRIBUNE, YOU PHILISTINE

Cheerless in Pottstown, PA

Retired, and now living easy in the tiny borough of Conneautville, Pennsylvania, the one thing I miss about working for thirty-some years in bustling Dallas, Texas, is reading the nationally syndicated "Dear Abe" column , which is carried twice weekly (still, I assume) in that area's major newspaper.

"Dear Abe," written by Dr. Abelardo Flatulotta, is an advice column for men, the putative counterpart of Abigail Van Buren's "Dear Abby" column. Hugely popular, it is printed weekly in the pre-eminent, leftmost column on the first page of the newspaper's sports section.

No question ever transcends the deductive power of Dr. Flatulotta's intellect. His answers, more than mere pearls of wisdom, are insightful Hope diamonds of psychological brilliance. He is a deviner, a soothsayer, an oracle, a Lake Tahoe of depth, clarity, and erudition.

I have saved many of his columns – some have yellowed with age – and almost daily I review one for inspiration and guidance. Figuring that many of my fellow locals are unable to avail themselves of the good doctor's irrefutably solid advice, I have repeated below the verbatim text of a few of his best recommendations, replies to questions posed by his distraught readers, offers of introspective counseling that would reward even the most balanced and fit among us.

Dear Abe: I work on an assembly line in a General Motors factory. My boss, when he walks past me, stupidly yells out, "Shoulder to the wheel, Herkimer, shoulder to the wheel!" (Herkimer is not the reader's real name.) The last time he yelled that out – about the umpteenth time – I jumped up and kneed him in the groin. Now he's upset with me. How do I get back on his good side? > Busted In Lansing, Michigan

Dear Busted: The only way you'll ever see your boss' good side again is by rolling him over in his casket! Your fish is fried, pal. Move on. Look for off-shore employment with the Yugo Motor Company.

Dear Abe: My problem is interminable erectile dysfunction. I've tried everything. Does acupuncture work? Please don't leave me dangling. > Limpid In Biloxi, Mississippi

Dear Limpid: My condolences, of course. Still, a renowned Thailand acupuncturist, Dr. Peng Pong, advised me that prolonged acupuncture treatment is indeed effective. Needle placement, he warns, is super critical. In a few rare cases the patients' voices cracked after the first treatment and for several months remained fractionally higher pitched. I suppose, however, if I was in your situation, I would learn to tolerate any negative side effect. Strive to keep your chin up – or whatever.

Dear Abe: I have this uncontrollable Dr. Strangelovian impulse to salute my wife whenever she insists I perform one of the tasks on her Honey-do list. Sometimes I even click my heels. Didrika can live with my occasional heel-clicking but my seig-heil salutes are over the top. Physical restraints absolutely do not work.
> Goose-Stepping In Fredericksburg, Texas

Dear Goose Stepper: Unfortunately, your affliction is not learned, it is, regrettably, genetic in nature. A truly understanding wife would quit ordering you around. Fat chance, but that's your only hope. Also, I must remark on the question of your basic honesty. You claim de Shicklegruber for a surname? Your ancestors were French? That's hard to swallow. I'll buy von Shicklegruber but not de Shicklegruber.

Special To Baffled In Costa Mesa, California: You bumpkin! No wonder your hemorrhoids swell when you have sex. Viagra is ingested, not supposited.

Dear Abe: My fiancée says I can't wear my John Deer baseball cap to get married in. I'd sooner be married with my boots off than bare headed. Her wedding gown will be a color she calls forrest green, so what in hell's her problem? Here's mine: if I don't give in she'll put on a long face, as she always does when she doesn't get her way, and ruin our wedding pictures. Still . . . she's not much to look at in the first place. > Thinking-To-Hell-With-It in Great Falls, Montana.

Dear Thinking-To-Hell-With-It: Because you left out vital information – and this is an important point that all you fans must remember – I can't insightfully answer your question. Are you bald? If your pate isn't well forested, you may have a point. Otherwise, I have to side with your fiancée, no matter how ugly she is. On the other hand, should you have lots of hair, wearing a hat all the time is indicative of a deeper problem. My monograph, "Dealing with Psychoses and other Odd Mannerisms," has helped thousands. (Email me at drabeflatulot@tapin.com.)

Dear Abe: My wife Caitlin has fallen in with the wrong crowd. Returning to college – we're empty-nesters – she began running with a gang of math majors and their gooney professor. She can't count to twelve without removing her mules, and she wants to be a mathematician? Ha, ha. What's a multi-function pocket calculator anyway? Some kind of sex toy? Anyway, she wants one. Also, what does the word algorithm mean? She's started throwing that word around a lot. If she knew rhythm from rat doo-doo we wouldn't have had the second set twins. > Doesn't-Add-Up in Philadelphia, Pennsylvania.

Dear Doesn't-Add-Up: As I also teach college–level mathematics, I take umbrage at your characterization of her math professors as goonies. Would you like it if I called you a grease monkey? Clean up your act, Sludge Mouth, and I'll re-consider your question.

Incredible! As I'm writing this, my wife, who is watching TV, pops into the room to tell me Dr. Flatulotta passed away late yesterday afternoon while in the care of an acupuncturist named Pong. No other details were broadcast.

My moral compass no longer has a north pole; I cannot go on, alas.

Sometimes saying only "Nuts!" just doesn't cut it

During the winter I bowl in a men's league one night a week. By and large bowlers are not card-carrying members of society's hoity-toity set, but none are ill-mannered louts either. Now and then I've heard a fellow Wednesday-Nighter utter an intense "darn," a heartfelt "dang," or even an edgy "shucks." But as for any intemperate or bowdlerized cursing, that's about it.

Imagine, then, my shock at reading in the newspaper that Vice President Dick Cheney had used a vile, four-letter F-word in suggesting to a political opponent that he perform a feat of personal acrobatics that we won't be seeing in this summer's Olympics (as some wag once put it).

Barely recovered from that blow to the solar plexus of my dignity, I read in the same news story that presidential candidate John Kerry had used the identical phrasing – in an equally salty grammatical imperative – while characterizing President Bush's Iraq policy! I might as well have been kneed in the groin and then, bent-over in agony, clobbered by a board-shattering karate chop to the back of my neck.

I did not immediately recover. But after finally restoring my composure (and thereby rallying my complexion), I took stock, spent a long hour mulling over this disgraceful business of politico grandees using unseemly language. I decided a little research was called for – perspective is important in these matters – starting with a better understanding of the self-contained physical act demanded of the affronted.

Professor Alfred Kinsey, in his 1948 ground-breaking study on the sexual behavior of men, reported that Americans of all kind engaged in unconventional sexual practices. He never once mentioned, let alone described, the act ordered by Vice President Cheney and Senator Kerry of their antagonists to perform in their moments of high temper. Possibly Professor Kinsey was blown away by the physical agility required. The omission, it seems to me, undercuts Kinsey's reputation for thoroughness, notwithstanding that he claimed his research encompassed more than 5,000 interviews.

Alas, the husband-wife team of Masters and Johnson, 1966 runner-up clinicians in the field of sexuality, were no help either.

Thwarted in researching the fundamentals, I decided to focus on the expression itself, expecting, nay, concerned, that I would soon learn that the command, "Go (bleep) yourself!" was a uniquely vulgar American idiom.

I checked around, read some cheeky women's magazines, cherry-picked the internet, and sampled TV talk shows that only middle-aged, forlorn housewives enjoy watching.

I shouldn't have. To my dismay, the trashy expression has gone international. Not only that, but politicians of other countries say it with more color, with flamboyance that American officeholders can't seem to master.

Here's how legislators of Great Britain's House of Lords suggest that a political foe should attempt the same comportment: "You can jolly well go (bleep) yourself, you bloody twit!"

See what I mean: is that colorful, cognominal "bloody twit" cool or what?

When an American legislator urges the same behavior, there's no heart, no charm, no pizzazz, just a lusterless verbalization of the three-word phrase itself.

German politicians – predictably as blunt as Americans – demand punctuality: "Go (bleep) yourself. At once!"

Spaniards, instead of straightforwardly appending the command as Germans do, add, fervently, "Arriba! Arriba!"

Japanese men, ever polite, respectfully bow before and after recommending that the focus of their anger get on with it at once.

Mexicans, who invented refried beans, say it twice rapidly: "Go (bleep) yourself! Go (bleep) yourself!"

Russians, claiming the expression for themselves, cite Joseph Stalin's indigenous version – Go (bleep) yourselfski! – penned, in Stalin's own hand, in a letter addressed to Leon Trotsky. At the time, Trotsky, a black-balled Bolshevik expatriate, was sojourning (more or less) in Mexico.

In France, where kinky sex is the norm, not the exception, the expression has died on the vine for lack of a fertilizing poignancy.

In any event, one thing is clear: American politicians should at least learn to express their potty-mouth sentiments more eloquently; they should give a little thought to punching up the basic phraseology: shouting a naked, "Go (bleep) yourself!" simply doesn't measure up to the piquancy inherent in the act itself.

As one might expect, on occasion an American military officer has found that that imperative, or a facsimile thereof, aptly represented his or her passion of the moment. I ran across reports of several such incidents while browsing 1,001 Things Everyone Should Know about American History, a book written by distinguished American historian John A. Garraty. I found one to be especially interesting.

Recall during World War II when the Germans overwhelmingly surrounded American troops at Bastogne, Belgium, during what came to be known as the Battle of the Bulge? And General McAuliffe's written response to the German high-command's order that he immediately surrender was a tepid, unworthy "Nuts!"?

Care to know what the General's spoken response really was? Uh-huh. You guessed it. And an aide said he followed up with a curt, "In spades, you hiny bastards." Professor Garraty, more discreet in citing the General's actual reply, allowed as to how ". . . what General McAuliffe [actually] said is thought to have been unprintable . . . ."

Of course, both Cheney and Kerry could have said "Nuts to you," instead of "Go (bleep) yourself!" But let's be honest here, "Nuts to you" is barely a light jab to the snoot, let alone a roundhouse to the old snot box.

I'll sleep better now, my ruffled sensibilities smoothed by publicly cleaning my breast of the disgust I felt at reading of the appallingly bad manners of two of America's prominent public servants.

God bless America, anyway.

Getting to the bottom of things

Dr. Corey Henry, resident proctologist at Baltimore's Johns Hopkins Hospital, calculated exactly the high-level of pain a man suffers during a digital examination of his prostate gland.

I had forgotten about the doctor's ground-breaking research until the other day when I read a story in the *Tribune* about the laudable efforts of several local men, all survivors of prostate cancer, who had come together to raise public awareness of that often pernicious disease.

Formulating the nature of pain as a partial differential equation and calculating the answer to three decimal places, Dr. Henry irrefutably proved that two rectal prostate examinations aggregate to the pain and agony of giving birth.

Dr. Henry reported his findings in a scientific paper written in doctor-speak (of course) in which he set forth his difficult equation and its solution in longhand script.

(Unfortunately, even Wong Font, the Wall Street Journal's master compositor, was unable to set the hyper-complex equation in type, which is also the reason Dr. Henry's findings have yet to be widely reported in the national press.)

Women, since Eve, have insisted that no hurt in the world equals the pain of giving birth. Endlessly misled, we men at last find out that the pain of childbirth is no more searing than the agony of two digital prostate examinations.

Moreover, Dr. Henry admits that he chivalrously rounded all decimal fractions down, which, of course, favors the women's position. Besides, he cast out examinations of even moderately tumid prostate glands, which are immeasurably tenderer than healthy ones.

Clearly, Dr. Henry, once and for all has lifted the mules, sandals, and spiked, sling-back pumps of feminine disinformation from the backs of men's necks.

Husbands observe their wives giving birth – squeamishly, perhaps – but stalwartly, nonetheless. Do wives ever look on while their mates suffer the unbearable pain of a rectal digital exam? Thereby forcing them to concede the truth of Dr. Henry's findings? Might as well ask if celery is fattening. (In fact, it is claimed by some that eating a stalk of celery causes a person to burn more calories than are gained by consumption of that vegetable.)

The Almighty got human anatomy right, by and large. But He sure messed up in fixing the location of a man's prostate gland: He might as easily have nestled it outside the body in the vicinity of kindred male genitalia. He didn't, however, and the cross we men shoulder is heavy. (It makes a man wonder if feminists are correct in challenging the gender of the Almighty.)

For convincing proof of Dr. Henry's myth-shattering research, I offer the following scene, which is typical of a middle-aged man's visit to his urologist. (Constitutionally, most adult males are simply unable to visit an urologist until their prostate glands have swollen to the dimensions of a medium-sized beefsteak tomato and have become tender as a long-festering boil – a condition, incidentally, that the good doctor Henry, in a parallel study, proved to be more enfeebling than the morning sickness of pregnancy.)

"I'm pretty sure it's my prostate," the patient says to his doctor. (Deeply imbedded, as that gland is, pinpointing the exact cause of misery isn't all that easy.)

The doctor nods understandingly and at the first opportunity utters the words that always mean, no matter his euphemistic phrasing, one thing: "Assume the position, Mack."

And whether "Mack" is an ornery Marine drill sergeant or a self-effacing haberdasher, he obediently drops his pants and shorts, rests his chest on the examination table, and waits with teeth clenched tight enough to dent a railroad spike. Meanwhile, the doctor, from somewhere behind him, snaps on a latex glove – with the crack of a spring thunderclap – preparatory to palpitating (doctor speak for mercilessly agitating) the patient's prostate gland.

The following monologue is typical of a digital prostate examination:

Patient (straining not to whimper): "About it, Doc?"

Silence.

Patient (eyes filling with tears): "That'll do it, huh Doc?"

Silence.

Patient (all composure gone): "Holy Mother of Pearl, doctor!"

The doctor, his patient now mewling shamelessly, finally withdraws his finger. It will be hours, however, before the throbbing of the man's prostate fades to the ache of an opiated knee misshapen by rheumatoid arthritis.

While the patient hitches up his trousers, the doctor writes a prescription: "Take two of these a day," he says, "until they run out. And I want to see you again in two weeks."

"Only," the patient replies through constricted teeth, "if you promise to give me a general anesthesia first." Trying to smile, he adds, "Or, a spinal."

The doctor, still a young man with a healthy prostate, laughs uproariously.

Head of PIA sits on press release of new spy gadget

The phone rang at exactly nine a.m. Struggling to fashion a silk-purse sentence from my wordy, inchoate sow's ear of an opening line, I wasn't thrilled at the interruption.

"What?" I answered sharply.

A woman's voice, stern and self-important, said, "Mister McClintock?"

"Not again," I replied wearily, figuring I was about to hear that my appointment with Dr. Verzygote had been moved back.

The woman continued as if my answer had made sense. "I'm calling on behalf of Hector Loy. Mister Loy would like–"

Vaguely recalling the name, I interrupted her. "Loy? From the PIA?"

The PIA, as you probably know, is the domestic counterpart of the cloak-and-dagger Central Intelligence Agency, or CIA. The "P" in PIA stands for

"Peripheral," that word chosen, apparently, in counter distinction to "Central."

"Mister Loy would like to be interviewed for a magazine article," the woman continued, tacitly admitting that her boss was indeed employed by the PIA. "Are you available?"

Interview the head of the PIA? I jumped at the chance. "When and where?" I shot back.

"Tomorrow morning in his office. Nine a.m. Sharp."

I reminded her that the PIA's address wasn't public knowledge.

"Are you alone?" she asked.

I said that I was, and she whispered an address.

Arriving at the main gate of the PIA complex, I was stopped by a soldier guarding the entrance. He patted a holstered pistol. "Park over there," he ordered ((pleasantly)), "and leave the motor on."

Note: I was instructed by a CIA operative to insert the word "pleasantly" after the word "ordered." Likewise, other CIA mandated words are enclosed in double parentheses (( )).

Empty enclosed parentheses ( ) represent omissions where the CIA operative instructed me to remove a word or expression; I may not even hint at the meaning of the expunged word.

I drove to the parking space where the soldier had pointed and stepped out of my car. A man wearing ((neat and spotless)) orange coveralls slipped behind the wheel. After twice loudly revving the engine, he sped away.

"I know how much gas I have!" I yelled after him ((redundantly)).

A burly M.P. who had quietly pulled up beside me in a golf cart wasn't amused. "You, McClintock?" she demanded ((respectfully)).

"Yes, ma'am," I answered.

I climbed into the passenger seat of the golf cart, and we lurched forward toward a boxy, two-story red brick building with narrow vertical slits for windows.

A Marine sergeant, cool and dapper in starched summer khakis, was waiting at the entrance. He and my driver exchanged glances.

"This way, Sir," he ordered, squinting suspiciously at my steno tablet.

Mr. Loy's office was situated on the ( ) floor in the ( ) corner of the building. The sergeant rapped solidly on the door exactly ( ) times. The words, "Come in," rang out

Pushing sixty (if not pulling it along) Mr. Loy's secretary glanced sourly once my way before bending to inform an intercom box of my arrival.

"Dang it Hortense!" a scratchy, high-pitched male voice rang out. "Couldn't you see I was on the encrypted line?"

Hortense, shrugging indifferently, gestured at the door behind her. I let myself into Mr. Loy's office.

Sitting behind a large wooden desk in a high-backed swivel chair, one leg folded under him, Loy slammed down the phone. His glare, when he finally looked up, scorched the wall opposite where Hortense was sitting.

Making his way around the desk, he stuck his hand out. Had he been taller and thinner in the face, he could have doubled for scrawny TV actor Don Knotts. In other words, the picture of an agent 007 he wasn't. After briskly shaking my hand, he returned to his chair, pulled a newspaper story from the center drawer of his desk, and held it up for me to see. "Have you seen this?"

The headline read: "CIA gadget museum no secret."

He waved toward an arm-less side-chair facing his desk.

"Yeah," I answered, backing into the chair. "Fascinating."

"Did you know the PIA also has a museum?" His question was stern.

"Afraid not," I said. "Where's it located?"

"That's a secret," he said. Sighing unhappily, he added, "Nobody's ever heard of us. I'm going to level with you, we–"

"Wasn't the PIA originally called the DIA, the Domestic Intelligence Agency?"

Loy slightly nodded. "That was before some PR flack stuck his nose . . . ."

"I'm going to level with you McClintock. Speaking strictly off the record, we always get the ((dark)) end of the Congressional funding stick. No one has ever heard of the PIA."

"Aha," I said understandingly.

He waited, seemed to be sizing me up.

"Okay then Mister Loy," I said, "let's cut right to the chase. I'll need a hook."

His flinty look turned into one of uncertainty.

I continued: "For my opening. A line that grabs the reader's attention – right away."

He reached under the desk and pressed something, a doorbell button I presumed. Shortly, a gaunt, stringy-haired man dressed in a white, ankle-length lab coat slunk into the room carrying a toilet seat, which he silently handed to Loy.

Loy's smile was fleeting but crafty. "This," he said, pointing to the seat's brass hinge, "is an antenna." He pointed at one little rubber bumper and then at the other. "Lithium batteries. And this–"

"That's all Percival," Loy said, interrupting himself.

Percival sidled toward the door where he had entered the room and waited. Loy glared, and Percival stepped through the doorway.

"Yeah," I said. "But what's it for? What's it do?"

"I'm coming to that," Loy snapped. "It's a bug, a mic and transmitter. Who'd ever suspect . . . in a john, yet!"

"Gives new meaning," I said, "to the old saying about getting 'caught with your pants down.'"

Loy gleefully slapped his knee. "Use that in your piece!"

Anticipating my next question, he assured me that privies were a hotbed of clandestine verbal intercourse.

"And other breaking activities," I mumbled.

He didn't hear me. "The presumed privacy and all," he went on. "I wish you could hear some of our tapes. You can't imagine."

"I think I can," I said.

After a few more meager exchanges, he asked suddenly, "Got enough material? I can't discuss specifics, you understand."

I fell back in my chair. "I'll . . . see what I can do."

His quick, hard nod suggested that he considered we had struck a binding deal.

"How," I asked, "does, 'PIA's latest gadget is a gas' grab you as a headline?"

"By God you're good, McClintock!" he exclaimed, slipping the newspaper story publicizing the CIA's gadget museum back into his center desk drawer. "Use it." He abruptly stood up: our meeting was over.

I spent most of my drive home trying to shoehorn the expression "southern exposure" into an eye-catching headline. It seemed to me that "PIA gadget gives new meaning to southern exposure" was passable. My editor thought otherwise.

De-tweaking the culture

Kathleen Parker, a syndicated newspaper columnist, writes that sometimes her articles, which she describes as accounts written to "tweak the culture," spin her audience counter-clockwise instead of in a gentle, self-improving clockwise direction as she intends.

I don't know how to "tweak the culture," but in my columns I sometimes kid people, and occasionally I, too, receive cranky, wholly unjustified feedback.

Apparently, it is not always clear when I'm only joshing. In any event, in this column, I take the bull by the horns and publicly apologize to readers whom I may have offended. My soothing, mollifying clarifications, I certainly expect, will once and for all slow down the inflow of barracudas waving such vacuous adjectival expressions as "an execrable excess." (At least writing a column is educational.)

Dear Donald W. (Onion City): In my column "Hooked on high-school football," I certainly did not have you in mind when I mocked a play-by-play account of last year's football game between Onion City and Conneautville. I tactfully suggested that some FCVC League announcers, although personable, bright, and articulate, wouldn't know an incomplete forward pass from a dangling past participle. If your letter is representative of your true nature, you have the disposition of a famished wolverine. My home address is none of your business.

Dear Jay M. (Saegertown): How could you not realize that I was kidding when I wrote in "More precious than gold" that bricklayers "would kill" for the chance to side houses with bricks trued-up on a metal-shaping machine? The expression 'would kill' is only a figure of speech, milling-machine breath! I've known a number of masons in my life, and none were homicidal. In fact, my mother claimed that her father (making him my grandfather, Jay), a thirty-second-degree mason could brick a house with the best of them. He passed from this life when I was still a toddler, and whether he was that good or not I am unsure since Mother was genetically programmed with the Irish gift of exaggeration. I understand that the old gent drank heavily and swore a blue streak, but that may have also been irrepressibly genetic as he, too, was full-blooded Irish. Anyway, your letter itself is a brick, Jay.

Dear Arlene K. (Cambridge Springs): I never wrote in my piece, "Besides, it should be called rolling," that being smart was a handicap to good bowling. I merely said that being smart could be a distraction. In your case, Ms. Gutter Mouth, it obviously isn't – not if you're as good as you boastfully claim to be. Incidentally, braggadocio is not becoming personality behavior, something you don't seem to understand.

Dear Ralph R. (Linesville): You wrote that my prose reads like the mutterings of a language-challenged Neanderthal. It's my fault that you can't tell honest laudatory prose from boastful gas-station bathroom graffiti? I think not. Your "subtle criticism," as you describe it, is no help at all, Ralph.

Dear Percival Y. (Cochranton): Lighten up, Percy! In the early years of our great Republic, characterizing an American politician as monarchical in spirit, if not in substance, truly was the whale dung of political insults. Portly John Adams was called "His Redundancy" by political foes. John Tyler, who succeeded to the presidency upon the death of William Henry Harrison, was slightingly addressed as "His Accidentcy." Frankly, I'm surprised you even know what the word "scurrilous" means let alone that you could work it into an exclamatory sentence. Besides, you used the impolite four-letter synonym for dung, not me.

Dear Francis F. (Rolling Hills Nursing Home): Had I known you were still alive, I wouldn't have described you in A Christmas card for Aaron as a blowhard. Actually, "blowhard" was my uncle's characterization. He was your next-room neighbor, Aaron, remember? So you see, I was only upholding a tradition, not starting one as claimed in the silly letter I received from your lawyer. Also, I can readily prove that I was not among the persons who hid your new lounger chair in the Home's off-site warehouse. So, stop whining and learn to merely bend with the wind of small jokes.

Dear Valerie K. (Meadville): Goodness, woman! Your name, "Valerie Crowe," is a splendid cognomen. Pretending in a column that I wanted to use the eponymic pen name Val Crowe was merely a trick that I once played on an editor who hacks up my deathless prose as if he's a fireman chopping into the roof of a house leaking smoke. And, since you asked: No, I would not go by the name V. Affpuddle Crowe, even though your great grandparents were raised in Affpuddle, England. (Naturally, I thought you made up the name Affpuddle, and I was surprised to learn otherwise.) Stick with Val Crowe, Dear.

As frequently happens, I've run out of space. In the interest of civility, however, I'll continue my apology in another column. Meanwhile, I'll consider whether a cutesy photo of me propping my chin on my fist, like the picture of Ms. Parker adorning her article, will set a friendly tone for my columns.

Okay, I've considered that possibility and decided that cutesy just doesn't work for a rugged, he-man face like mine.

THE FAR SIDE OF SCIENCE

Big Bang and then what? Big Pfft? And what about obtuse cats?

Science marches on, perhaps, and yet life's really big posers remain unanswered.

Where, precisely, is the "End of the earth"? Toast always falls to the floor butter side down. How come? What do women really want? Are cats naturally mulish or just dumb? These are life's real posers, but behavioral scientists don't have a clue.

Instead, what science offers is speculation on a lot of picayunish stuff, such as how and when the universe began. Human existence started with a "Big Bang?" Really. No one was around to hear it, so it may have only been a tiny whoosh. The time has come – actually the time is long past – for the smart people of this world, professors, farmers, and waitresses employed by fast-food restaurants, to get their heads out of the clouds and into real-world problems. Their dedication would save lives.

I like cats, and I love our aging tabby. Still, I'd like to know, is "Lucky" pigheaded or just plain stupid? It's something I've wondered about since my brother Silas, while mowing a hay field, rousted the sodden little guy from his hiding place and foisted him on our mother. At the time, Mother, widowed and eighty-six-years old, was living with my wife and me. The tiny beggar indeed was lucky to have escaped alive from Silas' usually omnidirectional hayfield mowing and he thereby acquired his name.

My brother Silas, incidentally, is so nearsighted that he once mistook a pole-mounted power-line transformer for a pineapple-shaped beehive. His wife stopped him from trying to dislodge it with a blast of water from their garden hose – likely, thereby, saving his children the embarrassment of admitting that their Pa electrocuted himself by water hose. Lucky must have sprung from his hiding place and somehow flagged Silas down, because Silas wouldn't have caught sight of any stray animal smaller than a moose heifer.

Lucky, when he finally stopped growing, weighed a whopping twenty-four pounds. He didn't walk, he swaggered – menacingly. He was so doggone big I worried that should a visitor misread his brooding – as was often his disposition after a futile night of courting – for want of a few pats of affection, the outcome could be bloody, maybe fatal.

Every time I turned Lucky out of the house, I half expected that shortly an irate neighbor would be marching our way, a willfully resisting, battle-scarred mutt in tow. Lucky, I was sure, could whip the health out of any bowser in the neighborhood.

While we were wintering in Dallas, Texas, Lucky, then two years old, became chummy with a cat named Sky that belonged to the couple living in the condo abutting ours. Perhaps "close to" is a better way to put Lucky's and Sky's neighborly dispositions than "chummy with," as their mutual affection was separated by a sliding glass door, the portal from our bedroom to an outside back balcony running the length of the four-unit building.

Sky and Lucky spent the better part of each morning doing everything but fondly embracing each other, which, of course, they couldn't accomplish through the door's full-length glass pane. After watching their bundle-board romance seemingly blossom into real, feline affection, I decided to slide the door open and thus push aside the obstacle to their affair of the heart.

Lucky, as I cautiously opened the door, made the first move, hauled butt faster than a prairie jack rabbit fleeing a hungry lynx cat and fixed himself so tight against the baseboard of the wall at the head of our bed that he couldn't have been dislodged him with a spudding bar.

Sky, for a second stared confusedly at the place where Lucky had vanished under our bed and then sprang nimbly over the sill and into our apartment, where he began rubbing up against my legs. As confused as Sky, it was a several seconds before I shooed him back out and slid the door shut.

A half-hour later, while I was reading in the living room, Lucky sauntered nonchalantly from the bedroom into the living room and stretched out lazily on the carpet in the middle of a splash of sunlight. By his manner, one would have thought that minutes earlier he had routed the 130-pound German canine brute owned by our neighbor in Pennsylvania.

That's the kind of puzzle, Lucky's inexplicably terrified reaction, that the consummate application of scientific methods would unravel in no time – not to mention reveal whether Lucky, and cats in general, hide their embarrassment or never feel personal mortification in the first place.

Personally, I think it's the latter. Cats are as lovable as warm puppies, but as dimwitted, it's clear, as retarded armadillos.

Lucky understands that our kitchen door is egress to the back yard, but in nine years he hasn't figured out which door jamb is hinged and which one is fitted with a latch. The presence of a doorknob isn't a clue at all. If he gets it right and parks in front of the latch jamb when he wants out, it is plainly a random choice.

Here's another reason why I think cats are stupider than your everyday groundhog (but would like to know for sure if they are). Our dog, naturally, can't tell time. But at least she knows the difference between nighttime and daytime. Lucky obviously does not. At night Lucky sleeps on our bedroom dresser, which is situated roughly thirty inches from our bed. No more able to tell daytime from nighttime than a hinge jamb from a latch jamb, he will, any time he's a tad hungry, launch himself from the dresser to the floor by way of our bed.

Trust me, when a twenty-four pound animal suddenly lands on your bed at three a. m. in the morning you and your wife will bolt upright – your wife's hair a fright wig and your's no less rumpled (if you have any) – certain that thunder had rolled and a lightening-struck tree had crashed through the roof of the house.

So, you're thinking: enough about cats already, right? Okay, then, wouldn't it be nice to know, say, the skinny on women? What they really want? For the record, even the late Dr. Sigmund Freud, the Austrian who originated psychoanalysis, wasn't able to figure that one out – despite, he claimed, thirty years of research into the feminine soul.

Freud, who lived to be seventy-four, died of his own hand, likely succumbed on his office couch during self-analysis. Most brethren of that calling believe he answered his own question, and after finding out what women really wanted, the revelation totaled his ego and the sudden onset of humility was too much for his heart.

On second thought, maybe deep knowledge isn't always a good thing. Maybe it's just as well that we know more about what goes on inside an atom than inside of a woman's head.

Yes, that's definitely a better plan; probably it has been God's thinking all along.

Yes, but Dr. Einstein never came to grips with relative pronouns

Genius, according to the late American inventor Thomas Edison, is more perspiration than inspiration – in a proportion of about ninety-nine parts sweat to one part cerebration.

A teenager when I stumbled across Edison's maxim, I was utterly baffled over why he believed the act of breathing mattered so little in the functioning of a creative mind. If nothing else, I figured that inspiration, the inhaling of air, should at least invigorate serious cognition.

Eventually, my sister, with typical sibling compassion, straightened me out by gently corrected my misunderstanding: "Moron. That's not what Edison meant by 'inspiration.' He meant, the spark to create something new, make something from nothing. Dummy!"

Four years my senior, Moron and Dummy were two of Jennifer's more endearing nicknames for me –

not to mention that she never got cuffed in the ear by mother at aiming either word at me.

My response, from the doorway, was measured: I reasoned aloud that she was also a dummy and equally stupid. She managed to get in my face, however, and I chivalrously bolted the room. "Then why," I demanded from the hallway, "wasn't he inspired to invent the fluorescent lightbulb? Instead of short-lived, hot-running incandescent light bulbs?"

Jennifer asked me if I knew what "expired" meant, and I picked up the pace.

Poets, creative in a way far different from inventors, are inspired by muses, by comely Greek goddesses who motivate them from time to time to arrange words in meaningless, unconventional ways.

Scientists and inventors aren't so lucky. They know darn well that no lovely Greek goddess (except possibly Urania, the muse of astronomy) will be paying them a timely visit in their hour of perplexity. Edison's observation about the character of "genius" makes this point crystal clear.

So, how did the great Dr. Einstein suddenly realize that time wasn't universally constant? How did he figure out, wacky though it sounds, that if you're traveling in a space ship, the dash-board clock ticks slower and slower as the vessel gains more and more speed? In fact, if you could soar along at the speed of light, an impossibility (or so he argues), time would stop altogether – and you would live forever! (Either that, or your heart would stop beating, and you would die instantly. I'm way over my head here.) Of course, the answer is that Dr. Einstein was inspired!

Dr. Einstein hit on his discovery in a spare moment while pondering why in the deuce time flies while you're watching a Marx Brother's comedy but grinds away at a snail's pace while you're walking your constipated pooch late at night.

"I was struck," he wrote in an endnote to his paper on The Special Theory of Relativity, "by the fact that time whizzed by while I was browsing lines of Dante's Devine Comedy, but came to a screeching halt during one of my proctology exams." (My German is poor, but I believe I've authentically paraphrased what he actually wrote.) Not known for his punning, I suspect "screeching" was his subconscious choice of words. I also suspect the story behind his flash of brilliance would have been widely reported had he included the anecdote in the body of his paper instead of burying it in the endnotes.

Dr. Einstein published his startlingly counter-intuitive paper in 1905. Can there be any doubt as to why it was millennia before someone first tumbled to the fact that immobile time ticked away relentlessly at the same rate while time on the move didn't?

Incidentally, not even the brilliant Dr. Einstein figured out where time "goes." His argument that a graveyard for time lies somewhere beyond our solar system has been roundly poohed by the scientific community – discarded as no less whimsical than the fiction of an elephant's secret graveyard. (A lesser physicist would, of course, been pooh poohed, not just poohed. Never mind.)

Dr. Einstein published his second paper on the subject of relativity in 1915. Mathematically far more complicated than his first, predictably the next day an article appeared in the New York Times asserting, ponderously, that only two men in the whole world were smart enough to cogently argue Einstein's propositions, a farmer in Iowa and, of course, a Times editor. After all, Dr. Einstein's mathematical formulations were merely novel expressions of the physical world, hardly more complicated than long-division arithmetic. Is the formula $E=mc2$ so tough to understand? Man has been calculating the areas of circles by the wholly parallel equation, $A=\pi r2$, since the famous Greek mathematician Chaos Demeter, in 608 BC, worked out that relationship while he was in charge of hoop circularity at Parthenon Cliffs Barrel Works. (Incidentally, the last Times' editor to let a grammatically simple sentence grace an article in that newspaper disappeared while on special assignment covering a mugging in a tough part of the Bronx.)

The Times newspaper reporter, apparently bent on jazzing up his story, seems to have overlooked the many obscure concepts of other disciplines of academia, of inscrutable, well-fertilized arguments blossoming fulsomely in the fields of psychology, sociology, astrology, and so on.

For example, Sigmund Freud's psychoanalytic theory of human nature was far more incomprehensible than the end results of Einstein's dabbling in the science of physical nature. In fact, Freud himself never fully understood his own research, finally admitting that after thirty years of study he still was unable to figure out what women really wanted.

See where am I going with this? If the readers of the New York Times were gullible enough to believe that only two men in the whole world understood Einstein's theory of relativity – and I don't for a minute think all the subscribers of that paper were that dumb – those same people would also have to believe that no one, not a single living soul, understood Dr. Freud's pioneering psychoanalytical theories, including, of course, Freud himself.

I rest my case (whatever it was).

Elementary, my dear Watson – and Crick

I was Christmas shopping when I spotted Don eating at the Wal-Mart snack shop. Don is a good friend, and he's very smart, which, I've come to realize, is an unusual combination. He was hunched over reading a newspaper article on the mapping of cancer's genetic makeup.

I sat down at his table. "Hi. Got a minute?"

He glanced up. "No, not really."

I nodded understandingly. "This thing called the genome. It's still a mystery to me. What in Hades is it?"

"What's the genome?"

"Exactly."

His gaze returned to the newspaper. "It's *only* the complete set of human genes."

He emphasized the word "only" as if he thought I couldn't hear adverbs very well.

"Ah," I said, gathering my thoughts, "much like a complete set of human teeth?"

He flinched. "Yes, Hugh. Only there are a few more human genes than human teeth. Some seventy thousand more."

I shook my head slowly. "Wow!"

He resumed reading.

I said, "Is jean spelled with a capitol j or lower-case j?"

He folded the newspaper and laid it aside. "It's gene, G E N E! It's a little speck," he said finally, "on a DNA molecule."

"Aha," I said. "Exactly as I figured. What's a DNA—"

"Hold on, Hugh!" He waved at someone behind me. "There's my wife. I have to run."

"You were a big help, Don!" I called after him.

The truth is, I have evolved my own way of understanding difficult scientific concepts, so I really didn't need Don's help. In fact, I'm thinking of writing a book, title it, oh, "Science Made Easy by Grammatical Analysis." The technique is almost too simple to take as gospel, as I will herewith illustrate.

Clearly, the word genome consists of two syllables. Coined in 1920 from the first three letters of the word gene and the last three letters of the word chromosome, geneticists pronounced genome as gen nom, that is, as a two-part word. Which is unfortunate because their way of pronouncing genome prevents a lay person from intuitively understanding what the word means. To circumvent this problem, one must realize that the word genome may also be – in fact should be – pronounced g-nome. Thus, correctly articulated, the first syllable of genome should be pronounced as in the horse-steering command, "Gee, Dobbins!" (And sometimes, "@#$%&*! Gee! Gee! Gee damn it, Dobbins" as, for example, when one is collecting hay into windrows using a horse-drawn hay rake.)

In other words, the first syllable of genome is not pronounced as if the letter g was plosive, as it is in the word "Giddyap." Exactly why, is a can of worms that I had best not open in this short column; no, I'll focus wholly on understanding the genome itself.

Whether genome is pronounced gen-nom or G-nome, the nerdy coconut who came up with the word itself blew it big time. "Nome" was originally the name of a province in ancient Egypt, and "Nom" has meaning mainly in French (as in "nom"de plume). Geneonomenclature would not only have been a superior coinage but also would have been self-defining. Like, who wouldn't know intuitively what the word geneonomenclature stood for? Besides, the word swings. It could even be the middle line of a really cool three-line haiku.

Perhaps the coco-noodle who invented the word genome just didn't like long words. Few scientists do. Even computerists won't abide any but bitty words. (No groaning over the word "bitty." Puns, remember, are the red corpuscles of muscular journalism.)

Again, this brief monograph isn't about language, and it especially is not about the craft of writing. Still, I would be remiss in not mentioning that when it was first coined the word genome was pronounced by radio newsmen as if it was a tri-syllabic word, that is, pronounced G-nom-ee.

To many people, G-nom-ee, even when clearly enunciated, sounded like, "J'ya know me," and, alas, when friends were chatting and the word genome came up, as often happened in conversations centered in duck blinds, around golf course greens, on croquet courts, etc., the listener, certain that he'd been disrespected ("dissed," as the kids say) had stormed off mad.

For example, in 1979 a group of Chinese, misinterpreting a Russian's tri-syllabic pronunciation of genome, "J'ya know me," as a brash put-down, bolted a meeting of geneticists who had rallied at the Walrus Palace Convention Center in Nome, Alaska.

The lone native Alaskan geneticist who attended was able to smooth things over, only to stomp angrily away himself when the Chinese balked at participating in the Eskimo practice of rubbing noses in gratitude.

Whatever. Back to the focus of this column.

As everyone knows, a speck is a very small bit, which is exactly what a gene is. Or, as my pal Don lucidly put it, "A gene is a speck on a DNA molecule."

A DNA molecule, though proportionately smaller than a grain of sand on one of California's mile-long

Pacific Ocean beaches, is still way too large to be classified as a speck.

I make this point because size perspective is fundamental to understanding genetics, DNA, etc. Next in importance is knowing exactly what the letters DNA stand for – which, unfortunately, is a sixteen-letter word that only chemists can remember. It's the same language predicament, incidentally, that for a long time squelched the widespread understanding of Dr. Einstein's "Theory of Relativity." (See title above: "Yes, but Dr. Einstein never came to grips with relative pronouns.")

Chemists, unlike most persons of a scientific bent, pig-out on long words. This is because all chemists have some German blood, and Germans always string together a number of existing words rather than coin a new one. (Creativity is not a hallmark of the German race.)

For example, the term water moccasin (the poison snake, not the water-proof sandal) translates in German to, mokassinwasserschlange, i.e., translates into footware/poison/water/snake.

There's collaborative evidence, by the way, that the Nazis may have won World War II, God forbid, if it hadn't taken so long to transmit and receive orders in the German language.

In fact, many historians believe Hitler didn't commit suicide at the end of the war but choked to death when he twice consecutively shouted, "Du schmutzigverrater!" (you dirty traitor) chasing after Field Marshall Herman Goering as he high-tailed it from his private bunker in Berlin to an awaiting plane. Whether or not Goering truly flipped Hitler a bird, as Goering's defense counsel argued in his War Crimes trial, is a moot point.

Darn, I've run out of space. Explaining all there is to know about the genome by grammatical analysis is taking longer than I had expected. Anyway, I feel I've at least covered enough for a discerning reader to realize that the genome, as one renowned geneticist made clear, is the haploid set of chromosomes and all the genes they contain.

Take that everyday word "haploid." It can be pronounced . . . oh, wait, I'm out of space.

Better Extant I than Sextant I

Jethro, my nephew, can program a VCR, thread a sewing needle, parallel park in one pass, even fix the innards of a worn doorknob. In short, Jed, as we call him, is both smart and dexterous. I doubt if he has *ever* lost money dealing the short-con "Three Card Monte," which con he learned in the Army.

There's a major hitch, however, in Jed's mental "git-along." He has no sense of direction and literally has circuitously wandered around in the interior of small woods for an hour trying to find his way out. If it was snowing, I doubt he could escape in a timely manner from a small city park, even one crisscrossed with well-trod paths of footprints. Jed could decipher a passage from the Rosetta Stone quicker than he could translate the sun's position into a direction for hiking home.

His father, Silas, bought him an expensive compass and taught him how to use it. The first time he put his new-found knowledge to use he broke out of a small forest directly opposite where he had expected to emerge. And that brand-new, high-priced compass was never seen again. Knowing Jed, I imagine he flung it, grenade-like, as far as he could.

In what was supposed to be a midnight, half-mile, naked swim across Conneaut Lake, Pennsylvania's small but nonetheless largest natural lake, Jed spent until 2:00 a.m. swimming an arc that ultimately carried him back to within yards of the dock from where he and his pals had pushed away. Jed grew up in the borough of Conneaut Lake, a village situated at the south end of the lake itself, and the midnight swim was a long-standing, high-school, coming-of-age ritual.

For a while, Jed blamed his slight myopia for his problem. His nearsightedness, however, was easily corrected with eyeglasses, and when he continued to get lost hunting the woods for deer and turkeys he reluctantly conceded that his faulty vision wasn't to blame.

Jed loved to hunt and trap, loved to roam the forests and marshes of rural Crawford County, where often as not he bagged the limit of whatever game was in season – and then traipsed around for an hour, weighed down by his harvest, his gun, wet hunting togs, and unspent ammunition, searching for a way back to his pick-up truck.

While in medical school – Jed is a dentist – he came to grips with the fact that Ferdinand Magellan he wasn't, nor ever would be, and one day he hit on the idea of developing a miniaturized inertial navigation system. He reasoned that other direction-challenged sportsmen could use one to hunt with and to find their way home after traipsing around in a woods afterward. (Inertial navigation devices work on a gyroscopic principle, and unlike GPS, for example, after geographic initialization they do not require external signals to calculate the host system's eventual positions.)

Jed and a friend, an electronics technician, worked evenings tirelessly for six months building a system from parts purchased at an Army-Navy Surplus store in Erie, Pennsylvania. Their plan was to construct a prototype, which they did, and call it Sextant X (X for unknown), and afterwards arrange with a local tool shop to produce it and a Pittsburgh or Cleveland advertising agency to promote it.

In form, the prototype Sextant resembled an encased, one-man oriental rickshaw. Its "load," which was centered over a pair of salvaged bicycle wheels, consisted of two stacked, interconnected, olive-drab metal boxes, one containing an ancient, six-volt motorboat battery, the source of power, and the other enclosing the electro-mechanical Sextant X itself.

Initially, Sextant X didn't work at all: Jed's friend, under the cover of night, trotted it back and forth within the neighborhood where he lived. It worked marginally after an evening of tinkering, however, and they decided it was ready for a real field test.

The neighborhood street trials took place on the Monday which, coincidentally, was the first day of buck deer season. Jed and his friend, eager to prove their invention, scheduled the "real" field test for midday of the coming Thursday, certain that there would be fewer hunters out on that day than at any other time during the two-week dear season.

Jed, canceled his patient appointments for that Thursday, and left by himself, informing his partner beforehand that he would take along his deer rifle, "Just in case."

Well, "Just in case" happened, and Jed not only saw a nice eight-point buck he also shot and hit it. He was sure he'd seriously wounded the big buck, but it didn't go down. Tracing blood spots, scuffled brush, and other signs, he found the deer, lifeless, five minutes later. While he was gutting it, a hunter stopped and congratulated him. Meanwhile, it had started snowing, and dark clouds had begun to roll in.

Not wanting to chance leading the hunter, with whom he was slightly acquainted, to where he'd parked Sextant X, and thinking he could easily retrace his path, he began dragging the heavy deer carcass in the direction opposite to where he'd left Sextant X.

Some hundred yards away, he slowed, listened intently for human sounds, and, hearing none, returned to the spot where he'd gutted his kill.

Jed looked around, and his heart tumbled from his chest: his path back to Sextant X was totally obliterated by snow.

After a long hour of futilely searching for Sextant X, he finally gave in to the weather, the imminence of a really dark nightfall, and the near certainty that his trek home would itself be an adventure.

Early the next day, Jed and his partner struck out for the place where Jed figured they find Sextant X. The morning was bright and sunny, but it had snowed most of the night. After hours of exploring the target area, they threw in the towel, an apt boxing metaphor as that morning they heatedly quarreled (for the first time) and then shortly headed for home; Jed's partner naturally led the way.

The men separately searched for Sextant X on and off for another week, but it had vanished without a trace. What's more, tired of each other, weary of working together most evenings for a half year, and, I suspect, dubious over whether Sextant X would ever truly perform as intended, their plans for fully field-testing Sextant X fell by the wayside.

To this day, neither Jed nor his co-inventor knows the fate of Sextant X. For his part, Jed no longer hunts deer alone. His boys, however – as neither is afflicted by their father's inability to tell directions – are two of the finest young hunters in northwestern Pennsylvania.

It's about Time

Dr. Einstein brought to light a thing or two that was previously unknown about our understanding of Time. Principally, he revealed that timed events happen measurably slower if the context is speeded up. In fact, your pocket watch stops ticking altogether if it is zipping along at the speed of light.

Say you're at the controls of a rocket ship on your way to the planet Mars, and you've really cranked that baby up. Compared to the wall clock in your kitchen back home, your wristwatch will be running slower than usual, acting like it badly needs a lubricating squirt of WD-40.

Einstein, however, totally missed the boat in the matter of Time's many other remarkable and well-documented properties.

For example, he never caught on to the fact that "Time flies when you love your work." Prehistoric cavemen figured that out while gutting, skinning, and quartering a day's hunt. Realizing that the activity was an enjoyable community task, they graciously allowed their mates to take it on.

Time, as everyone knows, is a great healer. Einstein, however, seems not to have appreciated Time's power, in and of itself, to work recuperative wonders.

And exactly what did he think was the agent that turned a tadpole into a frog? That metamorphosed fuzzy crawly things into beautiful butterflies? Gravity? Moonlight? A tender kiss? Hardly.

"Time will tell." How often have you heard that wisdom announced? It's all but unthinkable that Einstein wasn't aware of that innate faculty of Time. Most likely he turned a deaf ear, just plain wouldn't listen to what Time had to say. Scientists are uppity that way. Most even think they're smarter than farmers. My kid sister Coretta, who was forever telling Mother on us boys, should have been named Time.

Nowhere in his papers on relativity does Einstein mention the fact that "Time and tide wait for no man." (In the old days, the word "man," in sayings, proverbs, etc., meant all human beings, not just men.) It's possible, even likely, that he knew better, knew that Time doesn't wait for men but sure as heck waits for women.

Not to make an excuse for the great man, but in fairness let's assume he was always preoccupied and didn't notice Time's habit of discriminating on the basis of gender, those times that he and the Mrs. arrived punctually for a social event, like his Quantum Jumping Club's annual wild, baked raccoon dinner, despite her taking forever to "put on a face."

Time shifted into high gear, of course, if the upcoming social event was a birthday party for his brother-in-law. In that case, punctuality comes in second only to Godliness. If Einstein were aware of this sexist inclination of Time, he knew better than to let on.

There's no disputing the fact that "Time is money." Einstein showed mathematically how energy and mass are the same thing. So, how come he never got around to proving the existence of an equivalent relationship between Time and money? Since $E=mc^2$, shouldn't $T=\$c^2$. That is, shouldn't Time equal the product of money and the speed of light squared. Is that so hard?

Equalities pairing Time and other stuff are probably a dime a dozen. Only, thanks to Einstein's constricted understanding of Time, we may never know. Are you beginning to wonder, as I am, if Dr. Einstein truly wasn't a one-dimensional guy?

"A stitch in time saves nine?" I doubt Einstein did a lot of sewing, but, darn, that's no excuse for his overlooking the power of Time in underscoring the most boring of tasks. Tarry in heeding your wife's call to supper and you can bet the conversation around the table won't keep you in stitches. (Okay, I've misconstrued the meaning of that saying. Never mind. This piece is basically anecdotal, not one of my usual scrupulously researched, statistically unchallengeable, smack-on essays, so cut me a little slack here.)

"Time marches on" – glacially when you're behind a woman or an elderly driver plodding along just under the speed limit; "Time changes things," and we humans along with it: our skin wrinkles, hair vanishes, sagging happens, etc.; "Time is fleeting,' (see above regarding Time's swiftness while a man is dressing to attend a party for his wife's brother); and so on.

In other words, I've barely scratched the surface regarding the many commonly known powers of Time that Dr. Einstein negligently failed to research.

There's a "Time and place for everything," however, and this seems like the moment to end this long-past-due unmasking of the many shortcomings of Dr. Einstein's over-praised and exclusionary notion of the varied nature of Time.

Meanwhile, I may do a little investigating of Time myself. I'm retired and have plenty of Time on my hands. Besides, if "Time is money," why ain't I rich?

Moose on the loose

My friend makes a good living fixing personal computers. A sturdy, full-chested, fellow, his nickname is "Moose."

Moose's interest in computers is obsessive, and I kid him that his last name should be "Modem," as in "Moose Modem."

We met last Tuesday at a bar on North Street for a lunch of beer and Buffalo wings.

"Who won the game last night?" I asked as we settled into a booth. "I sacked out early."

Moose half drained his glass. "Computers, you know, really aren't all that complicated."

"Neither is Pick-up Sticks," I said. "Who won the game?"

He nodded. "When you get right down to nut-cracking time . . . down to the nitty-gritty, computers can't even count past two."

I internalized a "Huh," but I knew what was coming: one of his dull musings on the fundamental nature of a computer's mode of operation, but I couldn't stop myself. "Really? Can't even count past two, huh?"

"Nope."

"So, they just sit there going one two, one two, one two, one–"

"It's all the fundamental components do. Only they go zero one, zero one, zero one."

I mentioned Moose in, "Fancy that," another column. He is convinced that people who are as dumb as I am about computer fundamentals are not only congenital nitwits but also members of a sect of latter-day Luddites who one day will rise up and resentfully smash all the world's computers to smithereens. He seemed to think I was among the few worth saving. (Oh to be eight years old again.)

"That's all," I asked skeptically, "that the fundamental components do?"

"Indeed. All that the millions of tiny, nearly invisible transistorized circuits *can* do."

"Gracious," I mumbled, pretending to be impressed.

He nodded. "First, understand that the only thing any one group of those itsy-bitsy transistorized circuits can do is very simple arithmetic, either add or subtract. Literally. Any computer, from ENIAC, the world's first – which wouldn't fit in a gymnasium – to a lap-top that is barely half the size of a small briefcase."

I shrugged. "So. You expect me to believe that when I'm using my word processor I'm actually doing simple arithmetic?"

He laughed. "You? You couldn't add two small numbers together using a four-function pocket calculator! Alone in a sound-proof room! After a good night's sleep! No, you are not doing arithmetic. But the computer in your word processor sure as heck is."

Moose's voice, sounding, as usual, like a cricket with laryngitis, drives me nuts, so I tune him out at regular intervals. What follows are the parts of his babbling that I actually heard and remembered – more or less.

According to Moose, the heart, soul, and brain of a personal computer are combined in a processor that he went on to describe in terms nobody outside the business of designing computers understands, least of all me.

He glared when I asked, "What about its liver, spleen, and gallbladder?"

"Anyway," he went on, "if you pop the lid of a microprocessor, inside you'd find a chip of silicon, not half the size of a postage stamp, imbedding more sub-microscopic transistor amplifiers than there are people on earth, a place where the point of a straight pin – he emphasized the word point – would loom bigger than a football field, where time-wise one blink of an eye, relatively speaking, would seem to go on and on and on.

The "gazillion" (his word) impossibly small transistor amplifiers, all interconnected in one way or another, principally serve, it turned out, as a kind of many-page tablet on which numbers, letters, and other characters may be written.

He paused, waited to see if I was paying attention.

"Using a pencil or pen?" I asked shamelessly.

A tad less patient than a second earlier, he replied that characters in a computer are represented as sets of voltage levels."

"Really?" I said.

"That's right, Dolt," he answered sarcastically. "Voltage levels! A set of seven either high or low voltages for each letter . . . for each number, for a comma, for a hyphen, and so on. Seven voltages either high or low . . . seven binary voltage levels . . . seven separate voltages allow for up to one-hundred twenty-eight characters."

"Of course. But you used the word, 'written.' Why don't you computer nut-cakes say, 'characters are represented'? Is the English language that hard?"

He sighed. "Whatever, Hugh."

"Okay, and why seven voltages per character. Why not make elementary devices capable of ten different voltages? Instead of two? Wouldn't that simplify the design?"

"Very good, Hugh! The answer is a real-world reason."

I groaned. "Real world?"

Nodding, he said, "But, let me explain something first. Those gazillion little transistorized circuits? Like I said, all they can do is turn off and on, never settle somewhere in between. Think ceiling-light switches."

He gathered himself. "Now here's where you have to stretch your mind a little. Doesn't the physical switching back and forth between On and Off amount, in the abstract, to a form of counting . . . one-two, one-two, and so on, where ON corresponds the number 1 and OFF to the number 0?"

Totally clueless, I grasped my chin, squinted thoughtfully, and nodded slowly – very slowly.

He bought it.

"Those gazillion tiny transistorized circuits are wedged together proportionately about the same as grains of sand on a stretch of beach. And each is sitting on either a high-voltage 1 or a low voltage 0 waiting patiently to be switched to the opposite state – millions of times a second."

"I'll be darned," I said, slightly shaking my head. Sometimes I even fool my wife by blending those words with that gesture and then embellishing my simulated concern with clicks of my tongue.

I said, "Okay, I see how a number or a letter is represented, but how are numbers added together? And letters combined onto words?"

"Easy," he answered, "by algorithms, by long established algorithms."

"Oh," I said, clueless.

"Uh-huh," Moose said, "by a procedure that mathematically solves a problem . . . like the steps of long-division arithmetic."

"Pleased with himself, Moose drained his glass and pushed it toward the bartender. I finished my beer but shook off the bartender.

I said, "I'll take you at your word, that computers can only do simple arithmetic – you're not describing your golf game – but why binary arithmetic? Why not decimal? What's the big deal about–"

"Finally," he replied, sounding as if he'd been waiting a long time at a depot for a train to pull in. By his tone, I knew he meant that I had finally asked a half-way intelligent question.

"Because," he continued, "it's all but impossible to make an elementary, unified, ten-state semiconductor chip, one that doesn't eventually start misfiring. Sometimes the real world intrudes."

"Misfiring?"

"Yeah, like the engine in your Yugo, or whatever you're driving these days. Over time, ten-state electronic devices become, oh, eight-state devices."

"Ten states good, eight states bad, eh"

He nodded, more or less. "But, a two-state transistor operates at a rock-solid on-voltage or at a rock-solid off-voltage. Practically forever."

None of it made sense, so I said, "Makes sense to me. By the way, how big is a gazillion."

"A google," he offered without hesitation, "followed by six zeroes."

"Still," I said cautiously, "isn't binary arithmetic a lot more, ah, involved than digital arithmetic?"

"In a sense. If you only had thumbs and no fingers you wouldn't think so. But so what? Computers have speed and switches to burn. Light wouldn't travel a tiny fraction of a millimeter meter during a dozen binary math computations."

"Light moves pretty fast, huh?"

"Only about three hundred million meters a second . . . as Albert would tell you."

"You mean as Al would tell me. All the real scientists that I know refer to Doctor Einstein as Al."

"Yeah, like most people remember Sir Isaac Newton, as Izzy. Any more of your, ah, questions?"

"Yeah. Who won the game last night?"

AS THE TWIG IS BENT

Chances are, Lizzie Borden's mother was Irish

An old joke currently making the rounds by email reads something like this: "Tim and Patti, both in their early twenties and single, theoretically are living opposite each other on the same floor of an apartment building. Tim's Irish mother, her first visit to Tim's place, concludes that they are sleeping together. It is comportment that chills every cockle of her good Catholic heart. Tim and Patti earnestly pretend that they are sleeping separately, however.

Patti, a few days after Tim's mother returns home, can't find her sterling silver necklace. After ruling out all other possibilities, Tim telephones his mother and tactfully asks if she had seen Patti's necklace. "Yes, Timothy," she tells him, "I know exactly where it is. Check under the pillow on Patti's side of the bed."

Although the rhetoric misleads, it is pretty clear the moral of the story is that Irish mothers aren't to be trusted.

Centuries ago, the forming of McClintock clans began concurrently in Scotland and Ireland; our particular clan came into being in Ireland. It hurts to admit this, but nobody from either tribe amounted to a tinker's damn (the legacy persists). Worse, some members were just plain scofflaws, the most devious of the bunch having been elected to the Irish House of Commons.

I mention these details of my ancestry only to assure you that I know of what I write regarding the dark side of Irish motherhood.

Take the Irish word "shillelagh." Thought to have been named after a village in Ireland, further research has proven the word actually began life as a feminine pronoun. No joke. A feminine pronoun! (Instead of saying "She and I are friends," a Celtic forebear would say, "Shillelagh and I are friends.")

Although an account of exactly how "shillelagh" evolved from a feminine pronoun into the name for a small weapon is too involved to include here, there's no denying, however, that the progression made sense. Unfortunately, there's no chance that the factual history will be published. This is because women are now running America's literary agency business, and remotely sexist accounts of everything will never see the light of day.

For proof, consider this never-reported incident: Very late one evening a male journalist employed by the venerable New York Times, while working alone and furiously trying to meet a deadline, was caught by a guard relieving himself in a handy lady's restroom. Needless to say, he was forthwith blackballed from ever again dangling a participle for the Times or any other major newspaper.

But I digress.

Another fact will further illuminate the shadowy corner of Irish motherhood. Irish mothers spank their children, whale the health right out of them whenever they think it's warranted – which is any time one of their kids twice consecutively forgets to say, "Thank you" – provided the kid isn't bandaged head to toe in a body cast recovering in a hospital bed from a near fatal automobile accident.

I'm not exaggerating. Many times I petitioned God – racing home breathlessly from some late-running childhood game – to encourage Mother to undergo a "road to Damascus" conversion, not to Protestantism, but to Judaism, certain as I was that Jewish mothers limited their disciplinary blistering to assaulting their kids' ears.

Not that Jewish mothers are perfect either, but suffice it to point out there's no word in Hebrew even close to meaning the same thing as "shillelagh."

(On the other hand, the word "hectoring," traced to a line in King David's own hand telling of Bathsheba's incessant nagging – David was loath to make her queen – is Hebrew to the bone. Fairness and journalistic balance demand that I mention this Biblical fact.)

Irish mothers do not stop at mere spankings either. No less punishing is the merciless heaping of their children's dinner plates at supper time, the amassing of boiled green vegetables in quantities the Jolly Green Giant himself couldn't finish, even if each bite was pressed to his lips by a pretty nymph of the same ethnicity as old Jolly himself.

And, either you clean your plate slicker than a shiny new Corvette wheel cover, or you can wash and dry all the supper dishes by yourself.

Keep in mind that I'm talking about portions of food prepared by an Irish mother, not culinary delights whipped up by a female parent of Italian descent. I know what you're thinking, that the cooking could even be worse, that "Mom" could be of pure English stock. Or the food prepared kosher style, washed of every speck of flavor it ever possessed (which in the case of broccoli is not a bad thing). Or, heaven forbid, one of the vegetables could be a hefty portion of refried pinto beans baked to tastelessness. In any event, character development by forced ingestion of large quantities of spinach, broccoli, asparagus, and other greens, not one of which is a bit tastier than steamed binder twine, easily meets the Constitutional definition of cruel and unusual punishment.

I could go on and on, turn these few observations into a tiresome screed on the many failings of Irish mothers. But that is not my intent – far from it.

A saying – often a politician's rebuttal to criticism – has it that any jackass can kick a barn down but it takes a carpenter to build one. Admittedly, I don't work well with my hands. Still, I'm certain I could hammer together a shrine where every element of construction represented an honorable quality of Irish motherhood. Naturally, I would generously equip my monument with well-grounded lightening rods.

Hold on. In checking my draft of this piece, I now see where the moral of the story of Tim's and Patti's improper cohabitation as easily could be: "Never fib to an Irish mother."

The problem with that interpretation, however, is the implication that youthful evasions of the truth would slip right by mothers who aren't Irish. If you believe that, maybe you'd be interested in the long-term boarding one of our wonderfully behaved, half-Irish, teen-age grandkids – for almost any reasonable charge.

Second only to Drano

President H. W. Bush was "smack-on" about broccoli. ("Smack-on" is kid talk for correct, right, faultless, etc. Fish a brook for chubs with a grandchild and you learn these things.) Anyway, Mr. Bush said broccoli smells like an old tennis shoe and probably tastes as bad as it smells. Okay, I read a little into what he actually said, but the connotation is apt.

For a person of ordinary sense of smell, that is, for a person whose olfactory nerves faithfully carry the smell to his brain, the fumes alone bring on a fit of Montezuma's revenge. Dr. Kevorkian, it's believed, force-fed his terminally ill patients steamed broccoli so they'd beg for relief. The only thing that tastes worse isn't food at all, its castor oil.

Corporal punishment, when we were siblings – four of us, all grade-school students – was still in vogue. In most regards our mother was more or less indifferent to prevailing customs, but she lived that particular chastening to the hilt.

Every other week, on average, the calloused palm of Father's right hand turned one of our bottoms from ordinary, flesh-colored pink to a warmer shade of red. That's how it worked at our home: Mother decreed and Father dispensed.

It wasn't so much the thought of a spanking that set one of us to quaking, however, as it was to hearing Mother utter the words "castor oil" in a pronouncement that, somewhere along the line, imbedded the word "physic." Limp into her kitchen with a twisted ankle, say, and directly, under orders, you were hobbling for the bathroom in search of a smelly liniment of eye-watering potency with the admonition, "And don't forget the castor oil," clanging in your ears. No matter the affliction, rare were the times when she didn't append that command when ordering one of us to fetch a nostrum from the medicine cabinet.

Mother knew instinctively (and worse inarguably) that castor oil not only possessed the flushing power of an aircraft carrier deck hose but could also stave off malaria, dislodge pneumonia, and, by mere mention of its name, transform a nascent bruise into a purple badge of courage. Incidentally, she considered the nickname "Mom" no less a profanity than the lowest of four-letter epithets, an eccentricity I have obviously respected in this piece.

Suffering a "temperature," which degree of hotness Mother measured by cupping the calibrated palm of her right hand to a forehead, was the kiss of death, a sign from St. Patrick, if not from God himself, that not only good health but also salvation was certain only through the ingestion of a large slug of castor oil. Among us kids, the bad-luck number 13 had nothing on a number such as 101 – degrees Fahrenheit above zero. Houses in our neighborhood, all of economical clapboard siding, were built with only one bathroom, which was typical of the time and place. If a house had two stories, as was usually the case, the bathroom was situated on the second floor, central to bedrooms. And making it up the stairs from the kitchen – once the castor oil had begun its own relentless journey downward – wasn't all that easy, especially with one hand otherwise occupied and the other using the banister as a kedging anchor.

For a spell, Mother, sensitive to our caterwauling at her mere mention of castor oil (in the context of applying that universal curative), tried masking the taste of castor oil by combining it with orange juice and baking soda in what became a vile-looking slurry – and worst tasting one, too. One day our father, a bit under the weather but nonetheless intent on setting a good example for his kids, gulped down a half glass of the foul-tasting mess. He shortly threw up in the kitchen sink – and elsewhere. Mother, after Pop's splattery episode, returned to ladling out doses of straight castor oil. Plainly her heart was no longer in it, however, and when the castor oil ran out she turned to spooning us Epsom salts.

Originally the distillation of water from a well in Epsom, England, the salt – trust me if you don't already know – is no less powerful a cathartic than castor oil. (Epsom, incidentally, is a town in the county of Surrey where the English Derby is run.)

A Dutchman visiting the site in the late seventeenth century described the salt's effectiveness as "extraordinarily excellent," that during a long walk it "achieving the desired result of putting down sentinels in the shrubs in every direction." (Sentinels? Never mind.)

In its own way, Epsom salts tastes as bad as castor oil. Leave it to the English to come up with the Holy Grail of vile-tasting potables.

I now realize – alas, many years too late – that Mother could have passed a serving of steaming broccoli under my nose and achieved the same irrigation of viscera as she did in ladling a tablespoon brimming with castor oil down my throat. True, a saucer of broccoli is hardly a side dish of ambrosia, but it sure beats the taste of oil pressed from the poisonous leaves (true) of castor oil plants.

Having thought more about it, I'm now convinced that the first President Bush never once tasted castor oil. Likely, he ingested some sissy laxative such as Fletcher's Castoria. But, if he had, thereby affording him a chance to compare the smell of broccoli to the flavor of castor oil, he wouldn't have lost the big broccoli vote and may have been elected to a second term.

Baggage that comes with the name Hugh

By chance, good neighbor, did you read the recent AP story in the newspaper titled, "Manatees may be smarter than we think"? I hope not, because if you did you are worse off for it.

Clearly, the article's sole purpose was to denigrate the good and respectable first name of "Hugh." An etymologically challenged researcher gave that name to a 1300-pound manatee penned in a tank at a marine laboratory in Florida.

Grown manatees are essentially half-ton, water-dwelling slugs. They're not a bit smarter than slugs, either. For example, they pig-out on seaweed, imagining, no doubt, they're wolfing down bacon cheeseburgers. Slow-moving and stolid, some people – wholly indifferent to affronting bovines – call them sea cows. Odds are, manatees evolved from sunken logs.

Giving a dolphin the name "Hugh" at least makes sense: dolphins are sociable, acrobatic, and can swim circles around a manatee. But naming a manatee

"Hugh" is as far off-target as naming a great white shark "Cookie."

Probably the goober in Florida who christened that poor captive manatee never heard of King Hugh Unger II of Waxony. A great king, fair, etc., he ruled far longer than did most monarchs, including iconic Hugh O'Neil, the Earl of Tyrone, who was a power unto himself.

Alas, historians have little to say about King Hugh Unger II. This is because he was religiously monogamous and therefore – that personal trapping being about as exciting as a second helping of refried beans – was not worth the academic research.

The kingdom of Waxony eventually became a German republic, and the citizens began at once naming their children after the revered King Hugh Unger II. Traditionally, the name was given to a child born on Sunday. Nobody is sure why. Anyway, "Hugh" derives from the Teutonic word "hug" and means "heart" or "mind" or "spirit." (Of course, it may mean "craw," "spleen," or "bladder," too.)

My mother, God love her soul, thought that "Hugh" meant "smart." Her early appraisal of my physical qualities convinced her to try and pass me off as intelligent, hence my name. Around my sixth birthday, she would sometimes slip up and call me "Homer," which clearly isn't even marginally better than "Hugh."

I've learned a few things on my own about the name "Hugh." For one, it is an awful first name for a salesman or a politician; people just can't remember it. I know of this difficulty because my ever-present bunkmates in the service couldn't keep it in their minds. Then one began calling me "Mac" (short, if a bit skewed, for "McClintock") and soon everyone in the squadron was my friend. "Hi Mac," a fellow airman would say when we walked past each other. I would smile cluelessly and answer, "How you doin'!" or "How's it goin'!" or come out heartily with something equally anchorless.

In Korea I was called "Skoshi." I'm not sure of the spelling, but in the Korean language – actually it may be a Japanese word – it means small and is pronounced Sko she. In those days I weighed in at one-hundred-twenty-seven pounds and was in the best fighting trim of my life – okay, the best pinochle-playing trim of my life. Never mind.

At a stateside post I was known as "Hug-eye," literally called that by my fellow enlistees, not to mention being addressed thunderingly as "Private Hug-eye!" by the captain in charge of Supply, where I was briefly assigned.

A fellow supply clerk suggested the name. He remembered it from when a grade-school classmate who, reading an assignment aloud, pronounced the name Hughie as Hug-eye. The supply clerk attended grade school in Ohio, so it's not likely that he made the story up.

For the record, I never liked my first name. But then many people insist they don't like their given name, so I guess it's not the name Hugh itself.

As a matter of fact, my name's only saving grace is the song, "You, You, You," (I'm in love with you, you, you) which was a hit recording in the fifties (by the Mills Brothers?). Many listeners, especially those with a place for romance in their heart, thought they were singing "Hugh, Hugh, Hugh, I'm in love with Hugh, Hugh, Hugh." At any rate, that's what I thought they were singing the first time I heard it.

In fact, "Hugh, Hugh, Hugh, etc.," was the original title of "You, you, you, etc." until some genius advertising account executive – likely related to the bird-brain who named the hostage manatee "Hugh" – proposed re-titling the song "Hugo, Hugo, Hugo, I'm in Love with Hugo, Hugo, Hugo." The last anyone heard, he was eking out a living writing set-up instructions for Japanese–designed futons made in China.

Which reminds me: forty per cent of the world's Chinese population have only ten surnames. That's a fact. Zhou, pronounced as in "Zhou, Zhou, Zhou, I'm in love with Zhou, Zhou, Zhou," is one of the ten.

Where was I? Oh yes, the name "Hugh" carries a lot of baggage. Another time I . . . oops, I'm out of space, just enough room to float the name "Morris" as a becoming name for a manatee. "Morris the Manatee." Kind of sings, doesn't it?

Um, maybe not. Some oversensitive, narrow-minded new mother might take offense.

Food for thought

I do not work well with my hands; I have trouble screwing lids on canning jars and performing similar challenging tasks demanding extraordinary dexterity. You may remember my account of how, as a young, miscast apprentice tool-and-die maker, I flunked Tool Bit Sharpening 101.

My next-door neighbor could strop a wood chisel into a surgical scalpel in the dark, hanging by his knees from a rafter. I once sharpened a set of expensive, bone-handled steak knives, a splendid wedding gift given to Nellie and me, into a set of butter knives that looked as if they had tumble out of the back of a truck hauling trash to a dump. The last guy to sharpen my chainsaw suggested that I limit all my blade-sharpening efforts to hosing the mud off spades and shovels.

Behavioral psychologists are at odds over why some people have a knack for this and others a knack for that. Unfortunately, as persons of science, psychologists have this unyielding thirst for complicating matters, which explains how it is they miss the obvious.

Trust me, genuine natural ability of any sort is neither inherent nor something that can be learned. And certainly God has better things to do than oversee the apportioning of talent among the faithful.

Then what is the answer? Why can some men deftly carve an exquisitely baked Thanksgiving turkey and other men turn into a turkey trying to hack off one of its legs? (Which amputation – shades of the Devil – magically transforms the leg into a drumstick.)

The explanation is simple, and it's been right under our noses forever. It's a matter of what we eat. That's right: behavior depends on a person's nutritional regimen. Whoever wrote that "You are what you eat," hit the nail on the head.

Machinists – I know this first hand – are big on liver and onions.

The brilliant Albert Einstein wouldn't touch a meal that didn't include a side dish of boiled cabbage; in fact, often steamed cabbage was all he ate for supper.

Poets gobble down citrus fruits the way squirrels wolf down sunflower seeds.

Mathematicians eat a side of Grape-nut cereal with every meal, proving, thus, that they like to crunch cereal as well as numbers.

Farmers, who can do anything, eat everything.

I could go on and on, but the connection between diet and ability is crystal clear. Besides, this piece is about effect, not cause, about observable differences in raw talent, not about tracing those differences to obscure digestive processes.

My brother Silas can knock fifty well-flung clay pigeons from the air with fifty shots from a choked twelve-gauge shotgun. It would take me fifty rounds to shatter fifty clay pigeons still packed in their original carton. (Of course, I could sneak up on them.) The point is, Silas has this knack for hitting whatever he's aiming at, and I don't. What was his favorite snack? You guessed it: raw carrots.

Don, whom I've known forever, loves meat but hates fish. A golfer, he always reaches a green in two strokes – three at the most – his ball never stopping farther than a few yards from the cup. But to save his soul he can't finish a hole in one putt. He would even rim-out a cup situated at the small end of a big funnel. When he plays putt-putt golf, he confuses narrow angles with wide angles and generally withdraws from a game the second time a rebounding ball whacks him on the shin. Don, in other words, drives a little like Tiger Woods and putts a lot like Tiger Lilly, the Knoxville, Tennessee Bijou waltz queen. In short, diet giveth and diet taketh away.

Aunt Mildred, her soul now peacefully at rest – I presume – could decode a word cryptogram in her head, solve word jumbles at a glance, and finish crossword puzzles as fast as she could print the letters. Unlike Albert Einstein, she wasn't fond of boiled cabbage. But she never got enough steamed asparagus, which obviously worked for her in the same way that cabbage strengthened Einstein's brain.

On the other hand, Aunt Mildred couldn't judge volume, was never able to tell the difference between a four-once juice glass and a two-ounce shot glass. Living out her life in a nursing home, for years a friend smuggled vodka to her in cardboard orange-juice cartons. It took me a while to understand why she couldn't master writing poetry, given her prodigious ability with words, but I finally concluded that booze neutralizes the creative potency of citrus juice.

As a group, waiters and waitresses have uncommonly strong short-term memories. Think it's easy serving a table of eight diners and remembering which old biddy wants the cucumbers left out of her garden salad and which aging fuddy-duddy wants his half-order of French fries served on the side? Or keeping the different drink orders straight? Competent waiters and waitresses are always in short supply. Most, I'd wager, drink four or five mugs of caffeinated coffee every morning. I plan to check it out.

On the subject of serving food, I'm reminded of this related but little-known footnote to history. When Napoleon conscripted the flower of France's manhood to invade Europe, an enterprising restaurateur in Lyon, France, unable to hire competent waiters, came up with the idea of buffet dining. (And if buffet dining is not another good reason to flip France a bird, what is?)

I could go on and on, reinforcing anecdotally my theory of how diet makes the man. The problem is, I'm running out of space. And I hate leaving the impression that I'm all thumbs, as I may have in the opening lines to this piece. I'm not. I can hammer nails into wood (excluding the skinny, headless finishing kind), roll-paint walls and ceilings, inflate car tires, tread water, do a lot of things requiring above-average dexterity.

A little tweaking of my diet and before long I'd be changing the oil in my truck, not just checking it. Should I start pigging out on fruit, soon my columns would be stanzas of Miltonian poetry instead of paragraphs of barely workaday prose.

On second thought, give up wolfing down bacon cheeseburgers so I can change the oil in a car? Forego the joy of spooning my way to the bottom of a deep-dish peach cobbler to write poetry? It must be something I ate.

Could be my father was Custer's nephew

My father quit high school and went to work for the Erie Railroad Company – anything , I once overheard him tell a friend, to escape the drudgery of milking, haying, and slopping hogs.

In those days – the mid-1920s – Erie Railroad had a car repair shop situated in Meadville, Pennsylvania, the city where we lived. Father ran a complicated, belt-driven machine of decidedly unknown origin, which he also had to maintain. The Erie Railroad has since changed hands several times; moreover, the Meadville repair shop has long been history.

That's about all I remember hearing of my father's steady, first-paying job, except that over the years he was able to accumulate enough home-made tools to fill a wooden chest the size of a small steamer trunk.

A picture of a weird-looking, tool-like, something-or-other, which was recently provided to our local newspaper by a subscriber, reminded me of those times and in particular of the day I decided to inventory the contents of Father's tool chest. I hadn't started elementary school yet – grade school as we called it then – but the day wasn't far off.

When Father returned home from work that evening, I had all his tools – several were no less a mystery than the mechanical gadgets featured in the picture sent in by the newspaper reader – strewn about on the garage floor. I'm sure Mother secretly looked in on me now and then and likely each time tiptoed quietly away.

I perfectly recall the look of anger on Father's face at seeing his precious tools scattered all over the dirt floor of our garage. Grabbing the nearest tool, a ball-peen hammer, I asked innocently, "What is this, Father?" Even at that tender age I knew instinctively, as do all youngsters, that the best defense against an angry parent is a quick inoffensive question and that the name "Father" was more respectful than Dad or Daddy, which is how I usually addressed the "Old Man," er, ah, Father.

His features gradually softened, and seconds later his face took on the look of a person with something up his sleeve; it was a facial expression I'd seen before. Shaking his head thoughtfully, he took a deep breath. "That one," he answered somberly, referring to the hammer I was holding, "Goes back to the time when I was an Indian fighter."

Father wasn't predisposed to judge a person on his skin color or for that matter any other superficiality – an uncommon attitude of white males in the 1930s – nevertheless he somehow had it in his head that most Indians were fierce savages and that battling one in hand-to-hand combat was a paramount endeavor of male bravery.

Seldom did a week pass when a cowboys-and-Indians oat-burner wasn't showing at one of Meadville's three cinemas – almost weekly at the small Mead Theater on Water Street – and perhaps he drew inspiration from the advertising of those B-movie westerns.

According to Father, David Mead, Meadville's nominal founder, had single-handedly fought off a band of Mohawk braves bent on kidnapping all the tiny settlement's children. A few days after he told me that whopper – I believe I was seven – I regaled my grade-school classmates at story-telling time with this little known "fact" of western Pennsylvania history – to their rapt attention and, no doubt, to our teacher's secret amusement. Father, incidentally, was scrupulously honest except when he was plainly making stuff up.

"What's it called?" I asked, pretty sure the tool that I showed him was a hammer of sorts. As it turned out, it was a "ball-peen" hammer: I was bewildered over the thought of pounding nails with its rounded off-head.

"It's called a war hammer," Father answered. "It's worn on your belt. Give it here, and I'll show you."

Sitting on my legs – on my calves – I scampered to my knees and offered Father the hammer. He waved it menacingly over his head, and in the process forgetting that he was standing directly under the garage's middlemost single source of light, a bare, incandescent, 75-watt bulb suspended from a roof truss by a cord of twisted-wires.

His second swipe clobbered the bulb in the manner of a direct hit on a Mexican piñata and showered the two of us with tiny shards of frosted glass. Sparks flew.

Both of us jumped – being on my knees, I more flinched than jumped – and Father fled in the direction of the open garage door, warily assessing the situation over his shoulder on the way.

I was too young, at the time, to think of a snappy remark but have since thought of several: "Legendary Indian fighter scalps light bulb," or "Aged Indian fighter can't see the light," or "Misdirected ball-peen hammer fatally wounds light bulb," or "Fire when ready, Father!" and so on.

Father didn't read books, so a subtle barb such as "The Last of the Mohawks," a play on James Fennimore Cooper's acclaimed novel of a similar title, would have been wasted unless Mother or another better-read person had been around to hear it.

Father's sweeping blow with the ball-peen hammer not only destroyed the light bulb, it also – forever as I recall – sent packing the ghost of Meadville's legendary Indian fighter T. G. McClintock.

Father and I had most of the tools picked up when Mother strolled into the garage; he hadn't made known his arrival home yet from work, and I suppose she was curious.

"What are you bozos up to in the dark?" Mother wanted to know.

"Father," I volunteered hastily, "broke the light bulb."

"How in the world . . ." Mother began. She finished her thought with the observation that the rear garage window was "filthy dirty," a fact brought out, no doubt, by the faintness of light inside.

Father glanced sharply at me before asking Mother, "What's for supper, Dear?"

"Crow," Mother answered. "The first course will be humble soup."

I looked to Father for an explanation, but he was inventorying his jumble of tools on the floor, a slight smile on his lips. It was years before I understood what in the deuce Mother meant by her answer. I have since smugly used a derived version of her reply at opporture times.

On cooking breakfast and kindred adventures

Until recently, the kitchen in our home was the room that I indifferently ambled through on my way to the garage. The kitchen, as a place for actually doing something like, oh, cooking food, I topped out at fixing a bowl of Puffed Wheat, nuking a cup of coffee that had cooled, and, on a morning after a good night's sleep, toasting bread right the first try.

I've been on my own for several months now, long enough to come to terms with all our kitchen appliances. Frankly, our face-offs weren't always pretty.

In any event, I offer this column of "do's," "don't's," and "should-haves" to senior males who one day may travel the same gnarly road I stumbled along to become the accomplished amateur chef that I now am. Trust me guys, it's a path impossible to safely navigate without a map flagging all the ankle-twisting ruts.

Start slow. First, locate the anchor units of your kitchen. These are the sink, the refrigerator, and the stove – or range as women sometimes call a stove. The wall switch over the sink? It turns on a food grinder connected to the sink's drain. So don't expect that flipping it to On will illuminate the sink and surrounding area, and don't panic at the sudden unmuted growling sound it causes.

Move on to the cupboards. The one whose inside looks like it is holding seed junk for a scrap-iron yard? Those are your pots and pans. (At this point, do not attempt, under any circumstances, to remove anything from under anything else inside that cupboard. You do, and it's ground-zero right in your own kitchen.)

Generally, appliances sitting on the counter top are self-explanatory. The one that looks like it has no purpose in life is a motor-driven can opener. Look on the top-front for a sharp-edged disk about the size of a dime, and directly underneath a gear of about the same size. Slip the top, outside edge of a can – say of peas – between these two opposing parts and then push down on the lever on top. This action will rotate the can slightly and unintentionally dislodge it from the opener. Repeat these steps until the can stays in place, and the cutting disk has circumnavigated the top of the can. The lid should easily come off. If it doesn't, try a can of spinach. Persevere.

Study the contents of the refrigerator and food pantry. Take notes for future reference. (Now is a good time to toss out the vegetables you've pretended to like all your married life.)

Tackle the cupboard drawers last – cautiously. At least one will resemble Pandora's box, a drawer so overstuffed with utensils, and God knows what else, that the contents, when the drawer is opened, may fly out and injure a person lingering nearby.

Once certain of your way around the kitchen, you're ready to step up to the plate, so to speak, and prepare your first meal. Without a copilot, however, a cautious approach is best. And if heat is involved, you're pushing the envelope, pal.

My solo flight is illustrative. Rather easily, I must say, and without incident, I readied a bowl of Wheaties, a heftier, far less manageable dish than Puffed Wheat.

Thus inspired, the next day I successfully cooked up a bowl of rolled oats, serendipitously learning in the process that mashed oat buds are easily removed from the hood of a range by something called Soft Scrub. Steel wool also works but is a tad hard on the hood's paint.

Also, men, be aware that the cooking instructions on a Quaker Oats canister are impossible. For example, what in the heck is a "dash" of salt? Well, it turns out that it's far less than a teaspoonful, as I discovered firsthand. Cooked rolled oats, by the way, can be preserved by freezing, should you happen to cook too much the first attempt.

Naturally, man does not live by cereal alone, although I did for several weeks, before deciding I was ready for a culinary quantum leap: the preparation of a bacon-and-eggs breakfast! Okay, I actually used pre-cooked sausage. Close enough.

The trick to cooking up a meat-and-egg breakfast is getting everything properly cooked at the same time. The learning curve is steep and discontinuous, and it may take six to eight breakfasts. That's assuming you don't add potatoes to the mix. If you include potatoes, you'll likely burn the eggs, under fry the spuds, and end up eating each item of food consecutively, beginning with the toast and eventually consuming the half-raw potatoes.

The first time I fried potatoes for breakfast the yokes of my eggs, which were warming in another pan, turned into little round cushions suitable for protecting carpeting under the legs of our sofa. The metamorphosis was doubly disappointing because I had reached the point where a skillet of my sunny-side-up eggs no longer ended up on my plate looking like a white-and-yellow casserole – with an attitude.

Speaking of potatoes, here's something I'll bet your wife never told you: it takes a lot longer to boil potatoes than, say, to grill a hamburger patty.

Women intuitively know this. They also know that pot-watching prevents the water in a saucepan from boiling. I learned this on my own. Unfortunately, while so engrossed in thus educating myself, the lid for my frying pan welded to the pan itself, encasing forever a hamburger patty inside. Evidently the pan's Teflon coating out-gassed, as that polymer does at high temperatures, and formed a weld bead where the lid and pan came together.

Hoping for a little sympathy, I told of my misfortune to a lady friend. What I got back was, "You dumb donkey (family newspaper), why'd you put a lid on the pan in the first place? You never use a lid to grill meat." Yakkity yak.

Whatever, the pan had seen better days.

Of course nothing goes better with a bacon-and-egg breakfast than a short stack of golden-brown pancakes – not in my book, anyway. Pancakes are easy to make, and there's several kinds of off-the-shelf, pre-blended mixes. Preparation is simple. You measure a little of the mix into a bowl, add a (de-shelled) egg or two, pour in fresh milk, and stir to a fare-the-well. Thickness (think viscosity, men) is important, and you may have to experiment off-range before ladling the batter onto a hot griddle. If the concoction is too thin, it turns into a dark-brown crepe; if it's too thick, it accumulates into the beginning of a really tough biscuit.

You can also get fancy with the basic mix, that is, you can add a smidgen of almost anything that's not petroleum based.

Sour-cream pancakes are a tasty variation. I've been hankering to make some, but every recipe I've come across is written in code, typed in a shorthand that only women understand. Men don't know tbsp and tsp from tsar and tsarina. "Bake on a hot, lightly greased griddle." Right. Lightly greased with what? Vasoline?

I'll cover the risks of preparing lunches and suppers in another column – once I get the stupid little red light on my oven to stop going off and on.

More on coming to terms with household appliances

I explained in an earlier column how I mastered the operation of complex kitchen appliances, the running of which, until recently, was the exclusive province of my able wife. I offered that column for the benefit of senior males who someday, of necessity, must set off down the same pot-hole-filled road I stumbled along in becoming an accomplished amateur chef.

In this column, I offer kindred guidance in getting the hang of using other household appliances as well as proven techniques for efficiently performing chores that generally are inconsonant with male aptitudes – washing and drying clothes, for example.

Actually, laundering clothes is easy: just think basics.

When you can't get even one more pair of shorts into the clothes hamper, simply tote the hamper to the laundry room and dump the entire contents into the washing machine. Leave the clothes hamper close at hand and don't monkey with any of the washing machine's controls.

You'll find a large plastic jug in a nearby closet. Look hard on the front of the jug for the word DETERGENT, which will be printed in small letters on the label. Inside is liquid laundry soap.

Start the machine by pointing one of its control knobs to the word WASH. Only one knob will offer this selection.

Shortly, you'll hear the sound of running water. If you don't, try pushing in on the control. If that doesn't work, slap the panel a good one (think TV). And if that doesn't work, call an appliance technician. Ask him, after he finishes, to leave written operating instructions.

Pour a full cup of the detergent into the washer and leave the laundry room. Washing machines are the laundry-room equivalent of kitchen watch-pots: nothing happens if you hang around watching for signs of activity. Return when you hear a loud buzz.

Don't worry about thumping sounds while the machine is running. Any clanking noises, however, will be coming from a belt buckle, a ring of keys, a jack knife, coins, maybe a breast-pocket calculator. Ten minutes of the rhythmic sound of "clank, clank, clank" can get under a man's skin, so consider fishing the source (or sources) of noise from the tub. (Stop the washer first.)

When the washer finally runs its course, load the wet clothes into the drier.

Note: You won't be able to open the washer door until several seconds after all noise has stopped. This is a built-in safety feature. The lid can be immediately opened with a pry bar, but prying is sometimes hard on the finish of the washing machine, and I don't recommend that technique.

Start the drier. Don't touch any control.

Drying usually takes longer than washing, so enjoy a baseball game – at least until the seventh-inning stretch. If, in the meantime, a buzzer goes off, just ignore it.

Load the dried clothes back into the clothes hamper, carry the hamper to the bedroom, and dump the clothes into dresser drawers. You may want to carry the hamper on one shoulder to avoid knocking gizmos off tables on your way to the bedroom.

If the clothes seem a little damp, smell a little like newly spaded earth, chuck a mothball into each drawer.

Could there be an easier job? Hardly. Why women make laundering out to be such a chore is beyond me.

Running a vacuum cleaner is only a tad more complicated than laundering clothes.

First, put the cat out. Vacuum cleaners make only a little less noise than chain saws, especially old vacuum cleaners, and cats will knock over lamps, vases, and plants scampering for safety. My cat Lucky weighs twenty-four pounds (true), and he actually wobbles the sofa diving from it.

Roll the vacuum cleaner to wherever you've spilled the most potato chip crumbs, pretzel bits, and so on, and, if necessary, to where the cat has knocked over a plant.

Typically, the crumbs from the snacks will be scattered under the dining room table or strewn in and around the comfy recliner where you read magazines and watch TV, your throne away from the throne.

Unwind the cord. Vacuum cleaner cords are long enough to reach to a home's road-side mail box, so only unwind a third of it.

Plug in the cord, and then search for a way to start the machine. Look for a foot pedal. If there is one, step on it but be ready to jump back. If it's the handle-release pedal, the handle will fall away and whack you in the thigh – or nearby.

If the pedal activates the machine's attack handle, look for a second foot pedal. If there isn't one, you'll find an on-off switch in the handle. Snap it on.

Probably, the machine will inch forward slowly. This is normal, and does not indicate that a corner of the house has sunk, as, being a man, you will initially conclude. Instead, it means the carpet beater brush is spinning in a way to give the machine a bit of forward traction.

If the carpet brush doesn't spin, it's likely clogged with hair, string, dental floss, an inch or so of a worn shoe lace, etc., etc. If this is the case, turn the machine off (important), turn it over, and using a pair of side cutters and needle-nose pliers clear the housing. Wear latex gloves.

If the machine is functioning correctly, push it back and forth over the grungy areas of the carpet. If you're expecting company, you may want to move small pieces of furniture out of the way.

When you're through, turn off the vacuum cleaner, unplug the cord, and wind it back onto the machine's cord hooks. It won't fit, but never mind. Gather the excess cord in one hand, wheel the vacuum into a coat closet, and toss the cord in after it. You won't need the vacuum again for another couple months so push it into a corner behind the coats.

Even easier than doing the laundry, eh?

I intended to cover the operation of VCRs in this column, but I've run out of space. Meanwhile, I'll research why it is that my VCR won't stop blinking "12:00" over and over.

Please, Santa Claus, not even gold. And especially no frankincense or myrrh.

I've been around for seventy plus years, and there is absolutely nothing Santa Claus can leave me under our Christmas tree that I really want or need – short of, say, the deed to a free-standing, ocean-front villa in Malibu, California.

Okay, I truly wouldn't care to live in that land of fruits, nuts, and Hollywoodians , but with the proceeds from the sale of a Malibu villa I could buy season tickets to Steelers and Pirates games, hire a personal bowling coach (not that it would help), buy my wife the Massey Ferguson tractor she pines for, and pay a crackerjack chemist to develop a herbicide that will rid the world of broccoli, asparagus, cauliflower, and spinach. Ah, happy dreams. Never mind: back to the point of this column.

For a good ten years now, at some time during the week preceding Black Friday (the day after gobble-turkey-till-you-wobble Thursday), my nieces, nephews, and other militants of the shop-till-you-drop movement, begin pestering me for a personal Christmas present list. "We don't know what to get you," they plead. "You have everything," they complain.

Which is exactly the reason, I reply, that I don't want anything for Christmas.

I muster my arguments:

I could have founded a haberdashery with the new clothes I've left at the Salvation Army store.

I don't even know how to use some of my tools that were gifts.

I already own more bowling equipment than a real bowler would wear out in ten years.

My wife could make a cozy large enough to fit a sizable gazebo from my stock of Steelers' and Indians' pull-over jerseys.

My reasoning falls on deaf ears, of course, so I reluctantly make up a list, address it to Santa Claus, and very early the morning of Black Friday, hand it to my wife, who will circulate it among her fellow shoppers (see above) as they speed intrepidly north on I-79 toward the Mill Creek Shopping Mall elbow pads securely in place, steely eyes hidden by one-way sun glasses, and credit cards holstered.

It would be easier – for a reason even Santa himself can't explain – to match two snowflakes than to pair up the items on my Christmas list with presents bearing my name under the tree on Christmas morning. It's that way every year. (I'm not too quick, but I sure as heck know better than to mention the discrepancy, even to my infinitely understanding wife.)

Anyway, it struck me that, perhaps, by making my list for this Christmas a public letter to Santa, I could fix the problem once and for all. What could I lose? Little, if anything. So . . . the newspaper willing, and email working, here goes:

Dear Santa,

How are you and Mrs. Claus? Over your summer colds, I trust.

No doubt, Santa, that you and Peter Cottontail have resolved the difference in your itineraries that I pointed out in my letter last spring to Pete, the one I copied you on. Pete's all right, a little jumpy now and then, but he's a good listener.

I mentioned in my last two letters, in a very positive way, naturally, that the gifts you leave me seldom match the items on my list. I realize that Quincy Gimletti in Quality Control is getting along in years, but I also know that even really old elves don't make mistakes of that frequency and magnitude.

In any event, I've decided to reorganize this year's letter, as you will shortly notice, so as to include my list of gifts after offering my usual friendly suggestions concerning ways to tweak your already first-rate operation. Maybe that's the answer: putting the sleigh ahead of the reindeer, so to speak.

About Rudolph – God knows, my wife and I both love animals – but in all honesty, Santa, we're not that keen over being awakened at three a.m. on Christmas morning by Rudolph's glowing red nose. Sometimes he forgets and leaves it running in pulse mode, jolting us from a sound sleep thinking an ambulance has pulled up outside. Three years ago he forgot, and when we looked out later that morning vultures were still circling our house: somehow, they know.

I also understand that the issue of Rudolph's brightly shining nose has been aired infelicitously at temples in the area.

Incidentally—I think you'll get a kick out of this—Granny McClintock is under the impression that every mention of the name Rudolph is actually a reference to Rudolph Giuliani, the former Republican mayor of New York City. Somehow, she has it in her head that Giuliani suffers a chronic red nose from over imbibing. Granny, like that elderly woman of Southern folklore who claimed she always thought damn Yankee was one word, believes the word Republican, similarly unqualified, is a corruption of the English language.

On the subject of reindeer—please understand that this point barely rises to the level of a suggestion let alone to the loftiness of a recommendation—isn't it just possible that your high-spirited steeds would be more comfortable taking a breather at an Interstate highway rest stop instead of at our place? Or, should that be an inconvenience, perhaps Mrs. Claus could devise a rest schedule that rotates the homes in our area. Probably you are not aware, living as you do on arctic tundra, that reindeer poop is extraordinarily rich. True, it's nice being able to boast in summer of a great lawn, but it's a pain mowing it every two or three days.

Have you ever considered enclosing your sleigh, Santa? Taking a cue from the design of enclosed Amish buggies? I'm sure you're familiar with the fact that rosy cheeks aren't necessarily a sign of good health. I was a lad the last time I rode in an open sleigh. Frost didn't just nip at my nose, it chomped down so ferociously that the swelling hasn't gone down yet. My brother Silas was riding with us, and his ears, which have stood straight out from the day he was born (of necessity, he was delivered by Caesarean section) swelled to where incoming sounds gained ten decibels in loudness before entering his head. His ears never shrunk back, and to this day sonic booms still make his teeth rattle. Once, waiting to board a plane at L.A. International Airport, a boom dislodged one of his molars.

What I'm trying to say, Santa, is that frostbite can be a very serious health problem.

Almost as bad, picture yourself as a short fat guy with a huge nose and ears big as soup bowls, prancing around in red sweats with furry white cuffs and hems, and letting-go a hearty "Ho, ho, ho" every few minutes. See my concern? Mothers would need a tractor equipped with a front loader to maneuver their children onto your lap.

One final, very tiny point, Santa, something I'm sure you can easily clear up and address in a note to one of my nieces, which you might pin on her Christmas tree: why is it my gifts come in boxes with names like Neiman-Marcus, Bloomingdale, and Kohl's, but the purchase receipts are all from Dollar General and Big Lots? Doesn't that strike you as kind of odd? It does me.

You have a nice trip Santa, give my regards to Mrs. Claus and Quincy, and maybe suggest to Rudolph that he crank the wattage down a notch or two.

Very truly yours,
Hugh McClintock,
Conneautville, Pa.

PS. I have arranged the items in the attached list in descending order of my needs, of which I haven't any.

EITHER HIS PULSE QUIT OR MY WATCH STOPPED

On the wrong road again

A couple times a year Nellie and I take an overnight trip with another married couple, long-time friends who are also retired. If it's my turn to drive, Jiggs, our male friend, plots our route and navigates. If Jiggs drives, I do the paper work and the navigating. On the way, our wives, sitting in the back seat, chatter endlessly; we men, for their edification, keenly interpret the passing scene. Anyway, that's how it works in theory.

Alas, Jiggs, a plucky seventy-four, is slipping badly. He planned our fall visit to the NFL Hall of Fame in Canton, Ohio, and on the way dutifully alerted me to upcoming route changes – except for the U-turn we made after seeing the "Wooster – 20 Miles" sign: the city of Wooster is situated some thirty miles west of

Canton, that is, thirty miles beyond our planned destination.

Maggie, Jiggs's wife, got us back on track, which, on that particular trip, started their bickering. (Jiggs and Maggie are not our friends' real first names, neither is their last name Squabblesteen, but it could be.)

Jiggs would think it a disrespectful put-down if we didn't let him plan every other trip, so we take our chances. Besides, since we're all retired, unplanned side trips don't lessen the pleasure of our outings.

Jiggs also charted our recent trip to Seneca Niagara Casino, which is located in western New York State in Seneca Indian territory. Figuring Maggie had tacitly confirmed our route – largely a straight shot up I-90 from our little borough in northwestern Pennsylvania – I was comfortable following the course that Jiggs had laid out and Maggie had validated. I remember our trip this way:

Even before we near I-90, the women are wholly caught up in whatever topic is the current gossip du jour. Before long, however, my wife asks Jiggs where we'll be eating. Our travel routine – seniors are addicted to routine – includes wolfing down a big breakfast at about ten o'clock, skipping lunch, and eating a late-afternoon supper.

"Fredonia," he answers. "I know a good restaurant there. Not another damned chain, greasy spoon."

I glance in the rear-view mirror in time to see Maggie roll her eyes.

Nellie also sees Maggie's editorial gesture. Nevertheless, ever the diplomat, Nellie cheerfully endorses Jiggs' choice.

Neither Maggie nor I can persuade Jiggs that Fredonia is situated to the southeast of I-90, so we end up eating at a Denny's restaurant in Dunkirk. A city of some 15,000 residents, Dunkirk is roughly the same distance northwest of I-90 as Fredonia is to the southeast. Both cities are accessed from a common I-90 off-ramp – unfortunately.

Jiggs lets on that a Denny's restaurant in Dunkirk was his second choice. In any event, we all enjoy hearty breakfasts.

We're gathering speed on the eastbound I-90 service road, having left the Interstate proper for gasoline, when Maggie says excitedly, "Aren't those buffalo!"

"Where?" I ask.

Nellie answers. "On the right! Standing around that haystack!"

Jiggs begins erratically counting the animals out loud: "One, two . . . three . . . four, five . . . six . . . . seven . . . ."

Looking past Jiggs to see the animals for myself, I ask him if he's counting their legs and dividing by four. "No," he snaps. "I'm counting their horns (family newspaper) and dividing by two."

He has reached the count of nine – maybe ten – when the words, "Watch it!" boom out like a thunderclap from the rear seat. I wrench the car back into the right-hand lane. A speeding semi whizzes by, the long blare of its horn aggravatingly proving the physical reality of the Doppler Effect, the eerie change in pitch of a moving sound.

"It wasn't that close," I mumble, addressing no one in particular.

"No, not much," Nellie says.

"Was it that close?" I say to Jiggs.

"Was what close," he answers, still counting buffalo.

Another thirty miles roll by. Jiggs and I are caught up in making plausible excuses for our miserable golf games when Maggie blurts out that we're lost again. "I said at the time," she admonishes, "to stay on I-90. But, oh no, you–"

"We are not lost," Jiggs says sharply, half turning to face her. "My way is quicker."

"We're heading," Maggie snaps, "for Rochester, Jiggs." Her tone suggests she isn't taking any prisoners.

Jiggs abruptly pulls a map from the car door's side pocket, which is folded so that only a swath of western New York State shows. He scarcely studies it before quietly telling me to turn left at the next intersection. "A couple miles yet," he says. "We'll pick up I-190. Not that it would have made any difference."

Our wives, I'm sure, without looking, are exchanging knowing glances.

On that particular trip, we gambled until two a.m., very late by our usual habits, and met for breakfast at ten. None of us drink any kind of booze anymore, so our appetites weren't compromised by hangovers.

Only Nellie had money left from our night of gambling – something like thirty dollars – which Maggie helped her blow on the quarter slots before we left for home.

Maggie, younger than the rest of us by six years, volunteered to skipper our return. One of those super conscientious woman drivers who diligently heed all road instructions, suggestions, and warnings, Maggie wouldn't coast through an uncontested four-way stop in the middle of the Mojave Desert, would wet herself before exceeding the speed limit hurrying to a rest stop. In other words, behind the wheel of a car, Maggie drives other motorists nuts. I doubt, however, if she's ever been in a car accident, so my objection to her taking the wheel was more pretense than genuine.

In any event, Maggie drove us home, sharing the front seat with Nellie. Predictably, our return trip was totally uneventful, no tire-screeching stops, no screaming sirens, no missed turns, and no annoying blasts of trucks' air-horns – nothing.

Both Jiggs and I slept much of the way home, shamefully failing in our responsibility to instruct Maggie on the finer points of good-driver roadsmanship.

Luckily, we made it back without incident.

And how is, ah . . . your lovely wife?

More and more these days, I find myself approaching my workbench in the basement of our home with this unspoken question bouncing around in my mind: "What am I here for?" I'm after something, I tell myself. "What the heck is it?"

I remember eventually. Several times, however, I've begun an unrelated project before recalling, say, that I'm only in the cellar to fetch a screwdriver for tightening loose hinge plates on a kitchen cabinet door – hardly a mission needing an awesome feat of short-term memory.

My guess is that every senior's mind goes blank now and then: sometimes the light comes on when you flip the wall switch in an old house, sometimes it doesn't, and sometimes you have to wiggle the switch. Anyway, that's how the apparatus of my memory works anymore.

The fact is that becoming a short-memory dingbat may be the least of the scourges of growing old. True, some people are afflicted much later in life than others, but in the long run the misery of ding-battiness spares almost no one.

Here's a typical scenario. You bump into a young man (a person under fifty-five), an acquaintance that you met a years ago but rarely encounter anymore, and you can't remember his first name. His last name is Edson, not Edison you remind yourself. His given name, you're sure, is ordinary but it might as well be a long Slavic first name because your mind draws a blank. Worse, you really like the guy.

Let's say you are "Paul," and you're filling up at a gas station when he stops his Honda Civic alongside the next pump.

"Paul!" he exclaims, uncapping his gas tank. "Been a while. How's Elizabeth?"

Elizabeth, of course, is your wife. You can't manage a snappy greeting of your own as every cell of your brain is frantically engaged in rifling through a list of common first names.

"Fine," you answer. "Er, ah . . . just fine. We're both doing just, ah, really well."

You dress up your helter-skelter reply with friendly nods. You have no idea what young Edson is saying.

He's pulling away from the station when at last the light bulb flickers on. No wonder you couldn't remember his first name, it was a toughie. "Take care, George!" you yell after him.

George brakes and looks back expectantly from his driver-side window.

"Nothing, George!" You shake your head vigorously and wave him on. "Goodbye . . . that's all I meant George. Just . . . Goodbye!"

George, nodding slowly, drives away.

"Give my regards to, ah, your wife!" I shout.

If George heard, he doesn't wave or otherwise let on.

I have a niece named Michelle. I also have a "pretend" niece, a daughter of close friends virtually the same age as Michelle with the rather quirky first name of Jasminette.

When I come across my true niece, the name that invariably leaps into my head is Jasminette. I have no idea why. Moreover, neither love nor money can shake it from the place in my mind where the name Michelle should stand ready to heed my call.

Consequently, I end up greeting Michelle with a dumb remark such as, "My you're looking pretty today, Gal." A typical, young, semi-feminist, she always, somehow, favors me with a look that is a cross between a scowl and a smile.

Psychologists call the occurrence of people glomming onto the wrong name GCD, which stands for Geriatric Cognitive Dysfunction. Within the brotherhood, however, they quietly refer to it as LMS, or Lost Marbles Syndrome.

GCD (or LMS) is not necessarily an affliction of old age, but it correlates well. My situation has developed to where, at family gatherings, I often pull my wife aside and ask her who a certain young person is. This generally results in the following dialog:

"Who in heck is that?" I whisper, furtively gesturing.

"It's Paul!" my wife snaps, launching the name from the side of her mouth "He's your cousin!"

"My cousin?"

"Merle's son!"

"Oh." After a pause. "Merle who?"

During the winter I bowl on Thursday afternoons in a senior league at Plaza Lanes in Meadville, Pennsylvania. A Giant Eagle grocery store – one of over 200 of that large Pittsburgh-centered chain – is situated next door, and sometimes I shop there before returning home from bowling. My wife provides me with a shopping list, which seldom consists of more than a few items, as she has usually shopped earlier in the week at the small market in the borough where we live.

She hands me the shopping list as I'm leaving the house. Inevitably I say that I won't need it, reawaken her to the fact that my mind is a steel trap when it comes to remembering short lists of one- or two-word items. Typically, she gives me a yeah-right look and mumbles something."

I cram the list into my pocket, my contempt obvious; I will show her who the real brain in our partnership is by never removing it.

Okay, that's only a plan. Actually, I always check the list. Even so, once I forgot a box of Shredded Wheat that was way down the list, the fifth of five items.

"Where's the Shredded Wheat," my wife demanded, emptying the grocery bag that I'd just set down on the kitchen counter.

I nimbly explained that I couldn't make out her hand writing, said that the letters looked like they spelled "Shriveled Wherry."

"The next time," she said, "I'll stencil the letters."

Sarcasm, I told her, has no place in a loving marriage. She nodded sarcastically. (Wives, you know, can nod sarcastically, indifferently, grimly, etc.)

I take several kinds of medicine (everybody over seventy takes lots of medicine) some in the morning and some at night. My wife is also on several medicines. Once a week, she loads four small, compartmented plastic dispensers with our daily quota of pills and capsules. Her two dispensers are a different color from mine. Nevertheless, one evening I managed to take some of her pills instead of my own. (The frequency of so-called senior moments increases linearly with the hour of the day. Sometimes, from about nine o'clock on, two or three ordinary senior moments merge into a super senior moment.)

Our pharmacist is a family friend. Clyde – I'll call him – thinks he's a wit. In any event, he's smart and knows the purposes and side-effects of medicines with names ranging from Accupril to Zoloft. (No moaning!)

I telephoned him the morning after I accidentally took my wife's evening pills. I wanted to know: "Will Estrogen mess me up?"

"Are you suffering symptoms of menopause," he asked. "Ha, ha. It will help with your hot flashes. Ha, ha. You're lucky to still be alive. Ha, ha."

Where was I? Oh yes, did I mention that sometimes I set off for a destination and when I arrive I've forgotten my mission? Well, I do.

Fancy that

Alfred, Lord Tennyson, a nineteenth century poet, was one England's famous men of letters. A line in one of his poems affirms that "In spring a young man's fancy lightly turns to thoughts of love."

I guess his fancy turned slowly, not to say lightly, because it was fourteen years after he popped the question before he got around to marrying his beloved.

In any event, an observation on a subject as commonplace as a young man's amorous musings hardly seems worthy of versification, even by a poet of Tennyson's stature. I bet he would have been upgraded to poet laureate of England years earlier had he leveled on exactly what it is that an old man's fancy turns to in spring.

At seventy-four years of age, I certainly know what my fancy turns to when Spring rolls around: cogitations in bold, living color of nubile, scantily clad young maidens flitting about – in the kitchen whipping me up a scrumptious meal. (Actually, mine is more of a year-round fancy than an early spring fancy, but never mind.)

Figuring a tasty meal isn't the be-all and end-all of every old man's fancy, and since Lord Tennyson was no help, I decided to ask a few elders of my acquaintance what their fancy turned to upon spotting the first robin of a new year. Alas, in no time my earnest quest for sincere answers turned into unwholesome replies more appropriate to a game of liar's poker.

I bowl with the Wheezin' Geezers team in a senior league at Plaza Lanes in Meadville, Pennsylvania, fertile ground, I figured, for spading up an honest answer or two.

"Clayton," I asked loudly, rousing our team's seventy-six-year-old anchor man who was waiting his turn to bowl. "Spring is here, and I was wondering. To what has your fancy turned?"

We had already bowled two games and were about to begin the final game of the match. "I'm up already?" he thundered, rising unsteadily while focusing on the overhead TV displaying our team's running scores.

"No, no," I said. "Not yet. I'd like to know exactly what your fancy has turned to now that winter is over. I may write a poem."

He gave me a threatening look, a face I'd seen him favor his wife with as she walked away after they argued. "Did you say write a poem or read a poem?"

"Winter's over," I began again, "and I was merely wondering–"

"Sex," he said, interrupting my words of clarification.

"Seriously," I said, "What–"

"I am serious," he said, interrupting me again.

"Yeah," I said. "And I am the Cat Star." (Ahem: note my clever play on words; I could have replied, "You are not the Dog Star.")

Uncertain how to reply, he cut his eyes back to the TV display.

I said, "Sex, huh? I didn't ask about your fantasies, I asked about your practical thoughts."

He signaled it was my turn to bowl. "Envy," he said loudly as I headed for the ball-return rack, "is unbecoming a man your age Hugh."

"What do you mean by fancy," Roy, another teammate, asked me suspiciously. I had returned to my seat after failing to convert an easy two-pin leave into a spare. "I don't get the meaning of your question," he grumbled.

Roy is a heck of a bowler. However, remark on, say, Eve and Original Sin, and he'll sure as the deuce, scowl and say, "You mean Eve Johnson or Eve Vantussle?"

I explained to him that Tennyson, in using the word "fancy," was referring to a young man's testosterone-fueled imagination.

"Sex," he blurted out after exchanging glances with Clayton. "It's absolutely the main thought that enters my mind when I spot the first daffodil of spring."

I say, "And after sex, what? Trout fishing?"

"No," he says. "More sex."

After a moment I asked, "You don't ice fish?"

"Sure I do. On the days Pearl and I don't have sex."

"Of course," I said.

I decided to recycle an old joke. "You know how to catch a polar bear?" The look on his face told me that he hadn't heard the joke. "You cut a big hole in the ice, sprinkle peas around the edge, and when a polar bear comes to take a pea you kick him in the ice hole."

He laughed. "I could tell that one in church."

"Like, you ever go to church," I said.

"Like to know what my fancy turns to in Spring?" Clark, our number-three bowler, broke in.

"I'm polling our whole team," I answered. "Golf?"

I knew Clark was a golfer, a disastrously slow duffer on the links, according to both Clayton and Roy.

He shook his head. "Nope, it's sex. Golf isn't even a distant second."

I said, "You, too, huh?"

Nodding, he winked at Clayton. "Are you asking all this stuff for yourself or for your wife?"

"There's medicines for your situation, Hugh," Roy tossed in. "Therapy, too."

"I should be wearing rubber waders," I mumbled.

I have a friend who is a computer engineer. A big stolid man, his friends call him "Moose." I've mentioned Moose in other columns: he's the man who is convinced that persons as ignorant of computers as I am, are not only congenital nitwits but also socially maladjusted. I bumped into Moose at Hank's drive-up frozen custard stand on my way home from bowling.

"You're a young man," I said, once we had exchanged greetings. "I assume your fancy has turned heavily to thoughts of romance now that spring has arrived?"

"Is this your way," he answered, a skeptic look on his face, "of reminding me that spring has sprung?" He took a big lick of his two-dip cone of frozen custard.

"Something like that," I said.

He held out his cone, presented it more or less. "Soft ice cream," he said, grinning. "From Hank's. The best in the world. Since March, all I've thought about is Hank's ice cream. I dream at night of their Mexican sundaes."

"Mexican sundaes?"

"A paper cup of Hank's soft ice cream loaded with chocolate syrup and Spanish peanuts."

I joshed him about still being single. "Explains a lot regarding, ah, certain of your social inclinations."

His eyes sadly downcast he said, "Look at what marriage did to you."

Knowing better than to engage Moose in a battle of wits, I made up a reason for hurrying home, and we headed toward our respective vehicles.

I'm working on a poem, probably something in free verse on the acquired mendacity of old men. I should have a few stanzas ready in week . . . that I'll slip into another column. Lord Tennyson may turn over in his grave, but having short-shrifted us oldsters in the matter of our traipsing amorously into Spring – at least in our minds – he has only himself to blame.

Knights of the road, errant

After I bowl on Monday afternoons in a Senior Mixed League at Plaza Lanes, I sometimes shop for groceries at a nearby Giant Eagle store. Not one to fuss over a choice among brand names, I'm in and out in jig time, provided my wife's grocery list doesn't include an oddball item – say an exotic spice, such as cinnamon. Last Monday I ambled into the store's aisle of pet supplies and spotted Karl Shaginel near the middle of the aisle pondering a bin stocked with bags of Dad's brand dog food.

Shag, as he's called, works for Rigby Ford, a local automobile dealer. Sometimes his boss asks me to accompany Shag in fetching a new car or truck from another dealership; Usually Shag drives the new vehicle back to Rigby's, and I drive back the ten-year-old rattletrap we arrived in.

A usually reticent man, Shag was talkative that morning. Since we don't see each other often, I felt obliged to listen while he described all the wonderful features of his brand new John Deer riding lawn mower. Consequently, my usual jig-time shopping took longer than it takes to dance a French waltz.

Shag is a friendly guy, but like me he has reached the age where there's a noticeable ready-set-go delay between word-producing brain activity and the product thereof.

Consider the last time we fetched a vehicle for the dealership, which was more or less typical of every run we've taken. We're cruising along comfortably at 65 mph on Interstate 90 not far from our destination, a suburb of Cleveland, Ohio. I'm driving:

Shag, studying a road map: "I think we get off at the next exit."

Me: "Do what now?"

Shag: "We get off . . . we were supposed to get off here."

Me: "I'll loop back at the next overpass."

Shag, after we've driven a piece: "Two more miles."

Shag: "One more mile."

Shag: "We're here!"

Before long, that course correction made, and Interstate 90 behind us, we reach the intersection of the street on which the target of our pick up is located. Neither of us knows, however, whether we should turn left or right – to the explicit displeasure of the hothead driving the city bus behind us.

Abruptly I turn right, and after cautiously traveling a block – while Shag vainly scours the store-front businesses for addresses – pull into a self-serve gas station.

The clerk, perched on a stool inside a little windowed kiosk, congenially admits she never heard of a dealership that went by the name Hometown Ford-Mercury. A customer waiting behind me points and says, "It's about twenty blocks that way," which, by sheer luck, is the direction we're headed. I thank him and return to the car.

"We're okay," I say to Shag, who was on the verge of taking another nap. "About ten more blocks."

After a good twenty blocks we haven't seen any sign of a Ford dealership. I pull into another gas station and start to get out of the car, but Shag decides he'd better hear for himself. A minute later he's holding the gas-station door open, backing out, and nodding at someone inside.

"Just a little farther," he says, slipping into the passenger's seat. He's relieved if not out-and-out excited.

I drive another two blocks before we spot a customary blue-and-white, oval Ford Dealership sign. I park the car in a visitor's parking space near the show room, and we immediately take care of the most pressing business: we hurry off to the men's room.

While Shag tends to the paperwork, I attach a dealer plate on the recessed area of the back bumper of a brand new Ford F-250 pickup truck, which, for our convenience, has been left near the building's side entrance. Shag, his affairs inside settled, transfers a CB radio from our car to the truck.

Before starting home, we persuade ourselves, as usual, that the outbound trip wasn't as direct as we had expected that it would be, and we map out a different return route. (Even if we don't miss a single turn, it always takes us longer to get home than it took motoring to our destination. We never learn.)

Shag leads the way back and I doggedly follow in the rattletrap. Twice I am the target of a truck's long horn blast and the driver's vigorous one-finger hand message apprising me that by shear happenstance, in coping with one of Shag's sudden lane changes, I've cleared the front fender of the truck's huge cab.

Shag parks the new F-250 near the service entrance at Rigby's, removes the dealer plate, gathers his paperwork, and disconnects the CB. By then I have returned from parking Rigby's rattletrap, and together we head for the Sales manager's office.

Shortly, Smiling Jack Blodgett, the sales manager, briskly rounds a corner and asks of the nature of our trip. (Blodgett truly goes by that nickname, "Smiling Jack," which is not only an apt sobriquet but also one the dealership uses in newspaper ads and radio spots.)

"No problem," Shag answers breezily as Smilin' Jack slips into the chair behind his desk.

"A walk in the park," I add.

Smilin' Jack begins questioning Shag about the condition of the pick-up truck we brought back. I begin slowly backing away. "Keep me in mind for future runs," I say to Smilin' Jack the first chance I get. He says he will. Shag waves to me, and I complacently head for my own pickup.

A get-well card for Aaron

Uncle Ken, part Irish – and all blarney when conditions favor cajolery, sweet-talk, or exaggerated compliments – knew before moving into stodgy, tranquil Rolling Hills Nursing Home that his new accommodations called for an attitude adjustment – the Home's, not his.

Conscripting rumors and gossip as foot-soldiers, and deploying intricate pranks as long-range artillery, he soon mounted and launched his first attack.

The rumors I've forgotten. Most of his pranks, however, I recall. For example, once Uncle Ken and a crony in Maintenance carried off the brand-new leather recliner chair – a Christmas gift – belonging to the blowhard (Uncle Ken's characterization) living in the room next to his and left it in the Home's big outdoor storage shed while Blowhard was in the dining room eating lunch. The police were called – to no avail – and a report was filed. The next day, however, while Blowhard was eating lunch, the chair mysteriously reappeared in Blowhard's room exactly in front of the TV where it belonged.

Uncle Ken's pranks got wackier when Aaron Blodgett, a retired church deacon from Philadelphia – but in spirit a chap far more devil than angel – was moved in with Uncle Ken.

Both men were seventy-two years old, widowed, veterans of the Korean War, and avid pinochle players. In fact, virtually the only difference between the two men was their skin color: Aaron was black and Uncle Ken was white.

A son of the earth of decidedly white rural northwestern Pennsylvania, at first, Uncle Ken was uneasy over the idea of sharing his room with a "burr head" of uncertain "hygienic inclination." Long before falling seriously ill, however, he had learned a few sobering truths about the fiction of racial inequality. The two men, when Uncle Ken died, had become inseparable.

It wasn't long after Aaron became a resident before he and Uncle Ken had teamed up and were efficiently victimizing aides, nurses, fellow residents – and themselves.

Uncle Ken told me the story of Aaron's special get-well card at least three times – he was already teetering on the edge of dementia the first time – so I'll relate it here as a composite rendition. I've touched up – not to mention cleaned up – his language a tad, too.

One morning a week or so before Christmas, Uncle Ken came across "Linda" waiting for something or other at the nurse's station serving the wing of the Rolling Hills where he and Aaron shared a room. "How's Aaron," she asked, not even greeting Uncle Ken.

Weary of playing second fiddle to Aaron, who was the Home's only Afro-American and all but deified by the female residents, Uncle Ken answered that his roommate had seriously injured himself falling off the commode in their room's little bathroom.

He assured Linda that Aaron was using the commode exactly as it was intended to be used, but that Aaron had fallen asleep awaiting a second development. Peeved, Uncle Ken was no doubt much more explicit.

His account of the remainder of that evening I've set forth below, not in Uncle Ken's own words, but in a tighter dialogue that I think he would have approved. I've left out his frequent, ill-timed guffaws and his unprintable swearing.

So . . . imagine you're hearing an account of that evening told by a bedfast, crusty old timer with thinning, snow-white hair.

"It's evening, (he begins) and we're alone in our room. Aaron is propped up in his bed watching TV. I'm reading and have removed my ears (hearing aids). Suddenly Aaron mutes the TV and greets someone at our doorway, which – because the curtain dividing our room is half pulled out – is beyond my view. Linda and three other women, all in wheelchairs, push into our room. I insert my ears and hear Linda tell Aaron she's glad to see he's feeling better. I say to Linda that he's starting to watch TV again, a good sign. The other women express their concern. One woman asks Aaron if the commode in our bathroom is one of those high jobbies for persons who can't easily sit all the way down. Before he can answer, I shake my head vigorously, making it look like I don't want Aaron to see me intercept her question."

"To this point, Aaron has been sitting quietly with a dumb look on his face. Now, however, he realizes something is fishy, and he aims a brief but nasty, slit-eyed glare my way."

"For a little while, he was unconscious," I say. At the same time, I flash the women a don't-go-there look."

"Linda says that had to be scary, and I tell her I hadn't been as frightened since the night I got caught hoofing it against traffic leaving a N.O.W. meeting."

(Uncle Ken, whom I doubt feared anything or anybody, invented his story about the danger of finding yourself in the cross-hairs of a pumped-up woman driver leaving a National Organization of Women meeting, and he worked it into his conversation at every opportunity.)

"After a few seconds of cloudy uncertainty, Linda says to Aaron that they are all elated that he is up and about again. She hands him a big pink-hued envelope on which the words `In Sympathy' are neatly penned in large swirly letters. Aaron gives me another mean look and extracts the card. The graphics on the card are in the red-and-green hues of a Christmas scene, and Linda apologetically tells Aaron that they had to make do."

"I say, it's a beautiful card. Did you ladies make it? (Here, Uncle Ken always explained that some women residents enjoyed pasting together get-well, anniversary, and other similarly intended cards from parts of old greeting cards.) Linda allows that that indeed was the case. While Aaron is reading the card – all the while scowling as if he's peeling a rotting onion – I make my way for the door to our room."

"I advise the women avuncularly that a long visit would be therapeutic. A step into the hall I yell back, 'But, don't you overdo it Aaron!'"

Uncle Ken ended his story on that note (each time, as a matter of fact), punctuating the finish with guffaws and a distant, impish look on his face.

I doubt that either Aaron or Uncle Ken ever told Linda the truth. I was in their room, however, when Aaron avenged Uncle Ken's prank the following Sunday. I cover his retaliation in another column, "Caught on tape."

Uncle Ken and Aaron passed away only few weeks apart some twelve years ago; neither man was able to hold his ground against emphysema-related pneumonia. I was given to understand, reliably I believe, that

Rolling Hills Nursing Home soon recovered from their contrary residency, however, and again was soon a tranquil Home for elders living out their lives.

Caught on tape

Both Uncle Ken and Aaron were venerable residents of Rolling Hills Nursing Home. Each was seventy-two years old, widowed, and quartered in the same two-man resident room.

Physically hobbled but mentally sharp, they parried boredom and monotony by victimizing each other, Rolling Hill's staff, and their fellow residents with wacky, vandalizing pranks – as when Uncle Ken duped a female resident into believing that Aaron had injured himself when he fell asleep and tumbled off the commode in their private bathroom. The snookered woman rounded up a number of friends and together they wheel-chaired into Uncle Ken's and Aaron's room very concerned over Aaron's well-being – to his all-out befuddlement.

Both men have since passed on, Aaron, I'd bet, to the dwelling place of angels, Uncle Ken, I fear, to a far warmer habitat.

Aaron, thus victimized by Uncle Ken's silly hoax casting him as needing training wheels to use a commode, vowed he would swiftly get even for having to suffer the lead role in the comedic nonsense staged by his roommate. And he did, the following Sunday.

I was visiting Uncle Ken for one of our infrequent afternoons of checkers and small-talk when he told me how Aaron avenged his victimization. Aaron's daughters had taken him to a birthday luncheon in nearby Meadville, Pennsylvania, leaving me alone with Uncle Ken. Set forth below – smoothed a little and cleaned up a lot – is Uncle Ken's account of Aaron's well-planned retaliation.

"As you know," Uncle Ken began, "I'm a Pittsburgh Steelers fan. I wouldn't watch the stinking Dallas Cowboys play a football game unless it was the price I had to pay for having my foot removed from a bear trap."

(For the record, the Cowboys, promoted by that franchise's management as "America's Team," are hated by non-Cowboy fans no less fervidly than non-Yankee fans hate the nickname "Bronx Bombers" – as that New York baseball team was once boastfully called.)

"Aaron," Uncle Ken continued, "being from Philadelphia, is an Eagles fan. As pitiful a professional football team, last season, as ever there was."

"They played each other – the Cowboys and the Eagles – two weeks ago. Remember? The entire week before, that old fool (Aaron) couldn't stop bragging about his Eagles.

(To appreciate the true flavor of Uncle Ken's account, substitute more earthy profanities for expressions such as "dung," "dang," and "rotten.")

"I told Aaron," Uncle Ken said, "that the Philadelphia Eagles couldn't beat a drum if every member on the team had gong mallets for hands, let alone defeat the formidable Dallas Cowboys."

"We joshed each other, and, bottom line, ended up betting on the outcome. Not for money – he was once a Baptist preacher, you know – but the loser had to stand and sing a song in the dining room during lunch the Monday after the game."

"You know I can sing a little, Hugh, but Aaron couldn't carry a tune in a 10-gallon wash tub. Besides, I knew dang well the Cowboys couldn't lose. So right away I agreed."

"Aaron came up with a song that the loser had to sing, *The Three Blind Mice*."

At this point in Uncle Aaron's telling, one of the Home's aides rapped lightly on the door jamb, entered the room, and tacked a January event calendar to the cork bulletin board hanging just inside the doorway. Uncle Ken watched her leave, pretending, as usual, that he couldn't take his eyes off her butt, and then he continued, jumping ahead to the day of the game.

"The pre-game show is on, and we're propped against the heads of our beds arguing over the point spread when Aaron gets up and sticks a cassette in his VCR. He tells me his VCR will start recording at one o'clock sharp, adds that he intends to replay the game every night for a week – or some other baloney to that effect."

"Promise me," I say to Aaron.

"At one o'clock, the voice of announcer Pat Summerall interrupts a Budweiser beer commercial to say that a player named Ty Detmer will be quarterbacking the Eagles."

"I look at Aaron and say that someone at the TV station is asleep at the switch. No, Aaron counters, that's the way VCR's work in the record mode."

"Whatever,' I say. "Is the Detmer kid is any good? Aaron says, Let's just wait and see."

"First play of the game, the Cowboy's kickoff returner fumbles the ball, and three plays later the Eagles score to go ahead seven zip. Aaron right away begins humming the *Three Blind Mice* song – to the tune of God only knows what. I remind him that we didn't bet on which team scores first."

"At the end of three quarters, the Eagles are leading, 21-13. Worse, they're clearly beating the stuff out of the Cowboys."

"I tell Aaron that Dallas never gets down to nut-cracking time until the last quarter.

"Then, I'll be danged if the Cowboys don't tie the game their next ball possession. 'There must be another game on,' I say. 'This one's over.' Aaron shrugs and says we should wait and see."

Uncle Ken, who had this habit of peering over a person's head when he talked, suddenly lowered his eyes and said to me, "Do you remember the final score of the game?"

"No," I answered, "but I remember the Cowboys won." I had finished setting up the checker board and was waiting for Uncle Ken to make the first move.

"Yeah," he replied. "Then how come you had to sing that silly damn kid's song at lunch time the next day?"

I frowned, gave him a skeptical, you're-not-making-sense look.

He grinned and moved a checker. "That's right. You caught on yet?"

I shook my head.

"That Monday afternoon," he continued, "I couldn't find a Tribune newspaper anywhere – the reason being that Aaron and Kitty (Uncle Ken's seventy-something-year-old, preserved in-alcohol, resident girlfriend) had hid them all."

"The next morning, Tuesday, I spotted a Monday USA Today in the wastebasket inside our nurse's station. I took it back to our room, and I'm reading the sports section when Aaron – he's writing a letter – starts to giggle. I told him they got the score of the Cowboys-Eagles game all crapped up, and he giggles louder. I say, 'you're writing about me losing our bet, huh?' He shakes his head and just sits there. His pen is poised over his writing tablet as if he's thinking of what to say next.

"I kept on reading . . . 'The paper,' I say to Aaron, 'says the Cowboys won.' He goes nuts, thought that was the funniest thing I had said since he moved in with me. I asked him what was so stinkin' funny, but he's laughing so hard he can't answer me."

Uncle Ken paused. "It finally hits me," he says, shaking his head in admiration. "You know what the little peckerwood did?"

"I think so," I answered, grinning.

"We watched the Cowboys-Eagle game of 1996 – one he had saved on a video tape!"

I asked Uncle Ken who all knew about Aaron's little charade. Only the whole stinkin' Home, he answered.

I'm half-deaf, fella, not half-witted.

I'm slightly hard of hearing: a touch of deafness runs in my family.

My maternal grandfather was all but deaf. After retiring he enjoyed listening to baseball games on the radio, which he did by setting the volume so loud that neighbors living a half-block away protested. (According to grandmother, the slamming of neighborhood windows when he turned on the radio sounded like an artillery barrage.)

My mother couldn't hear well either. Among other duties, she had to wait on customers at our family-owned bakery. More than one customer, before mother began wearing hearing aids, discovered that the mere act of driving home had somehow morphed a banana cream pie into a Boston cream pie or a cherry pie into a box of chop-suey cupcakes.

The first day Mother wore her new hearing aids at work she suddenly heard this rumbling noise, which kept getting louder and louder. Hurrying to the back of the store, imagining she would see the big, floor-model dough mixer unsteadily lurching her way, the daytime set-up baker, after several moments of utter confusion, explained that a big military airplane was passing over the borough. It was a sound she hadn't heard in years. I suppose that kind of thing happens often to persons wearing a hearing aid for the first time.

I remember some of my similar little embarrassments as a grade-school student. Our third-grade teacher at First District Elementary School threatened loudly to tape my mouth shut if I didn't stop replying "Huh?" to her questions. In a penmanship class at Neason Hill, I was roundly scolded after walking away from the blackboard where I had just scripted a big, lower-case letter p with fat ascender and descender loops instead of the straight vertical lines the teacher had apparently warned the classroom to use. Nor does being asked twice by a teacher – sternly the second time – to erase the blackboard earn a young student brownie points.

Okay, so sometimes I just wasn't paying attention. Never mind.

Musing over those happenings reminded me of a piece printed last year in the Tribune about the incidental perils of partial deafness. The article was written by a hard-of-hearing writer who lived in Rhode Island. Since most of us elders don't hear all that well, this Senior Scene insert seems like a good place to remind readers of her wry observations.

People get snippy when they're constantly asked to repeat something. Aware of this, the writer, Eleanore Devine, nevertheless advised hard-of-hearing people against simply smiling and nodding at persons who rarely speak above a mutter. Instead, she counseled, they should smile while listening, but all the while half nod and half shake their heads. Otherwise, she warned, they'll risk conceding something they wouldn't agree to, such as donning concrete boots before climbing into a small boat heading to a deep part of Lake Tahoe. (I have slightly exaggerated her warning.)

Does anyone besides me see a market here for big red lapel badges saying "I'm losing my hearing, not my marbles?" Or a printed command for jerseys that read, "Please don't explain again. I'm old but I'll get it.?"

Ms. Devine mentioned that another line on that poster urged, "Don't take any notice of Grandma. She is deaf as a post and a bit batty."

The poster's real tidings, as she pointed out, are not that Grandma should be ignored, but that she will likely, if she's dissed, as the kids say, feel rejected and isolated and may set up camp in a far away parallel universe.

I go one step farther. I smile genially while nodding my head and frown thoughtfully while I'm wagging it – being especially careful to pause explicitly between those contrary sentiments so the person after my ear won't be looking around for my keeper.

Ms. Devine mentioned seeing the caption, "She's losing her hearing, not her marbles" below the picture of a stooped older woman cupping a hand to her ear. Both funny and poignant, the message was the subject of a poster on display at the York Deaf Society in England.

The skinny about human organs

Many a young whippersnapper has volunteered the meaning of a big word he'd just used while I was trying to figure out what the word was, not what it meant.

Psychologists informally refer to geriatric battiness as "Elderly Lost Marbles" (I may have explained this in another column; I can't remember), which all but obligates me to mention that during a school semester in which our grandchildren lived with us, we appositely nicknamed the seven-year-old "Little Big Horn" and the ten-year-old "Lost Marbles." (Clearly, deft segues are second nature to me.) The boys are descendants on my wife's side (as if you hadn't already assumed that).

It used to be Nellie could hear a pin land on a carpet. Now most of our evening conversations play out something like this:

Me: "What's on the TV, Hon?"
Nellie: "Do what now?" (She's from the South.)
Me: "What's on TV?"
Nellie: "What's on TV?"
Me: "Uh-huh."

Nellie: "You have the remote. Check and see."
Me: "What?"
Nellie: YOU HAVE THE REMOTE!"
Me: "Oh."

Frequent, unplanned naps are also a nuisance of old age. Nellie and I watch a little bit of TV most nights, and all too often I doze through crucial scenes. I swear that one minute I could be watching a live broadcast of the Titanic scraping that wayward iceberg and the next minute staring at an open sea and asking myself what in the devil happened to that large magnificent ocean liner.

I've slept through dozens of what had to have been exciting Cleveland Indian and Pittsburgh Pirate rallies.

By and large, sports are well covered on TV. Moreover, seniors, especially, benefit from the fact that athletic contests can be enjoyed even with the audio fully muted. Some TV sports announcers are pretty good, but many, in truth, are just pretty good-looking. Unfortunately, if you're an elder and you don't like sports, most of the time you'll find yourself up the once-called "vast wasteland" of TV without a paddle.

There's a saying: "Lead with your best wine." Ms. Devine's best offering – it seemed to me – came near the end of her article: At a high-school reunion, her friend, after finally isolating a long-ago crush, looked up at him – only to frustratingly mumble, 'My [hearing aid] battery's just gone dead.'"

There's a saying: "Lead with your best wine." Ms. Devine's best offering – it seemed to me – came near the end of her article: At a high-school reunion, her friend, after finally isolating a long-ago crush, looked up at him – only to frustratingly mumble, 'My [hearing aid] battery's just gone dead.'"

Cheers! Uh, CHEERS!

The skinny about human organs

It takes a modicum of creativity to write a humorous newspaper column, but nowhere near the flair required to make a saucepan of perfectly seasoned "Texas Red" chili or to whip up a serving dish full of savory potato salad.

In any event, trying to write funny stuff sets me to wondering about such things, about what Eric Hoffer, America's "Longshoreman Philosopher," characterized as "Discontent translated into art."

Moreover, now that I'm well into my seventies, I read with more than my usual interest a recently published Associated Press story on how aging affects a person's creativity.

Not that it's only the fault of the writer, but the AP story hashes over some really bad science. Mainly, it reports on misdirected research resulting from experimenters' ignoring evidence clearly proving that a person's bodily organs all age at different rates.

As bad, if not worse, it is clear that not one member of the research team profiled in that article was abreast of recent investigations probing the likelihood that different parts of the brain itself age at different rates. A person's brain, remember, is highly compartmentalized, and many parts – at least in my case – slumber inertly for days at a time. I suspect that the neurologist running the show was a youngster still in his forties – possibly older. In any event, consider my situation. I'm seventy-four – according to my birth certificate. Most of my organs are exactly that age. On the other hand, two are functionally much younger, while others, by any measure, are indisputably older. (A full scientific explanation is beyond the scope of this piece; diet, predictably, plays a part, however.)

It is entirely possible that my spleen is physically younger than my chronological seventy-four years of life. Doctors haven't a clue as to a spleen's real bodily purpose – "variously functions to modify the blood" – yeah, yeah, yeah, so I can't say for sure. We're all in the same leaky boat on that one.

It is also possible that, biologically speaking, my liver hasn't even turned seventy yet. Once thought by philosophers to be the seat of desire (honest), mine still secretes bile at a pretty good clip, which effluent indirectly bears on a person's regularity. Generally not given to boasting, nonetheless I must mention in passing how unswerving regularity is one of my prouder geriatric attainments. I mean, I could set my clock, accordingly.

Of course, my lungs aren't nearly as powerful as they once were. In truth, I haven't won an argument with my wife in a dozen years. (Persuasion, as most couples learn early in marriage, only works in romance novels and soap operas: loud shouting is the trick to winning a spousal argument.)

Likely, if I hadn't been a heavy smoker when I was a young man, I could still out shout Nellie. Incidentally, it's a peculiarity of human lungs that the right lobe ages faster than the left, explaining why long races at track and field events are always run counterclockwise. (Think it through, and the connection becomes obvious.) I estimate the age of my lungs – the average of both lobes – is seventy-five, plus or minus six months.

I'm certain my bladder – strictly speaking not an organ – is the oldest vital component in my body. At one time it was capable of easily expanding to the size of a softball, now it protests in a most disconcerting way when it reaches the volume of a golf ball. As a functional unit, I judge that it is rapidly approaching octogenarian footing.

A well-designed human waste system would include a relief valve and overflow tank. (Not that I'm finding fault God, it's just something for You to think about when You start over after You allow the next Big Bang or Big Pfft, or whatever.)

My kidneys haven't unduly aged at all and are in perfect synch with my official age. I know this because they dispatch urine at the tempo of a runaway nuclear reactor, same as always. (See above as this relates unfavorably to the matter of my slowly vanishing bladder.)

Skin – yours, mine, and the rest of God's creatures – is more a well-contoured container than anything else. Still, medicos classify skin as an organ, give it the same prominence as kidneys, lungs, and so on. I blame dermatologists on the deception: charge an arm and leg for treating a mere container? You jest.

Measured against other old timers, I'd say my eyes and ears are exactly my chronological age: I wear trifocal glasses, and I'm shopping for hearing aids, looking for a make that can amplify the purring of a cat and simultaneously attenuate the roar of a nearby rocket lifting off.

My sniffer, unfortunately, hasn't caught up with my eyes and ears. I say unfortunately because a whiff of steamed broccoli still affects me in the same way as a good slug of castor oil. Embarrassed early in life, I avoid restaurants on St. Patrick's Day, afraid I'll be seated next to diners who have been served plates heaped with corned beef and cabbage.

It may simply be that a nose the size of mine wears out piecemeal, that some sections age slower than others, and that mine, therefore, is still quite efficient at picking up the smell of ratty old sneakers, etc.

Dr. Werling Allspaugh, quoted in the AP story mentioned above, claims aging of the human brain doesn't in the least diminish one's ability to create. Dr. Allspaugh is head of Poultry Behavioral Sciences at a large state university close to Sioux City, Iowa. He bases his argument wholly on experiments related to the art of painting (by humans, of course, not chickens), which is where he takes a wrong turn.

But what about other common endeavors of exceptional creativity, Doctor? Composing political speeches, for example? Disguising the effort to improve a golf lie? Credibly explaining to your wife why, back from the grocery store, you forgot the corn starch.

Just as different regions of the brain control our various organs, different parts of or brain manage our creativity. You'd think a neurologist, especially one with a PhD from a well-regarded state university, would know that, would understand intuitively that parts of our brains age at different rates in the same way that each of our organs grow old at their own pace. Sadly, it's apparent that Dr. Allspaugh, thinking he'd wove his way some ninety-plus yards to a touchdown, actually fumbled the kickoff.

Sweating the small stuff

I've become a worrywart. Age does that to people. Piddling things, the petty stuff that I wouldn't have wasted a second fretting over when I was younger, keep me awake at night.

I should have seen it coming.

Uncle Rodney, not long after his wife died, sold his home and moved in with my parents – with his sister, my stepmother, and my father. He was seventy-eight at the time, in good health, easy going, and quick of mind, although wholly undomesticated.

The elderly widow living next door to my folk's home did not own a car, and she encouraged Uncle Rodney to park his six-year-old, spotless, exemplary, four-door sedan, in her driveway.

One day, out of the blue, Uncle Rodney announced he had driven his car for the last time. He didn't explain the reason for his decision, but true to his word, he never drove it again. Likely, he either caused an accident or nearly caused one.

Every Wednesday morning, however, beginning the week after his sudden surprise announcement, he checked his car's oil level, measured the pressure of every tire, including the spare, ran the engine ten minutes, pulled ahead a few feet, backed up a few feet, wiped off the guava, and so on and so forth. This went on for months. And then one morning the car wouldn't start. It groaned several times but that was all. My father jumpered the car's battery, but it still wouldn't start.

Uncle Rodney was a tough, self-assured old codger, not one to brood over life's minutiae. Still, the mere possibility that his car, which had barely been moved for almost a year, and which he planned never to drive again, needed the attention of a mechanic kept him awake the whole night. The next morning he had it towed to a garage and fixed.

In a word, Uncle Rodney was suffering from progressive senioritis, a disease of many symptoms and no cure brought on by the slow, life-long transformation of a person's funny bone into a worry bone.

Worrying, simply put, is a progressive and unavoidable malediction of old age. And, wise or foolish, rich or poor, healthy or infirm, the curse prevails.

Nowadays, our family bills are fewer and more easily managed than ever. We can afford hobbies: I bowl (kind of) and my wife plays bingo (competently).

We enjoy an occasional excursion on a tour bus, taking in a Cleveland Indians' or Pittsburgh Pirates' baseball game, blowing a few bucks at a casino, touring a site of historical importance, meander the disordered paths of a botanical garden, and so on.

Our house is solid and every appliance practically new. We're retired, so neither of us gives a hoot if the weather forecast calls for a day of warm sunshine or ten inches of snow. In fact, my wife, born and raised in Alabama, would about as soon watch wind-whipped falling snow as a drama on TV.

So, what's left for me to worry about? Well, health for one thing, mine and my wife's. The fact that we're both in good physical shape for two old geezers is totally irrelevant. Here's what I mean.

Seniors get lightheaded easier than young folks – most of us do anyway – and a few weeks ago, noticing that my first unsteady steps after rising too fast from a chair were not only getting wobblier but also lasting longer; I visited our family doctor.

A slight woman in her forties, Doctor Serum (close enough) is not only smart as a whip she also has a bedside manner that the late etiquette maven Emily Post could have featured in one of her books. Of course, I let on it isn't my idea that I'm there (it's a male thing), and after describing my symptoms, I declare solemnly that my wife was concerned.

Dr. Serum nodded and said nice things about my wife, who is also one of her patients. While explicitly ruling out a few possible causes, she snuck in the fact that I was seventy-four years old – somehow making it sound like an achievement – and in words that would calm a junkyard watchdog on a windy night, suggested my problem was geriatric in nature and not worth the expense of investigating medically.

"Geriatric vertigo?" I asked brightly, pleased with my coinage for light-headedness.

"Your words," she laughed, "not mine."

I was certain – my next visit to Dr. Serum's office – that the sore on the back of my neck was no less than a pus-filled carbuncle and more likely the wellspring of dangerous basal-cell carcinomas. After all, it was the size and color of a ripe cherry, my wife's Lilliputian assessment notwithstanding.

I looked up the word "pustule" when I got home and found out it was doctor jargon for "pimple."

Perhaps the loose skin on the bottom of my right foot isn't the beginning of leprosy, but then again, maybe it is. All the same, I'll sleep better if Dr. Serum takes a look.

THE BONE YARD

The turkey has landed

In an episode of the TV show "Everybody Loves Raymond," which is now in reruns, Raymond's wife Debra somehow wrests the privilege of preparing the family's Thanksgiving Day dinner from her domineering, self-important mother-in-law, the world's greatest mother, cook, and housekeeper.

Debra's choice for the entrée? A two-foot long, twelve-pound, Atlantic cod!

I like fish as an entree. But for a Thanksgiving dinner? The show's writers could have come up with another screw-ball entree – vegetable pizza for example – but the choice of fish was a real howler.

For years my wife very ably cooked Thanksgiving dinner for our extended family, for a gathering of our relatives at our place on that festive November Thursday.

I carved the turkey for her first-ever thanksgiving dinner.

Surviving that assignment unscathed (I'm irreparably unhandy), I proudly set the big tray of carved meat in front of my place at the end of the table and waited confidently for the compliments that I knew were sure to follow.

My sister Coretta was the first to remark on the way in which I had deftly disunited the bird's parts.

"Picasso!" she blurted out, scrambling to her feet as if trying for a better perspective. "Your tray of turkey, Hugh, it somehow reminds me of an abstract Picasso painting. How clever!"

"As if you'd know a Picasso painting from a checkered watercolor with little coded numbers all over it," I replied. Girding my loins, I added, "Like, anyone here knows a Picasso painting from a tossed Italian vegetable salad." (Actually, I girded only one loin, but they didn't know.)

Jasper, my brother, who is an accomplished trout fisherman despite a soft spot in his heart for night crawlers, broke the silence. "Nice job, Hugh. What'd you carve that big boy with, your chain saw?"

A cousin wanted to know exactly what kind of exotic bird it had been pre-mortem.

On that one, Nellie, my wife, leaped to my defense. "A nineteen-pound turkey. Honest."

"I always thought," another cousin piped up, "that turkeys came with big legs. You sure it wasn't a woody duck, Hugh?"

"What counts is the taste," I mumbled.

Sensing that our family's congenital faultfinders were ganging up on me, my loin ungirded, I silently bent to the task of apportioning the meat on each plate of an awaiting stack.

I have not carved a turkey since that day, and Hell will freeze over before I carve another.

My humiliation that Thanksgiving, though painful and obviously unforgotten, falls short of the embarrassment of a friend on another Thanksgiving Day dinner at which I was a guest.

At the time, I was recently graduated from college, still single, and living alone in a furnished apartment in Santa Monica, California. Three other guys, each also twenty-something, single, and launching professional careers, lived in the same building. Evenings and weekends we hung out together, etc., etc. (Here isn't the place to elaborate on exactly what we did, suffice it to say we were all in our twenties, dating, etc.)

George, an engineer employed by Hughes Aircraft Company, like to cook. And on the occasion of our first Thanksgiving together he invited us to his apartment for a turkey-and-trimmings, BYOBeer dinner.

Wearing a yellow apron featuring a furiously sweating gobbler making tracks for a distant forrest, he greeted us enthusiastically and waved us into his living room where he had set up four TV trays.

All the apartments in the building were three-room units consisting of a tiny kitchen, a living room, and a bedroom. The kitchen and living room were separated by a wall just long enough to shield most of the kitchen from occupants of the living room. The bedroom could be reached from a door in the rear wall of the living room.

George had the NFL, Thanksgiving Day football game on the TV, and we three guests took seats together on the sofa, leaving an overstuffed chair for George to sit in.

The sofa faced the TV set and more or less looked out on the opening into the kitchen.

We had settle in, and during TV commercials we were teasing George over his dawdling cooking ways when suddenly, out of the blue, a basketball bounced from the kitchen into the living room, stopping just short of the sofa.

Only, it wasn't a basketball. It was George's nicely browned, fourteen-pound, stuffed turkey, the entrée for our Thanksgiving dinner. Somehow, in transferring the bird from his oven to a kitchen counter, it slipped from his glove-protected hands.

So help me, that bird bounced three times before coming to a rest on the living room carpet in front of where we were watching the game.

Startled, and while we were still wondering what in the deuce was going on, George, still with a large, quilted glove on each hand, ran into the room, scooped up our main course, and high-tailed it back into the kitchen.

"Luckily," he shouted over his shoulder, "I have a backup-turkey in the oven!" Shortly, we heard water running.

Regaining our senses, we began shouting wisecracks:

"Hey, we weren't in that big a hurry, George."

"Personally, I'd of set up a buffet, George."

"Did you hit the frothy a little early today, George?"

In any event, a half-hour later we were loading our plates with tasty slices of turkey, mashed potatoes, and cornbread dressing and passing around a small salad bowl of cranberry sauce.

I also remember that the stuffing was a tad dry and somebody saying that he loved it because its consistency reminded him of his favorite candy, peanut brittle.

Looking back, I at least have to credit George for knowing how to carve a turkey. Only he kept the drumsticks for himself. I guess.

More precious than gold

Early in the 19th century a throng of mill workers in Nottingham, England, went bananas over the prospect of losing their jobs, and they smashed the mill's new, automatic machinery. Led by one, Ned Ludd, the rampage spread to other cities, and members of the movement became known as Luddites.

So far, so good.

The historical account soon jumps the track, however, beginning with early newspaper reports that wrongly suggested the piston of Mr. Ludd's mental steam engine had rusted tight – as Brits characterized battiness during the Industrial Revolution. Furthermore, contrary to initial reports, the workers' rampage positively was not a protest against the technological changes underlying the mill's new labor-saving machinery.

Mr. Ludd wasn't a nut, nor were he and his co-workers enraged over the likelihood of losing their means of living. The simple fact is they lacked the technical aptitude to run the new machinery. And being typical adult males, they weren't about to admit to any in-dexterous shortcomings of that sort.

I'm certain that's what truly happened because in the late 1940s I tried my hand at running complicated machinery. How in the deuce I, a young man who couldn't screw a nut on a bolt without referring to a drawing, slipped by the tool-and-die-making apprenticeship committee at Talon, Incorporated, is something only an astrologer could explain. Talon, at the time virtually the world's only mass producer of zippers, employed some two thousand workers in Meadville, Pennsylvania, alone.

In keeping with Talon's rigorous four-year apprenticeship program, I spent the first two weeks in a basement room studying the hardness, plasticity, adaptability, and so on of various metals and the next two weeks in a first-floor cage full of expensive hand tools, a secured room that a silver-backed gorilla packing a crowbar couldn't have busted into.

The porridge hit the fan the first Monday of my fifth week of apprenticeship, my first day "on the floor."

Guided by my boss, we stopped next to where a blocky, unpretentious-looking machine the size of a growing buffalo lurked ominously.

"This is a shaper," my boss said.

Respectfully silent, I waited.

"Basically," he went on, "it shapes metal into rectangular blocks. A moron could run it."

Appreciating his gift for understatement, I nodded shrewdly.

"It won't bite," he said, gesturing at a well-shielded red button printed with the word ON.

I bent forward and pressed the button. A heavy electrical motor began whining and shortly the whole top of the machine, about a quarter ton of cast iron, began moving ponderously back and forth. Before long, it reached a steady-state speed of maybe fifty strokes a minute.

"Whoa," I said edging back for a better perspective. "That's really something!"

My boss, after a quizzical look at some ill-defined distant object, explained the purpose of each of the machine's four controls. Briefly, here's how it worked: Mounted on the front-end of the part that rumbled back and forth like a 500-pound battering ram was a device called a chuck. The chuck held a tool, called a bit, which was ground to the likeness of a miniature plow blade. A vise mounted at the front of the shaper's base held the work piece, a block of rough-cut metal somewhat larger than called for in the schematic of the final product.

Once the machine started, the bit began shaving slivers of metal from the work piece. The vise holding the work piece was nudged crossways incrementally on each return stroke, and before too long the whole top surface was shaved down a tiny fraction of an inch. The piece was turned over, and the bottom was similarly machined. Two more rotations resulted in a finished job of right-angle exactitude that brick-layers would kill for.

Nowhere in the world is there a simpler, less complicated motor-driven machine, and inside a week I was well on my way to becoming a world-class shaper operator.

Alas, something the boss didn't tell me was that a shaper bit eventually dulls from use. Nor did the wily rascal explain that it was my job to sharpen it.

The three-dimensional aspect of grinding a shaper bit is what done me in, was the Achilles' heel of my makeup that kept me from becoming a machinist of tool-and-die-maker caliber. Try though I might – I secretly wasted enough expensive tool-bit stock to armor a Sherman tank – I never got the hang of grinding a shaper bit to where it didn't lose its edge a few dozen strokes into a job.

When a shaper bit dulls, the shavings it produces turn blue from the heat of friction and the cutting oil starts to smoke. In my case it happened so often that whenever I started a job a veteran machinist would make a big show of standing by with a fire extinguisher.

A fellow apprentice once showed me how easy it was to make a shaper bit. Whisking a two-inch length of bit stock this way and that across a fast-turning grinding wheel, in no time he handed me a finished product. Sonny, I'll call him, was so indifferent to his

God-given genius for things mechanical that he acted as if he'd just unwrapped a package of chewing gum and offered me a stick.

I used the bit on my next job. And my next job. And for the first time in my life I realized that gold and silver were not the world's only precious metals.

That priceless little tool bit and a slackness of business – I was shortly moved from the shaper to a catchall job called "bench work" – saved my job. What saved my dignity was the onset of the Korean War, which gave me the opportunity to gracefully quit the Talon, Incorporated, Tool and Die Making apprentice program and enlist in the U.S. Air Force. After my discharge, I attended college on the Korean War G.I. Bill, majoring in the far less challenging field of electronic engineering.

"Everybody wants ta get inta da act!"

"Why," Nellie asked, "are you making faces at yourself in the bathroom mirror?"

I didn't know she had returned from shopping.

"I'm practicing," I said.

"Practicing? Practicing what?"

"Did you see the ad in the Tribune about the Chippendales?"

She shrugged. "The male dancers who'll be performing at the Stable Pitt and Pub restaurant? Yes, I glanced at it. Why?"

"The ad says they're the hit of Las Vegas."

"So?"

"So, now that I've reached seventy-five, the tipping-point age for athletes, I've decided to give up bowling and become a male dancer."

Nellie didn't say anything for several seconds. "How do those hobbies connect," she asked finally, "to you standing in front of the bathroom mirror in your Jockey shorts tossing your head around and squinting your eyes?"

I said, "Take another look at the guys in that ad, Dear." I gave my head a smart, ain't-I-pretty tilt. "I'm perfecting their sexy come-hither look."

"I see," she said. "And suppose it works. Then what?"

I ignored her cut, her belittling of my masculinity. "Then . . . I have a plan."

"A plan?"

"At this time," I muttered, "I'm not saying what it is."

I turned from the mirror, showed her a new visage of sultry, bedroom eyes, a likeness of the face of the lead Chippendale. "What do you think?" I said.

"I think," she said, "you're about to fall asleep standing up."

I glared (gently – respecting my marriage vow) and turned back to the mirror. "Are you going?"

"Take in the Chippendales? It depends. If tickets are discounted for seniors. And there's a reserved section – up front."

She may have been putting me on. Anyway, I told her I'd call Wanda, the restaurant's owner, and find out.

Wanda Ramaley runs the Stable, Pit & Pub. I know her slightly from a bowling banquet I got stuck with arranging and decided, a few years back, on her pub for the meal.

Wanda has been cool to me, however, since I asked if her kitchen's red-hot Hungarian stuffed peppers were the very last meal eaten by the model for the big plastic horse in the restaurant's anteroom. Its mouth is agape and its lips are cast forever in a last desperate whinny for water. My friend ate one of the peppers, and he swears it melted his fillings.

I dialed the restaurant's telephone number and whoever answered said to hold on a minute. In a few seconds, Wanda picked up and asked how she might be of help.

"Wanda!" I replied smartly. "It's Hugh!"

"Oh," she said, adding after a second, "Uh, which Hugh?"

"Hugh McClintock! You remember."

"Oh, yes. You bowl – kind of – don't you?"

"Whatever," I said. "I see where you've booked the Chippendales. Aren't they something!"

She said, "Their agent called me."

"No matter," I said. "I'm calling, Wanda, because I've been thinking. You could easily – considering the demographics of this area – double the attendance at the show if you'd work in a skit for seniors. What do you say?"

"Um . . . a skit for seniors? I'm not so sure, Hugh. What kind of skit?"

"A dance number, of course. A little something I worked up."

"Right. Who'd do the dancing?"

"I'd be the lead. I have three friends in mind that I'll cast as second bananas."

She asked me if I had looked closely at the ad. "The Chippendales are all husky, flat-bellied young men. With lots of long, thick hair."

I said, "We needn't get into details just yet, Wanda. But you can rest assured that I've worked all that stuff out."

"Really?" she said. "And what do you call your act? 'Shock and Awe?'"

Chortling politely, I said, "That's a good one, Wanda. No, we're The Davenports—in keeping with the furniture theme. Cool, huh?"

"The Davenports?" she said. Asperity had crept into her voice.

"Yeah," I said. "We kicked around The Sofas, but the term Sofas is just not show biz."

She said, "No, not like The Davenports, that's true. What would you charge me?"

Three hundred dollars, I answered. "After expenses, that'll leave us—"

"Expenses?"

"Little things," I said. "But they add up. Support hose, orthopedic dancing shoes, wigs, tights . . . Advil. We'll spring for our own music."

"Your own music?"

"Yes. Something upbeat but dignified. I have a Jo Ann Castle tape of "Westchester Cathedral." We'd coordinate our dancing with the oh-bo-de-o-do lines. I ran the idea by Maud and Floy, bowlers on my team in a mixed senior league at Lost Lanes in Cambridge

Springs. They didn't say much (possibly for the first time in their lives), but I sensed that they approved."

Wanda said, "Westchester Cathedral? By Jo Ann . . . ?"

"Jo Ann Castle," I said. "She was the lead pianist on the Lawrence Welk TV show. Boy, could she –"

"Hugh, the bottom line is, that I just couldn't afford . . . the Davenports."

"I see. Well . . . Wanda, we've been friends a long time. So I'm going to cut you a deal. The Davenports will pay for their personal gear. How does that strike you?"

"Honestly?" she replied. "Like a mud pie in the face."

"It sounded as if you said, 'Like a mud–'"

"I'd still be way over budget, Hugh."

"Boy, you are tough, Wanda. My final offer: two-hundred bucks and we also pay for the personal stuff?"

"I've got a call on the other line, Hugh. I'll get back to you."

"That'll work. Before you go, will there be a reserve section in front at the show? Nellie wants to know."

"Um, I don't think so. But that could change."

Wanda hung up as I was asking another question.

The woman knows show business like I know brain surgery.

By any other name, it's still blather

Blatherology is, of course, the study of blather. If you're a philologist – a word hound – you probably already know that blather is a synonym for flapdoodle. The terms blarney and malarkey are linguistic first cousins of blather. And bamboozle is blather kicked up a notch.

A two-syllable word of barnyard ethnicity that regularly seasons the speech of gandy dancers, drill sergeants, and newspaper editors, is also another word for blather. Whether a bovine or equine stem, the use of either version is considered to be in bad taste except, of course, by the incurably adolescent Hollywood crowd.

Serious blatherologists insist the word blather is meaningless outside the context of an American presidential campaign. They may have a point.

In this Country, the first recorded, clearly obvious blather was penned by super-patriot Thomas Paine. In a snit – as he often was – Paine accused President George Washington of private treachery and public hypocrisy, claimed he was an ungrateful lout and almost certainly an impostor. At least Paine had the common sense not to charge President Washington with being a summer soldier or a sunshine patriot (No groaning.) In any event, blather has ever since been part and parcel of every American presidential race, as the examples gathered here will, I believe, convincingly illustrate.

Think back just a few years. Al Gore's followers claimed that George W. Bush didn't have brains enough to drain lemonade from his cowboy boots (I've cleaned that saying up a little) let alone run the Country, while Bush's supporters assured us that Gore was merely a bookish policy wonk, a man long on talk and short on deeds. Both accusations are pure blather – tepid as blather goes, but blather, nonetheless.

In the early years of the Republic, describing an American politician as monarchial in spirit was the whale dung of political effrontery – the vilest kind of low insult. Portly John Adams suffered the indignity of being nicknamed "His Rotundity." Political foes of John Tyler, who succeeded to the presidency upon the death of William Henry Harrison, referred to Tyler as "His Accidentcy."

Why Democrats haven't dubbed President Bush "His Fraudulency," as they did Republican Rutherford B. Hayes who won the office in the disputed election of 1876, is unclear. Likely, it's because the specter of British royalty no longer haunts the collective mind of America's hyper-patriots.

For the same reason, calling President Bush "His Redundancy" probably wouldn't work even though Democrats are certain vice-president Richard Chaney hovers 24/7 just outside the oval office and is the real power behind the big chair of American politics.

President William Clinton was a bright man. But he was a dim bulb when it came to managing his personal life. Reports of his postnuptial meanderings were characterized – ironically by a member of his own staff – as "bimbo eruptions." Catchy, the phrase will no doubt follow him to his grave and may even end up in one of those two-inch-thick tomes of immortal phrases. (Never mind that use of the word "bimbo" was a try at misplacing the culpability of Clinton's extracurricular activities.)

John F. Kennedy was caught on tape describing Richard Nixon as a "filthy lying son-of-a-bitch." "Not blather at all," Democrats insisted, only a keen insightful observation. In any event, it was uttered before Nixon's proven involvement in the Watergate burglary, explaining, perhaps, why Kennedy minced his words.

Presidential campaign slogans are often cleverly transmuted by opponents. Republican candidate Barry Goldwater's 1964 motto, "In your heart you know he's right," was recast by backers of Democratic candidate Lyndon Johnson as, "In your guts you know he's nuts."

In the 1968 presidential race, Democrats pasted a Republican campaign banner proclaiming, "Nixon's the one," onto a billboard-size poster bearing a photograph of an Afro-American woman pregnant with what had to be a very robust, final-trimester fetus.

Lyndon Johnson, among other politically savvy Democrats, enjoyed slyly suggesting that Jerry Ford, when he was a lineman for the University of Michigan football team, played the game without his helmet. Although Ford himself never publicly denied the charge, his fellow Republicans insisted Johnson's remark was little more than an air-headed canard. Again, probity isn't necessarily a hallmark of blather.

President Harry S. Truman assured America that should Dwight Eisenhower become our president his leadership would make President Grant's scandal-scarred administration look like a model of Christian rectitude. (Ever a scrappy fellow, Truman also promised a music critic, who had panned his daughter's singing debut, that he'd soon need a "new nose, beefsteak for a black eye, and perhaps a supporter below.")

Mining history for passages of campaign blather is as easy as finding oil under a desert of Saudi Arabia: the reserves are vast and all but begging to be tapped. The product, of course, must be broadly refined – same as newly produced oil – for public consumption.

John Quincy Adams' pithy summation of James K. Polk's shortcomings is a typical extraction. Polk, according to Adams, "[had] no wit, no literature, no point of argument, no gracefulness of delivery, no eloquence of language, no philosophy, no pathos, and no felicitous impromptus."

History doesn't record whether Polk truly was bereft of "felicitous impromptus," but the fact that he didn't challenge Adams to a duel strikes me as telling.

I personally am not an accredited blatherologist. I do research for a friend who is, however, (PhD, Harvard, 1974), and I'm chomping at the bit waiting for the 2004 presidential campaign to begin in earnest. The great East Texas oil field discovered in 1930 was soon producing over a million barrels of oil a day. I expect each of the upcoming party conventions will produce noxious oily political blather at about the same rate.

A few short hops to peace on earth

As unbelievable as it seems, I was a handsome child: oodles of curly blond hair, alert blue eyes, and a smile so endearing that it set mature women to gushing baby talk as if it was their native language.

Then my genes kicked in, puberty struck, and I grew up. Now a balding, near-sighted, fat, sour-faced old wobbly, that a stranger would guess to be a retired high-school algebra teacher who grumps over everything from unsheathed woman's legs to un-diapered tree crotches.

Actually, I've never taught anything, let alone a subject as difficult as algebra. My brother Silas, on the other hand, was a public school teacher all his working life.

Silas is even uglier than I am. Back when I was courting, I'd fix him up (as we used to call arranging a friend a date) so we could double date, making me a handsome escort and him a homely chaperon. If it wasn't for Silas, I'd be a sulky hermit troll living in a corrugated box under a bridge salvaging my ego by jumping out and frightening passing women.

Although my brother and I would finish one-two in any contest of the ill-favored, we are way different in our interests.

Silas likes to hunt, fish, and trap. I couldn't hit the wall of a barn from inside with a sawed-off 12-guage shotgun; I've never cast a lure where the fish weren't fasting; and when I tried running a trap line the only thing I caught more often than a worthless possum was my thumb.

I like to bowl and golf, and used to be half-way decent at tennis. Silas roams a good half of his side of the court playing a tennis lob, staggers around as if he's suffering from senescent vertigo. When he finishes a game of bowling, the gutters are as dust free as the table tops in a spinster's home. Once at a golf driving range he beaned a golfer practicing by herself at the end of the hundred-foot arc of driving tees.

It makes sense, then, that when it comes to physical activity our interests are oil and water. So we compete in other arenas. Why do we compete at all? Because we can't help it, because we are congenitally predisposed to lock horns at every opportunity. That's how brothers are. Heck, it's the way men are. (Of course, women are competitive too, some even more than men. But this piece isn't about the proclivities of my wife and her friends.)

Centuries ago Lao-tzu, a Chinese philosopher, postulated that greed was the worst of all disastrous behavior. Perhaps he was right. But certainly the vice of naked competitiveness (I don't mean nudist camp volleyball) is right up there too, at least as tragic as wearing a brown pin-stripe suit to interview for a job at IBM.

Competitiveness, as a human trait, isn't necessarily all bad, however. A world without golf courses to putter around on? Badminton given the bird? Archery quivering away to strolling in the woods? Senior-center bakeoffs that don't rise to the occasion? Life would be duller than setting through a reunion of spousal relatives in a picnic shelter on a rainy summer afternoon.

Which brings me to the subject of this piece: rivalry is a good thing – up to a point. Unfortunately, that point is often reached all too soon, it being that the seeds of human nature took root long before Neanderthals Toom and Moog squared off arguing over who speared the most fish, a situation aggravated by the fact that neither man could count past the number two.

So, what's the answer, the solution to the problem of wanton human aggression? Clearly, the "Big Thinkers" don't know.

In the short run, farmers may offer a solution. Farmers know everything about everything because they must to survive. Resolving a dispute by taking a two-by-four to a stubborn mule is indisputably effective. Equipping one end of the table at corporate meeting with a three-foot section of a wall stud, however, isn't practical and might tend to inhibit forthrightness on the part of subordinate corporate officers.

The long-term solution, which Silas and I stumbled onto, is so obvious, so uncomplicated, so easily implemented that it's hard to believe it's remained undiscovered until now. In short, by chance, we found a harmless way to deal with unrestrained belligerence.

The answer: Chinese Checkers.

That's right, the venerable game of Chinese Checkers. Disputes would be resolved by games played at neutral sites among heads of states, winner take all.

Reason with me here. First, the playing pieces, tiny marbles, are ineffective as hand-launched missiles; second, up to six people can play at one time (just try a little sneaky slight-of-hand with five people watching); third, the game itself is language independent, and fourth, it's so simple to play that none but a child would boast of winning – although, as this is an academic quality, expository piece, it would be wrong if I didn't mention that I seldom lose to Silas.

Merely consider the fact that the game is language-independent or, more precisely, that it is language-neutral. Let's say, the American and French presidents are playing, and in the heat of the game the American, a Texan, slips up and calls the French president a shameless goat roper. A quick follow-up smile by the

American and likely the French president would think he just heard himself characterized as a beneficent shepherd.

Sir Isaac Newton allegedly deduced the existence of gravity when he was hit on the head by a falling apple. Silas and I discovered an equally powerful force, also by chance, playing Chinese Checkers at a family gathering on a rainy Thanksgiving afternoon.

We expect that scientific recognition will follow publication of our in-depth sociological study, "On Conflict Resolution by Chinese Checkers," which only awaits the working-out of authorship, that is, whether the author's line should start with my name or Silas's. Our lawyers are honing their arguments.

Me? A Baron? Awesome!

I've slightly known, maybe, five lawyers in my lifetime, none of whom struck me as a snob.

Then I see the words Preston Q. Wordbin, Esq., or Elmo Chatty, Esq., or Harry Garrulous, Esq., in an advertisement or on a promotional letter, and I have second thoughts about the instincts of persons drawn to practicing law.

The abbreviation Esq., of course, stands for Esquire. Why attorneys are more deserving of a snooty title than, say, auto mechanics or house painters, isn't all that clear to me.

What's worse, in America the title "Esquire" smacks of the most egregious of social pretence, of having chucked the appellation "working stiff" for an imposter fellowship in the British system of peerage.

The stem (the "squire" part of "esquire") originally meant a propertied country gentleman. Over time, however, the meaning changed, and the term squire eventually came to stand for the young males who helped medieval knights dress for battle.

Thus, the demanding job of personal manservant to a knight – I presume donning a suit of mail is a tad more arduous than slipping into a pair of jogging sweats – was eventually judged worthy of the title of squire, the entry-level position of British gentry.

The practice of law is a gender-independent calling, as all vocations should be, and the word esquire entitles both males and females. I make this point only because several years back a well-meaning but socially ignorant male lawyer championed suffixing "Esquire" with "ette" at a N.O.W. meeting in Denver, Colorado. The poor misguided bugger hasn't been heard from since. Rumor has it there's a connection between the man's disappearance and the rampant building construction – in particular the digging of foundations – underway in Denver at the time. According to a brief mention in The Denver Post, his disappearance remains a mystery.

So, lawyers feel they need a distinctive title of their own. Okay. But why one that reminds of British aristocracy? Meeting with a lawyer compares to an audience with royalty? Hardly.

What's wrong with the tidy, straightforward designation "Preston Q. Wordbin, Attorney"? Institutionalized hoity toity, implied or otherwise, is downright un-American.

Phil, a long-time friend, suggested lawyers use the neutral title "Blatherskite," as in, "Preston Q. Wordbin, Blatherskite." Clueless as to that word's meaning, I looked it up in my college dictionary. Abbreviated BS, and pejorative to boot, I rejected it out of hand. Phil at the time was licking his wounds over the legal thrashing he took in a divorce battle, which no doubt prejudiced his attitude.

Isn't there an association of lawyers that convenes periodically to formulate policy and pass around trial defense strategies? "Trial Attorneys against Sensible Laws," or some sort of brotherhood of that name? I think so. Who better than members of that estimable body to consider a new, less patronizing appellation than "Esquire"? (On second thought, who worse?)

If it makes sense for lawyers to use snooty peerage titles, why shouldn't all professionals append their names with similar uppity handles?

The grades of British peers, ranked top to bottom by degree of snobbery, are: duke, marquis, earl, viscount, baron, knight, squire, and page. Actually, knight, squire, and page aren't truly titles of nobility, but the distinction is small. The feminine inflections are: duchess, marchioness (marquis), countess (earl), viscountess, and baroness.

The reason Brits chucked the title Earless is obvious (compare Earless in Dublin to Sleepless in Seattle). But "Marquisess" isn't all that bad, taking into account that marquis is pronounced mar-key, and therefore, marquises is pronounced mar-key-ess. At any rate, permutations go begging.

It takes six years of higher-education and a passing mark on state "boards" to become a pharmacist. Clearly, druggists, if anybody, are deserving of their own stagy title.

Respecting the depth of a druggist's formal preparation, and replicating the legal profession's custom of using titles of British peerage, it stands to reason pharmacists merit the rank of "Duke."

Instead of "Peter F. Buckly, Registered Pharmacist," Mr. Buckly would simply sign his correspondence, "Peter F. Buckly, Duke." Is that cool or what?

The name Peter F. Buckly, which is a dressed up alias, brings to mind a remark I recently overheard at a big gathering of family and friends. Standing near a cousin nicknamed "Buck," who was petting his Shar Pei – undeniably the world's ugliest dog – I heard a passerby say from the side of his mouth that if it was his dog he'd teach it to walk backwards.

It usually takes five years of college to become an architect, and proportionality, it seems to me, demands that upon graduating, architects should be awarded the title of Viscount or Viscountess.

Employed by J.P. Jones, Naval Architects, Jenny Sackett's business card would inform prospective clients that she was Jennifer T. Sackett, Viscountess at Naval Architecture.

Even practitioners of the lowly vocation of engineering, of which I was once associated (theoretically), would deserve their own titles. Personally, I favor "Baron," as in Hugh J. McClintock, Baron. The title of Baroness, for female engineers, of course, is also cool.

Naturally, in printed form, an engineer's specialty, such as "Board Certified in Ball Bearings," would have to subtend his name: engineering, like medicine, is a discipline of unnumbered, high-paying fields, of specialization.

Certainly craftsmen, those who deign not to call themselves professionals, deserve courtesy titles of their own. The head of a major labor union could start the ball rolling.

Hold on! I lost my head, got carried away picturing myself as a tweed-jacketed, steed-mounted baron graciously accepting the heartfelt applause of devoted field hands lining a back road of my large Highlands estate. The individual who personally suggests applying a nose-in-the-air title to the likes of any carpenter, plumber, auto mechanic, or other tradesman, whom I've ever known, had best offer the guy (or gal) a barf bag at the same time – and be ready to dodge a poke in the old bazoo.

Antlers and horns and tusks? Really, Sir.

Most of my adult life I lived in two large concrete, steel, and glass cities, Los Angeles, California, and Dallas, Texas, and my idea of roughing it amounts to dining late at night on the balcony of a high-up room at an expensive Las Vegas, Nevada, hotel. (Okay, wolfing down cheeseburgers on the second-floor overhang of a cheap Reno hotel. Never mind.)

An upshot of my misspent adult years is that I can barely tell the difference between a wild pheasant and a white, barnyard rooster. The closest I've come to spelunking a real cave is groping my way to an empty table in the smoke and darkness of a big-city basement bistro.

Put another way, I can't talk turkey – in a manner of speaking – with most of the men in these parts. Silas, my brother, would welcome Typhoid Mary into his duck blind sooner than he'd ask me to join him.

Here's where I'm going with this: being a certifiable idiot about outdoorsmanship, I read with the intensity of a young student every article appearing in the *Tribune* written by "Outdoors" reporter John Crooks. Crooks is not only a fine writer, his stories are always interesting and informative.

His recent column, "Think like a turkey, sound like a turkey," was first rate as usual. Regrettably, I can't say the same about one of his earlier pieces in which he reported on the lost art of searching the carpeting of forests for antlers shed by deer.

Imagine. He began that article in the middle! Far better had he opened by vetting the issue of why it is that certain of God's animals must seasonally suffer the agony of bony projections sprouting from the tops of their heads.

Think about it, Mr. Crooks. What terrible original sin did caribou, deer, and moose ever commit? It never occurred to you that I and others who read your always first-rate columns are entitled to know the answer to that question?

I've never immersed myself in the Bible, but I've read enough Scripture to have figured out what actually took place during the creation of those poor, accursed ruminants.

To begin, I reject out-of-hand the notion – advanced by some scholars of the Old Testament in explaining the inchoate nature of manatees – that God rested (dozed off anyway) near the end of his six days of non-stop creativity, as reported in Genesis, and lost

His place in His "Handbook On Everything." That explanation simply doesn't wash.

What likely happened – I've pretty well thought this through – is that He outsourced the job of creating certain animals, deer among them, to a start-up temple in ancient Mesopotamia and turned quality control over to an aide, possibly the same nitwit who allowed, nay, encouraged, Eve to pig-out on fruit plucked from the Tree of Knowledge.

Of course, I can't say for sure who that aide was. Remember, however, that both Noah and Abraham were among His principle worldly helpers. And, let's be honest here folks, neither man is remembered for his competency – not to mention that both were hard of hearing.

I will bet that when God first saw those pairs of deer, moose, and other antlered beasts trudging up the gangplank into Noah's ark there was all heck to pay. "Abraham! You fathead!" Etc.

One thing we know for a certainty, it was around that time when Noah offhandedly coined the phrase "wrath of God." Furthermore, his coinage could not have been in reference to fast-rising waters as God had forewarned him that thunderstorms were on their way.

Another shortfall of Mr. Crooks' article, "The saga of deer antlers," would it have killed him to explain why in the deuce antlers are made of different materials from horns? He could have spelled out why it is that antlers are solid and horns are hollow. Worse, he didn't mention "tusks" at all.

Surely, whitetail bucks could spar as effectively during rut time with antlers structured of ivory as with antlers made of bone.

Take elephants. Think they'd be an endangered species if their tusks were made of bone instead of dentin? The question answers itself. Furthermore, I'm convinced that bone steer horns would dress up the hood of some rich Texan's 1960 Cadillac convertible as handsomely as regular keratin horns – and might even be shinier.

Incidentally, you can buy designer furniture fashioned from the antlers of longhorn cattle from the main Neiman Marcus department store in downtown Dallas: see page 46 in the Company's 2004 Christmas catalog. Better telephone first, however.

The point I started to make was: Why so many different materials for basically the same animal body part? Regrettably, Mr. Crooks turned away from explaining that one, too.

I hate to sound like a scold, but, again, it's pretty obvious that God was at fault here. The same hard material – a rust-proof metal, perhaps – would have worked just fine for antlers, horns, and tusks; Lucifer himself would have killed for horns of titanium.

Most likely God tried to fix things up after the fact, glanced up from reading His "Handbook On Everything," saw it was almost midnight of the first

Saturday ever, let go a cosmic-shattering yawn, and grumbled, "The heck with it."

Imagine, had it only been, say, ten p.m. when He broke from reading the Handbook, it's entirely possible no animals – none living on this planet anyway – would ever bear the cross of bony protrusions growing out of their heads, while in all likelihood we men would sport a brand new crop of hair every year, each harvest a magnificent mane of color-fast, progressively thicker tresses than the last.

And women . . . their feet would stop growing at the onset of puberty and for the rest of their lives shrink incrementally five millimeters in all directions every year on their birthday.

Where was I? Oh yes. You're a splendid writer, Mr. Crooks. Only you should aim higher. And I'm not talking about shooting turkeys roosting in a tree, something I know you'd never do, although likely that's the only way I'd every bag one.

Ten? Only ten, Moses? Are you sure?

Ongoing research will soon inarguably confirm the validity of the assertion that I have set forth in this column.

The Ten Commandments of the Old Testament? <u>There were originally fifteen</u>. That's right, five additional core commandments! And I don't mean that picky follow-up stuff bruited about by the latter-day prophets.

Most likely it was Moses who blew it. Engraved on tablets of stone, an embroidered slab large enough to impressively hold even smallish, four-word law number five, "Thou shalt not kill," would weigh upwards of fifty pounds. Trudging down a long winding, mountain path while shouldering a fifty-pound rock is hardly a walk on the beach, as Moses no doubt discovered early on.

True, men were used to hard manual labor in biblical days, but even Moses, reportedly a big man, could not possibly have hiked all the way up Mt. Sinai and back down more than ten times in one day – not hefting a 50- to 100-pound rock each downward trip. Moses was the only cosigner on the paper work transferring the ten edicts, so there's a good chance he was alone when he met God's messenger to take ownership.

In other words, the circumstantial evidence plainly indicates that Moses left some commandments behind. The exact number is most likely five, but a final reckoning will have to await the ongoing inspections of the caves and crevices along the several trails flowing downward from the pinnacle of Mt. Sinai.

So why didn't Moses seek help? Probably he did, even likely tried to enlist his pals. Still, let's be real here. Would even his best friends have volunteered to likely herniate themselves carrying home fifteen new rock-inscribed law-and-order laws? Talk about a scattering of people, does the word Diaspora come to mind? Never mind that Moses' buddies were nurtured by Hebrew mothers, mankind's domestic law-enforcers extraordinaire: the hefting far transcended ordinary household lifting.

Something else researchers are now agreed on: Moses fetched the Ten Commandments in the wrong order – likely saved the heaviest ("Thou shall not covet thy neighbor's wife, etc., etc., etc.") for last, figuring along about his third trip that God would notice his uncertain lurching and dispatch help.

The familiar listing of the commandments on a single slab of stone by Moses' friend, Matzo the Mason (as he promoted his business), is assuredly the same order they were fetched, and plainly that is not right. The commandment "Thou shalt not commit adultery" nestled between "Thou shalt not kill" and "Thou shalt not steal"? No way.

Not only is the order wrong – reckoned on the degree of potential immortality – but the cadence is also lousy. This matters because the whole nine yards of un-metered Mosaic law would be easier to remember if it wasn't for the likelihood that Moses (no David, he) had a tin ear when it came to rhythm – unless, of course, he was duped into believing that free verse was some kind of highfalutin poetry. It may appear that I have it in for Moses. I don't. From all I've read, Moses was a good man: clever, learned, a natural leader, possibly even a shaman. Remember, however, that he was no spring chicken when he received his marching orders from God.

Not as pressing, but relevant is the issue of every commandment beginning with the archaic "Thou shalt not," especially in this age of American teens believing the word "like" is an all-purpose English language conjunction. I admit this is nit-picking. Words, however, are important, and when thoughtfully penned, are mightier than the sword – some nut said.

Perhaps dressing up every commandment along the lines of, "Like, don't swear, Dude," would better catch the ear of youngsters. And a crisp, "Like, never lie," proscribes bearing false witness against a neighbor – or anybody else, anywhere, anytime.

The rule, "Like, don't crave another person's belongings" seems a bit wordy – until you compare it to the original: "Thou shalt not covet thy neighbor's wife, nor his manservant, nor his maidservant, nor his ox, nor his ass, nor (much of) anything that is thy neighbor's." (For thoroughness of exposition I added the words "much of.")

I ran my thinking past Ted Galeforce, a lawyer friend, and he told me I was crazy – not for suggesting we tinker with anything as sacred as the Biblical Ten Commandments but for believing that laws consisting of a bare minimal number of words would do the job.

"Terse and pithy," he explained, "aren't something we lawyers abide gracefully."

He pulled a heavy book from a shelf behind his desk that was sagging with heavy books, opened it near the middle, and began reading aloud.

"Ah, ha," I interrupted, after enduring the longest five minutes of my life, "I see your point!"

Snapping the book shut, he mumbled something to the effect that a law worded along the lines of "Don't unlawfully appropriate another person's property – not unless you want to leave your teeth in a glass of detergent at night, or not unless you prefer hearing sounds filtered through cauliflowered ears, or not unless you'd like to begin walking with backward-turned feet

– would cut it." But, he said, "certainly not a law shortened to a mere, 'Don't steal.'"

He returned the book to its place on the shelf, taking long enough for me to reach his office doorway. I offered a polite, "Later, Ted," over my shoulder.

So far, according to Google, of the five new commandments already discovered only two have been fully restored. Number twelve reads, "Thou shalt not mention in public thy wife's real age nor shalt a wife publicly mention thy husband's distinguishing sizes, especially his belt size." And number fourteen reads, "Thou shalt neither cook nor serve broccoli except as tiny, uncooked, barely noticeable morsels mixed into a garden salad that is to be eaten on a cold, windy day outdoors."

It's easy to see why Moses ditched number fourteen, the one about engaging in unseemly coveting: that darn law is longer than the original number ten and likely the raw tablet itself weighed over a hundred pounds. Its location is still a mystery. (At least one notable biblical scholar believes it's buried in mud at the bottom of the Gulf of Suez, thought he's sketchy on how it got there.)

Researchers have yet to fully agree on the exact text of commandments eleven, thirteen, and fifteen; I'll write a follow-up column once I hear.

Maybe the name Hugh isn't so dorky after all

Nearing the end of completing my winter Honey Do list, I decided to take the time to lightly research the subject of people's names, and I stumbled on a book written by Paul Dickson titled What's in a Name?

In the first chapter, Dickson briefly defines anagram as a word or phrase made from another word or phrase by rearranging its letters, and then he alphabetically lists the names of people, places, and things that he characterizes as "flipped and scrambled."

In 1975, a pooch named Cilohocla began winning big at Florida's Derby Lane greyhound track. As the name began appearing often in the press, its source became a question of interest to area newspaper readers. Was the name Italian? Gallic? Portuguese? The mystery was finally solved when someone read it backwards. (After which, no doubt, some wag said, "I'll drink to that.")

A residential developer in Santa Ana, California, perhaps a soul mate of the owner of Cilohocla, named a street Initram. The people living there successfully petitioned to have the name changed. Yes, in swinging California! Maybe it was a Mormon neighborhood. Or, maybe – no less stodgy – a hard-shell Baptist enclave.

The idea of spelling names backward intrigues some people. Most housewives in America know that Oprah Winfrey named her TV production company Harpo.

Pat Boone, a pop singer in favor in the 50s and 60s, named the second of his two record companies Agoom Agooc, a backwards spelling (more or less) of his company Cooga-Gooma Enterprises. Incidentally, Cooga Gumya (not Cooga Gooma) is a euphemism for God. (Honest.) You've probably come across it in such postulates as "You can't serve Cooga Gumya and Mammon." Or, perhaps in warnings such as Puritan preacher Cotton Mather's, "Thunder is the voice of Cooga Gumya!" For a perspective on Pastor Cotton's personality – insight into why he was a gung-ho supporter of the Salem witch trials – you must remember how one morning, after an evening spent leading celebrations of the Eucharist at a number of neighborhood churches, he woke up to find a witch under his bed.

Considering that in this day and age political conservatives sometimes wake up to find communists sleeping under their beds, and political liberals aren't able to chase from their bedroom closets the specter of talk-show host Russ Limbaugh lurking inside, perhaps the good pastor shouldn't be judged too harshly.

Ak-Sar-Ben is Nebraska spelled backwards. Once in my early twenties I skated in an ice rink in Omaha by that name. Unable to circle the rink twice consecutively without landing on my keester, the experience convinced me that Ak-Sar-Ben was an all-time dumb name. It didn't help that small kids, skating as if "to the rink born," snickered openly as they zipped past me.

Years ago, guesting on the Tonight Show, Lisa Minnelli used the name Dyju Langard, an anagrammatic rendering of her mother's name. Her mother, of course, was the late Judy Garland. Could be, Lisa was a couple bubbles off plumb even back then.

Walter Schroder named his hotel in Fond du Lac, Wisconsin, Retlaw, his given name spelled backwards. I mentioned in another column how my brother Sherman had christened his purebred Shar Pei dog "Walter." Following Mr. Schroder's lead, when Walter sired pups, Sherm could name one of them Retlaw. Then he could name one of Retlaw's pups Walter. And so forth. Elevate that scheme to the level of naming humans, and the less than inspiring appendage "Junior" would eventually disappear from the English language. Some first names would be natural candidates for generational flip-flopping – Leon and Noel, for example.

During the decade of the '60s I mainly worked for Hughes Aircraft Company in California. Founded by the enigmatic Howard Hughes, HAC, in spite of the word "Aircraft" in its name, was, and I presume still is, exclusively in the business of manufacturing electronic parts and systems.

Mostly, I hung out with a few of the company's engineers. One, Palmer Arnold, was an employee of a Hughes' subcontractor. Palmer or "Pal" as we called him, often flew commercially to business appointments, and sometimes a crowd would be waiting when his plane landed, the people who had gathered assuming, of course, the name on the flight's manifest was that of golfing great Arnold Palmer. Although a handsome chap, Pal no more favored Arnold Palmer in looks than I resemble Arnold Swartzenegger in build.

The manager of a department in the division of Hughes that made satellites was named Blue Green. Mr. Green went by the nickname "Red." True. I never met Mr. Green, but I assume he came by his nickname honestly, I mean, that he was a red head.

My wife, who at the time also worked at Hughes, reported to a chap with the double last name of Reynolds Price. It wasn't until years later that I learned there was a prominent Southern writer of the same name.

Those names, for rather obvious reasons, have stuck with me. A few days ago they percolated to the top of my mind when I stumbled onto a piece about the RJ Reynolds Company's controversial Joe Camel ad campaign.

Certain names are well-suited to their owners. These are called aptronyms, a word coined by the late journalist and radio personality Franklin P. Adams. Mr. Dickson opens his chapter on aptronyms with several gruesome examples:

A Montreal window cleaner named Will Drop died in a fall; Messrs. Willburn and Frizzel were fried in the Florida State Prison electric chair in 1941; and Dr. Robert Fry was the official who pronounced convicted felon Linwood Briley dead after his electrocution in 1984 by the State of Virginia.

Medicos with apposite names, selected from among nearly five dozen listed by Dickson, include: Akin Frame (a chiropractor), Ann Looney (a psychologist), Zoltan Overy (a gynecologist), and P. P. Peters (a urologist).

Prominent linguist Dr. Steven Pinker writes of a woman who gave her newborn daughter the name Meconium, positive it was the most fetching English word she'd ever come across. Too late, she learned it was a medical term meaning the first bowel movement of an infant. And, I've always thought the name Hugh was pretty crappy. (No groaning.)

Regrettably, some family surnames – often of non-English derivation – are the butt of jokes merely because of the unflattering connotation of common English words of the same or similar spellings.

Thumb through a few pages of a telephone directory of any size and you'll come across such honorable family names as Boozer, Bratt, Buzzard, Fink, Gaul, Grimier, Hickey, and Muck.

The respected surname Hooker is a slang synonym for prostitute. "Hooligan," according to author Dickson, was originally a surname. Talented hockey forward Corey Pecker skated for the Erie Otters during the 2000/2001 season.

Audley is the given name of a nice man who lives nearby. I can't help but silently append the word "Enough" to his name whenever I hear it spoken, making "Enough" his middle name – that is, making him Oddly Enough Smith (Smith isn't his real last name).

A phrase no less worn to gossamer thinness than "oddly enough," is the tiresome, "Enough already!" which probably is what an editor at the Tribune silently grumbled when he reached this point in my rough draft.

More a favor than a Christmas gift

Frank Fletcher makes a living as a freelance writer of non-fiction "How-To" pamphlets and magazine articles. Automobile mechanics everywhere sleep better at night knowing their shelf of technical manuals includes Frank's classic monograph, "How to Read a Dip Stick."

We're friends, Frank and I (Fletcher is not Frank's real last name), though he's usually about as amiable as a gaseous mother bear watching over her cubs. When I told him I had decided to use a pen name for my newspaper column, he advised me, in his typically warm avuncular way, that that would be idiotic.

"How so?" I snapped right back

Turning from his computer, he took a few seconds to gather his thoughts. "I don't have the time."

I nodded but held my ground.

After another few seconds he added, "Whatever you do, don't use a pen name."

"You use one," I said. "Why shouldn't I?"

He glared past me for a long moment and then swung back to his computer. Typing furiously, he missed my friendly parting wave.

Frank is a heavy drinker, favoring Cutty Sark scotch over other libations, and while driving home that morning I concluded he was suffering one of his typical industrial-grade hangovers. Nevertheless – presuming he knew something I didn't know about the use of pen names – I decided to wait a couple weeks, hold off until Christmas rolled around before pitching my idea to Edgar Mitchell, the op-ed page editor of one of the newspapers that I submit my pieces too. (Mitchell is not Edgar's last name, which, approximately, is "Mitchkabibble.")

"Mitch" is not nearly as fun-loving as my friend Frank Fletcher. Figuring if I was ever going to catch him in a good mood, the holiday season would be my best chance. Moreover, I could argue that I wasn't asking for something as grand as a Christmas gift, only a small favor.

"I've decided to use a pen name," I said when he finally returned my call. An upbeat version of Winter Wonderland was playing in the background.

"Why?" he demanded irritably.

I had anticipated his question. "On the advice of counsel," I said.

Of course he knew better. "That's baloney!" After a long pause he added, "But, humor me. What name did you come up with?"

He should never have mentioned the word humor, as my brain has this odd tendency to glom onto any word suggesting jocularity and process it into an irrelevant response.

"Val," I answered.

Actually, I had cool-sounding "Tracy Sinclair" in mind for a pen name.

"Val?" he said. "Hugh Val? That's pitiful. Hugh Valley might work, but–"

"No, no," I interrupted, "Val would be my first name."

"Your given name?"

"Uh-huh. Has a nice masculine ring to it."

"Masculine! Really, Hugh. Every hear of the name Valerie?"

"Ever hear of the name Edna?" I shot back.

He tried beating against the gale of my persuasion with a ninety-degree tack. "There's a movie actor named Val, isn't there?"

"Could be," I said dismissively. "From the geniuses who gave us Biff, Bo, Rip, Rock . . . and Tab? Probably. So?"

"So," he said, "Val sounds phony . . . much too Hollywood."

"Not to me. It sounds–"

He said to hold a minute. Back on the line, he wanted to know what I had in mind for a last name.

"Crow," I answered. "You know, like in, `As the crow flies.' Only, I'll end it with the letter e." I spelled the surname stressing the last letter.

After a moment he said, "Remember that Nixon dupe named Egil Krow?"

I answered that I didn't remember any Nixon staffer of that name.

"You wouldn't," he said, quickly adding, "But I do. And I think you should use Eagle Crow . . . E A G L E C R O W"

"Right," I replied with a hint of disgust. "Why not Crow Eagle?"

Obviously temporizing, he said, "Isn't there a movie actor named Crowe?"

I said, "We wouldn't have the same first name."

Our conversation was interrupted again at his end, and for a while I was entertained by a background chorus of youngsters singing Frosty the Snowman. He returned and asked me how I had settled on that pen name.

I drew a deep breath, a long inhalation meant to suggest weary resignation. "Well," I said finally, "I really like the name Tape for a last name. It's crisp and all. And uncommon. But no way would I go with Duct for a first name. Also, it seemed to me–"

"Duct?"

"Sure," I said. "Duct Tape. It's catchy."

"Duct Tape," he repeated feebly. "Are you . . . .

I think he started to question my sanity. In any event, his next word, "Velcro," was anything but feebly uttered. In fact, it was bellowed, as was my full real name, which, along with several newspaper-inappropriate words, followed on the heels of his loud exclamation of the word Velcro.

His voice finally trailed off.

"I kind of like the name Elmer," I said, moving the handset back to my ear. "But Glue for a last name? No way. Glus, maybe, but certainly not Glue" – I paused for a second – Val Glus? No, I don't think so. What's your opinion?'

He didn't answer.

"I couldn't decide if Epoxy was a better first name or a better last name. Epoxy Epperson resonates. On the other hand, Rocky Epoxy swings, too."

"What name would you like etched on your head stone?" Mitch asked softly. I pretended not to hear, and he repeated his question, adding, "Because that's the only place you'll ever see your own pen name while I'm at the *Tribune*."

He hung up, and I took stock. I can live with 'Hugh McClintock', I said to myself, resigned to using my real name. On the other hand, `H. James McClintock' has a kind of authorial ring to it.

I called Mitch back. Exactly what he said to me is unimportant, but it wasn't any words jolly old Saint Nick ever uttered.

In broad daylight, too

It is not simply getting ripped off that flusters my wife and me, it is knowing for certain that the dirty little thief is a close neighbor. In fact, there are signs of collusion between two neighbors – both miscreants live nearby – and sometimes there's a third party involved, a confidant, evidently.

Naturally, we've reported the thievery. Our borough policeman hasn't so much as lifted a finger (anyway, not in the clean sense of that saying). A little due diligence on his part and I wouldn't feel obliged to make public our problem: Conneautville, after all, doesn't need the bad publicity any more than, say, Linesville, Saegertown, Cochranton, or any other nearby borough.

Yesterday we just missed catching Spike heisting the goods. We were watching from our kitchen window.

"Look at him," Nellie said disgustedly as Spike trotted smartly from our yard. "He's a picture of innocence. He thinks we can't see that he's got Puffy in his mouth."

I agreed. "You can tell by the way he's holding his head."

Actually, Spike's head slightly wobbled in cadence with his high-stepping. As would most married men, however, I recognized I had been cued to offer positive confirmation of a spousal remark, and I responded accordingly.

Holly, we knew, would be heartbroken. About half the size of a football, Puffy, a stuffed doll in the likeness of a puffin – enormous orange beak, short fat neck, and a duck's body – was a Christmas gift to Holly from my brother and his wife.

Once before I had seen Spike slink home with another of Holly's stuffed dolls. Lesser booty, it was probably a trial run. I took chase, but was thwarted by a neighbor's dog, an eighty-pound German shepherd with a mouth full of teeth a white shark would kill for, and a window-rattling bark ten decibels louder than the report of a small Army cannon. I knew if "Bear" saw me in hot pursuit of Spike, he'd misread my intentions, and seconds later I'd be reminding anyone watching of another meaning of the expression southern exposure. Once aroused, I doubt a logging chain could restrain "Bear."

We continued to watch as Spike met with Scotty near the back steps of the house where Scotty boards. We're all but certain that Scotty is the ring's mastermind. (Of course, Spike and Scotty are fictitious names.)

Although neither of us saw Spike pass his loot on, their sneaky glances in the direction of our place were dead giveaways. Furthermore, the weasely looking character that arrived just before they went their separate ways had "fence" written all over him. Short-legged, glossy-haired, and constantly preening, he hung around only long enough to exchange Puffy for – what? The going booty rate? One-fifth of the little doll's true worth? He wasn't a local, we were sure of that.

Yesterday was the third time we know of that Spike hit our place. Chances are we're not his only victim. The sneak applies all his cunning to stealing only one thing: stuffed animal toys. Confinement for a long day in old-fashioned stocks would be suitable punishment for the unfeeling little low-life.

We've scolded Holly – often since "Lump Lump," her stuffed hippo, turned up missing – over leaving her toys lying around outside. We've even gone so far as to return one of her fleecy dolls to her mouth as often as necessary for her to worry it back to our rear porch.

Holly's plenty intelligent – we fancy her old man was a street-smart poodle – but I have to concede that expecting she'd understand the potential consequence of leaving one of her toys outside was a few too many dots to connect, even for Holly. A pup from the litter of a friend's part-dachshund bitch, we adopted Holly a few days before Christmas. The season suggested her name.

I've talked to Spike's owner, subtly pointed out his pet's congenital predisposition for thievery. Howard (not his real name) flat didn't believe me. Worse, he couldn't stop grinning, seemed not to appreciate the gravity of the situation.

Spike, as I made my case, sat quietly at Howard's feet.

"Spike!" Howard says to him sternly, "have you been burglarizing the McClintock's place?"

Suddenly the center of attention, Spike began flouncing about excitedly, acting as if he wanted Howard to pick him up.

"I'm afraid," Howard says to me, "You've fingered the wrong dog, Hugh. But I'll, ah, keep an eye out."

"Howard," I later explained to my wife, "said he'd make damn sure Spike never filched from our place again."

"Good," Nellie said, knowing she'd been cued to offer positive confirmation of what was likely spousal hyperbole.

"Still, I went on, "to be on the safe side, let's gather Holly's toys whenever she returns from circling our little quarter acre."

Nellie's words followed me as I walked from our kitchen into the mud room on my way to the garage. "So, Howard didn't believe you?"

"Not really," I answered. "Remember, Hon, Spike is an only dog."

Hardly a shaggy dog story

Nipper, our family pooch of my adolescent years, was a Heinz-57 mutt, the offspring of another mutt of incommodious parentage who was the offspring of another mutt of incommodious parentage, and so on ad infinitum.

Nipper followed my brother and me everywhere – slept with us, ate when we ate, involved himself uninvited in all our outdoor games, and so on. Smart, the only command Nipper didn't understand was, "Go home!" Our little pal died of old age several years after I had reached adulthood.

When Nipper passed away, our cousin, who married into a family of veterinarians, gave Mother a boxer dog. "Slugger" was a purebred and all, but superbly maladapted for showing: one of his ears pointed up and the other hung down. Mother, bright but a rustic to the bone, could not have cared less.

(On the subject of family pets, Mother maintained to her dying days that Samson, the favorite of her two parakeets, became furious and wouldn't sing if she lined the bottom of his cage with any part of a newspaper except a selection cut from the editorial page. Once my sister, as Mother told it, thoughtlessly lined the bottom with a folded Classified Ads page. Samson clammed up tighter than a spinster's change purse, and he wouldn't sing a note until the lining of his cage was changed. Mother also swore Samson could chirp the song, *Home, home on the range*, but she claimed he got nervous in front of people and wouldn't try. Mother didn't hallucinate, but as I pointed out in another column, all her forebears were of "talkative" Irish stock.)

Anyway, our cousin's gift of Slugger elevated our household overnight to a higher social standing: no other family in the neighborhood could boast of owning a dog of unmixed parentage – at least none of the families with children.

A story recently published in the *Tribune* reminded me of those long-ago days. Written by the paper's fine West Correspondent, it was about a Conneaut Lake, Pennsylvania, woman's love affair with showing her dogs. Conneaut Lake, a borough of fewer than a thousand permanent residents – the population swells in summer – is situated eight or so miles west of Meadville.

Among other achievements, one of the woman's dogs, a Shar Pei, won a Best of Breed blue ribbon in a show sponsored by the Kennel Club of Buffalo, New York.

A Shar Pei – if you haven't seen one recently – begins life bundled in a loose-fitting fur coat that is piled fold upon fold upon fold over most of its body. In fact, a well-known American Shar Pei kennel goes by the name, "Chinese Shar Pei Von Wrinkles."

A Shar Pei's head differs from that of a hippopotamus only in size and hairiness: shrink the head of a hippopotamus tenfold, cover it with prickly bristles, and you'd virtually replicate a Shar Pei's box-like head. Ears that are dinky, flat-lying cabbage leaves, a mouth and tongue charcoal in color – not the pink of most canines – and sunken eyes that are duller than agates of soot, collude in a way to ensure that the world's handsomest Shar Pei wouldn't make the cut in a beauty pageant for wart hogs. The expression Shar Pei puppy is a three-word synonym for ugly.

However, beauty, as a proverb has it, is in the eye of the beholder. It's my guess that owners of Shar Peis can see as well as any of us but psychologically compensate for what their eyes make out.

(My brother has a Shar Pei, his second one, and it's pretty clear to me that Silas has convinced himself he owns a boxer. The human mind, it's a well-known tenet of psychology, works in mysterious ways to keep the body healthy. Though much uglier, a Shar Pei has the same full muzzle and deep chest as a canine Boxer, which is likely the reason for Silas' confusion.)

Mrs. Fuller (not her real name) christened her award-winning Shar Pei "Ma's Shawnee Shining

Through." Giving high-bred dogs long, unusual names is a tradition of show-dog ownership. The name of the first authentically registered Shar Pei was "Down-Homes China Souel." (Honest.)

Soon weary, however, of issuing whole-name orders such as, "Fetch, 'Ma's Shawnee Shining Through!'" Heel, 'Ma's Shawnee Shining Through!'" and asking, "Do you have to go, 'Ma's Shawnee Shining Through?'" before long Mrs. Fuller was calling "Ma's Shawnee Shining Through" simply "Ma's." (Admittedly, here I'm reading a little more into the story than was actually reported; my conclusion, however, is sound, even if my inferential reasoning rings a little hollow.)

The diminutive nickname "Ma's," among other salutary benefits eliminated a two-second, word-unbundling delay between one of Mrs. Fuller's commands and the dog's response.

For reasons better left unreported, no one in the Fuller family applied the nickname "Ma's" while Mrs. Fuller's mother was visiting. (Again, I'm interpolating, drawing what seems to me to be a reasonable deduction from the reporter's well-honed story.)

My brother named his Shar Pei "Walter." It's not that Silas has no imagination (he's both part Irish, naturally, and an irremediable fisherman), rather, as an owner of a half-dozen hunting dogs he favors short, practical names. He christened one of his Labrador retrievers "Pete." Imagine if he had to order a dog named "Czar Peter the Great" to fetch a duck he'd just shot from the sky. If the duck wasn't dead when it hit the water, it'd die from laughing at Silas' command. And "Pete," had he ever been addressed, "Czar Peter the Great," would have altered his retrieval path so other dogs would think he had charged out from a different blind, one manned by out-of-state hunters. Naturally, "Walter's" nickname is "Walt."

Mrs. Fuller told the Tribune reporter that her star Char Pei, now almost 13 years old, missed showing his stuff badly at a dog show, and that "Ma's" positively knew the difference between strutting down a runway and walking a street of the little borough of Conneaut Lake. Bestowed, however, with the name "Ma's Shawnee Shining Through," there's no doubt in my mind that "Ma's" knew from puppyhood she was destined for dog-show greatness.

On the other hand, I wonder what Silas' Shar Pei thought when he first learned he'd been named "Walter." I imagine he wasn't very pleased, probably wondered if he was a step-dog: "I'm destined to guard junk yards all my life? Only chase stupid groundhogs away from the backyard? Do no more than growl menacingly from inside a pickup truck cab?"

My wife and I will be naming our next dog – conceivably a snow-white poodle – Cleopatra Queen of the Nile, Mistress of Julius Caesar and Mark Antony. It is a show-stopping name if ever there was one.

We'll call her "Cleo," however, and only the three of us will ever know her full name – at least until Cleo wins Best of Breed at a New York Kennel Club dog show.

Your Lordship? Hmm. I've been called much worse.

I have a serious reservation about the Hindu religious belief of reincarnation, but if the rebirth of my soul in another human body should happen, chances are I'll return as a low-life con artist.

Here's why: There will always be good and evil in the world, and cosmic balance, it stands to reason, demands that I be reincarnated as an endlessly evil person. Furthermore, if Hinduism is even a marginally sound religion, I'll be reincarnated as a strikingly handsome man, tall, square-jawed, lots of hair, broad shoulders, a tango dancer nonpareil.

Ultimately, my fate will rest solely with the Hindu cosmic law that works these things out, the ordinance that accounts for and ministers to the belief of plenty of human good here, a little human evil there. A crazy law, as spiritual statutes go, if it wasn't a two-parter, if it didn't address both good and bad behavior, presumably there would only be good in this world: no wars, no coveting of thy neighbor's spouse, no incontinent pets, no broccoli-cheese soup, and so on.

Anyway, con artists – my certain future if Hinduism prevails – do not have it all that bad. Sure, they get beat up, shot at, and they're arrested off and on. So? Small tribulations can be brushed off. Still, living on the edge, as they do, is the one thing about men that invariably attracts the attention of women, i.e., that tempts otherwise decent young women to fall off the wagon of chaste prudence. Remember The Sting? The movie starring Paul Newman and Robert Redford? Two really cool, handsome con men, right? And likely as not, representative of the breed.

For one reason or another, some Americans are overly impressed by persons with an accent. Among the upper-crust of urban America, cultured English turns heads faster than Lady Godiva's second nude horseback ride, the ride where she worked both sides of the street after bobbing her hair. Can you imagine cushier pickings for a con man than the upper-crust citizens of New York City's Manhattan Island? Can men imagine the lovely Godiva cantering sidesaddle down the main street of Coventry? Do birds have skinny shins?

If I am not reincarnated as a Brit, I'll become one, add expressions such as "old chap," "bloody," and "twit" to my workaday vocabulary. And I'll learn to sniff haughtily at any side dish except haggis pudding, which I'll let on is tastier than a double-bacon cheeseburger.

I know that particular ruse – the trick of misrepresenting one's native citizenship – would work because it has in the past.

A Scotsman, passing himself off as an English lord, swindled financier Jay Gould, one of nineteenth-century America's wealthiest men, out of a million dollars – at the time, a thousand dollars was a small fortune. Gould took the hit while he was engaged in a struggle for control of the Erie Railroad, at the time, one of the longest railroad lines in the world. The Scotsman, deceiving his fellow countrymen into believing he was "Lord Glencairn," ripped off a jeweler big-time in Edinburgh, England, fled to America, and took up residence in Minneapolis as "Lord Gordon-Gordon." (The name "Lord Glencairn" is cool, however, so I may reprise it for myself.)

After picking clean the bank accounts of a number of well-off Minnesotans, the phony Lord Gordon-Gordon met Jay Gould in New York City, where he snookered Gould into believing he held securities that could be pledged to gain control of the Erie Railroad. Gould paid extravagantly in cash for the non-existent securities. No sooner had "Lord Gordon Gordon" pocketed the money than he cut and run for Canada, which, in those days, had no extradition treaty with the U.S. Clearly the swindle involved no heavy lifting. And I could certainly live with that.

God forbid, however, that I should have to go by the title "Lord Hugh-Hugh." I can already hear the brutal asides:

First man: "Ho, ho! Here comes Lord Hugh-Hugh."

Second man: "Do you mean Lord You-You? Ha, ha."

Nor is Lord McClintock-McClintock any less sappy. Spoken without pause, the repeated pronunciation of my last name sounds like the galloping of a horse in a Hollywood oat burner: Maklinok, Maklinok, Maklinok, Maklinok. (The letter t is silent in the surname McClintock.)

Hold on. I got carried away. Me? Reincarnated as a suave Englishman crafty enough to work a swindle the magnitude of the one that snared Jay Gould? That is roll-around-on-the-floor funny.

If I do come back as a con man, likely as not I'll be a sham free-loader outfitted with a tin cup and very dark shades. Or, at best, a dealer of three-card Monte plying slight-of-hand trickery on a scruffy side street of Las Vegas or Atlantic City.

Maybe I'll learn the Pigeon Drop Con. In fact, now that I think about it, living out my next life as an itinerant practitioner of the lowly Pigeon Drop Con is probably my certain destiny. This is because I've seen it worked first hand, giving me a pretty good sense of the fundamentals.

Years ago, in Dallas, Texas, my 70-year-old mother was targeted for a Pigeon Drop. The culprit, a neat, modestly dressed middle-aged woman, knocked on the front door of her home and flashed a billfold that she claimed was lying on the front sidewalk. Bulging with money, she wanted to know if it belonged to my father.

No, Mother told her, he had passed away. (I'm betting that when the woman heard Mother was widowed her eyes began vibrating like a pair of matched ruby lasers.) Then, she wanted to know, could she use the telephone to contact the owner? Whose name and telephone number was conveniently available on a card that all but fell out of the billfold. Lo and behold, the telephone service at that address had been discontinued.

You can guess the rest of the con. Essentially, for a two-hundred-dollar "finder's fee," the woman allowed as how she'd split the bundle of money with Mother – after all (1) the owner had clearly disappeared, (2) probably he was very wealthy, and (3), the clincher: likely as not it was drug blood money. While she divvied up the money, Mother could round up the two hundred dollars.

Had the crook known beforehand that Mother was not only honest to a fault but also tighter than the bark on a young maple tree, she'd have sailed by the house faster than she would have zipped by a home tented to exterminate pests.

The point is, I intuited stuff from Mother's potential misadventure that will make me a world-class Pigeon Drop Con artist. Given a few years of hitting big-city neighborhoods and I'd have pretty, lissome, blondes, brunets, and redheads crashing my pad every night.

I expect, of course, that when I'm reincarnated I won't look at all like I do now.

Where goes Peter Cottontail?

Great! Just great! Ol' Peter Cottontail missed our house again. He left Easter baskets for the kids across the street, so I know he visited the neighborhood.

As usual, a few days before Easter, I decorated our yard with colorful, life-sized, wooden silhouettes, cut-outs of sprightly children and beribboned lambs romping happily about our flower-wreathed flag pole. I even laid out a small rock garden in a likeness of the Star of David – just to make clear my ecumenical side. Still, the furry, bob-tailed little rascal never showed up.

Somehow, he seems to know that children no longer live at our house. I suspect he exchanges an address list with Santa Claus. I presume he also checks it twice. I have no idea where he spends the off-season, but unless he's crazy as the usual March hare, you can bet he is not freezing his stubby little tail sharing living space at the North Pole with excitable, airy-fairy Rudolph, the reindeer of red-nosed fame.

Neither, was it ever clear to me, how it is that Pete favors eggs as gifts to children. Eggs would make sense if that hoppy little icon were an Easter chicken. Certainly the name "Penny Plumage," or Queenie Quill resonate with the same rich overtones of joy and happiness as the name "Peter Cottontail." Moreover, where is it written that the Easter Bunny is indisputably a male rabbit? In Playboy magazine? Certainly the name "Peter Cottontail" could as easily be Patti Cottontail, and Patti could just as easily go ". . . hopping' down the bunny trail" as Peter Cottontail – who, anyway, loaded down with all those candy eggs, probably does more lurching than hopping – not to mention constantly pulling over to furtively hitch up a hernia belt that is likely fitted with shoulder straps. Why haven't feminists weighed in on this macho malarkey? (Incidentally, the famous Russian proverb, "Better to go hungry than suck an egg on Easter Day," cleverly glosses over the question of the Easter Bunny's gender.)

So . . . I can't prove irrefutably why the Easter Bunny skips our place, but I'm leaning toward my wife's theory that he ineptly spars with Santa Claus while mapping his route.

On my own, however, I ran across a few related facts of more than passing interest.

To begin, the notion of an Easter Bunny had its origin in pagan fertility lore a long time before Christ was born. (And you thought my front-yard Star of David decoration was dumb, didn't you? Ha.) The rabbit, at the time the most fertile animal known, was taken as a symbol of, ahem, "new life" during the spring season.

The first recorded mention of an Easter Bunny was discovered by a monk in a German monastery searching for dirt on Martin Luther – although the monk adamantly denies that wasn't his primary interest. Germans, therefore, can legitimately claim the distinction of having invented the Easter Bunny.

During the Cold War, Germany's claim was challenged by Russia, however, whose scientists, we learned back then, invented everything, including rocks and trees. A cultural cooperation subcommittee of the United Nations is considering Russia's challenge. They'll announce their decision the year 2020.

Apparently, the first candy Easter bunnies were also made in Germany – sometime in the 19th century.

German settlers, arriving in Pennsylvania Dutch country during the 1700s, introduced the Easter Bunny to American folklore. From a child's viewpoint, a visit from Oschter Haws (roughly, the name translates into Peter Flaxenbottom) on Easter rivaled the wonder of Christ-Kindel pussy-footing by on Christmas Eve.

Children were told that if they behaved, Peter Flaxenbottom would lay colored eggs in their discreetly hidden nests, which the boys formed from their hats and the girls from their bonnets.

Over time, parents assumed the responsibility of building and provisioning the "nests," which have evolved into elaborate wicker baskets that are filled with everything from colored eggs and chocolate rabbits to radio-controlled toys. Rumor has it that next year, in addition to their famous Christmas catalog, the Dallas-based Neiman Marcus department store is publishing an Easter gift catalog featuring children's Easter basket fillers ranging from bred down Shetland stock to wee, nuclear-powered HUMMER rip-offs.

Maybe the Easter Bunny doesn't sit down with Santa Claus over scheduling his stops; maybe logistics simply aren't his long suit. Or maybe he's a little too jumpy to listen well. In any event, next year I think I'll address my usually wasted thank-you note to Ms. Easter Bunny.

If that doesn't work, I'll initiate a class-action law suit: McClintock et al vs. the Easter Bunny. Aware that the Easter Bunny's vast refrigerated warehouse of stored eggs would be worth millions, American law firms would move mountains for the opportunity to take it on.

In bad taste

I'm only seventy-four but the part of my brain that remembers recently mentioned names, addresses, telephone numbers, and similar trivia, evidently is much older.

My kidneys are actually a few years younger than seventy-four (something my unforgiving bladder doesn't seem to have picked up on), while my gallbladder is exactly my chronological age. Tests on my heart, lungs, and liver are pending.

The human spleen is still an organ of mystery to medical science – at least doctors no longer regard it as the seat of warm, intimate emotions – and I'll likely never know the true biological age of mine. I wouldn't be surprised if it had stopped its activity years ago – whatever that was.

The fact that a person's organs age at different rates was discovered in 1996 by Dr. Klaus von Rettich, a German biologist who, at the time, was moonlighting as a mortician in a crime-ridden Berlin slum and selling pre-owned caskets on the side. I mentioned a consequence of his astonishing discovery in an earlier column titled, "At least I'm not growing old all at once."

A human organ is basically tissue that is made up of cells, which are the microscopic, structural units of all living organisms. Cells, in turn, are constituted of several other things. It follows, therefore, that the oval-shaped clumps of cells covering the surface of a person's tongue must be taste buds. (My short-term memory may be shot, but given all the facts I can still reason my way through a gnarly technical poser as deftly as any young scientist.)

I touch on these biological relationships as a way to ease into explaining the effect of aging on taste buds, a subject recently examined in an article published in a big city daily that was written by a respected, registered dietician of national credentials. Without citing one iota of scientific proof, the author rashly claimed that as persons grow older, their ability to distinguish between flavors diminishes proportionately.

As luck would have it, she's right; so I've decided to cover her duff by explaining why all flavors tend to go vanilla as the years pile up, as she should have done in her piece.

Remember as a kid how your mother made you eat everything she put on your dinner plate? That started it. That's when your ability to taste began receding to where by seventy years of age it's sheer happenstance if you can tell a snort of gin from a slug of hair tonic, or a

Belgian waffle from garlic toast, or egg noodles from chitlins. Only last week a friend that is my age, who was awaiting cataract surgery, mistook a bowl of Boston baked beans for lumpy chocolate pudding and couldn't taste the difference. Later that day she overdosed on Gas-X pills and spent the next two days in forced isolation, under guard, at Meadville Medical Center.

The human body has several natural defense mechanisms: the charge of energetic white corpuscles' rushing to defend against a bacterial invasion comes to mind immediately.

An equally powerful protective reaction occurs when an individual chomps into a helping of food that his mind perceives as less than a toothsome victual. The process is not fully understood but somehow it involves the secretion of tainted saliva by an individual's large posterior salivary gland. Why one bite of nasty tasting food – in some cases a mere whiff – instantly transforms that gland into a raging, rogue tummy part is still unclear: Dr. Rettich several months ago turned his penetrating brilliance from researching the aging of human organs to the aging of human cells, and it's still a mystery even to him.

Dr. Rettich compares the affect of aging on a person's taste buds to the spraying of an herbicide on weeds: some survive, some croak in hours, and others slowly shrivel away. He panicked an audience of Harvard pre-med students when he off-handedly suggested that the ones dying a slow death produce the dark-brown taste that over-imbibers experience the morning after they close a pub.

Based on a poll of 1,096 adult Americans, part of the research whose work was funded by Philadelphia-based Scrapple Foods Corporation, a team of three respected botanists has isolated and ranked ten foods most likely to trigger an involuntary upchucking, victuals (grub is a better word) so disagreeable in taste that vomiting is all but unavoidable.

Broccoli tops the list. (No surprise there.) Boiled cabbage – think New England boiled dinner or dressed-up corned beef – matched up with boiled turnips for second place. Both calf's liver and anchovies ranked high among non-vegetables, as did buttermilk. Oddly enough, sauerkraut didn't make the cut. (For a complete, ranked list of the offending foods, log on to http://www.phewy.org. Each item on the list affects a person's salivary glands in a way that Dr. Rettich has compared to the explosive seeding of a water-saturated storm cloud.

Presumably, the dietician who penned the article mentioned above isn't aware of Dr. Rettich's pioneering work. In any event, she treats the problem of diminishing taste as an unavoidable end-stage affliction of human life, merely the inevitable consequence of aging. From that standpoint, her recommendation to counteract the loss of taste by enhancing the food we eat makes sense.

If, however, she intends the word "enhancing" to be a synonym for "improving," she's saluting reality while simultaneously poking her thumb in a good eye. Plain and simple, flavor substitutes don't cut the mustard.

To cite a few examples: there's two kinds of butter-flavored seasonings, bad tasting and wretched tasting; no souped-up blend of herbs and spices can ever hope to compete with a measured sprinkle of salt and pepper; a pinch of salt substitute is indistinguishable in taste from a pinch of bauxite ore (in fact, I'm pretty sure some salt substitutes really are bauxite ore); monosodium glutamate tastes as bad it sounds.

The final result of Dr. Rettich's ongoing study of the aging of human cells will no doubt prove as compelling as his trail-blazing research into the aging of human organs.

Nevertheless, it would be wrong, even dishonest, if I didn't mention that his findings have yet to be independently corroborated by other researchers. And until then – and it almost certainly will happen – readers may want to heed the advice of Roman statesman Pliny the Elder (nee, Clyde Pliny), and mentally ingest this column "with the sprinkling of a grain of salt," the old toga-traipsing naturalist's way of gently challenging an opponent's veracity.

Sometimes it was the best of times

"It was the best of times, it was the worst of times . . . ." is the well-known opening line of Charles Dickens' novel, *A Tale of Two Cities*. It pretty well defines my four-year hitch in the U.S. Air Force.

Over fifty years have rushed by since I doffed my service khakis for civilian mufti. My relatively few bad times in uniform have become dim memories, so I'll just let those few happenings wither on the vine.

What I remember as the good times were by and large incidents of low comedy, a "Three Stooges" level of nonsense that twenty-year-old males think is double-knee-slapping funny. I've cleaned up most of our ribald mischief for this column and dressed up the rest – hopefully, with a minimum of humdrum verbiage.

After basic training, I spent the better part of 1951 learning how to fix radars at Keesler Air Force Base. Keesler shares a length of its eastern boundary with a border of the city of Biloxi, Mississippi. At the time, Biloxi was the residence of some thirty thousand uncompromising "Y'all-hurry-back" Southerners. I haven't returned to either Keesler or Biloxi since leaving those places late in 1951.

In 1951, if you stepped inside any business in downtown Biloxi, walked into a barber shop, ice cream parlor, drug store, haberdashery, bakery – any place but the Christian Science reading room – you'd bump into a slot machine and often as not have to thread your way by a stand of those one-armed bandits to make your way to a clerk.

The gambling was so shady and commercially rooted that slot-machine-eradicating Congressional hearings were held while I was stationed at Keesler. The city was soon placed off limits to all Keesler airmen, some 15,000 of us, and before long – that gushing money spigot turned off, the consequence of our monthly pay being stopped – the slots were trucked away to greener pastures, to Las Vegas perhaps. Restricted to the base during the hearings, and afterwards for another several weeks, most of us enlistees – all in our late teens or early twenties – wished to hell Senator Estes Kefauver, who chaired the investigating committee, had minded his own damn business. Ah, youth.

Biloxi in the summer is hot and humid, and our wooden, two-story barracks were not air conditioned, an uncommon amenity of most residential living in 1951. Billeted in double-decker bunks forty men to a space that was not much larger than a modern double-wide mobile home, the air was not only hot and humid it also reeked irrepressibly of the odor of a gymnasium locker room after a hard-fought basketball game.

The airmen of our particular squadron, some six hundred enlistees, attended electronics class from six a.m. to noon, the first of three, daily six-hour shifts, and we often had the rest of the day to ourselves – except, of course to fall in and march to a mess hall for supper. In the afternoons we sacked out on the springs of our bunks wearing our cotton, khaki-colored boxer shorts. If we wore T-shirts or slept on any part of the mattresses, the woolen blankets, or the uncased pillows, those garments and the mattresses, would be soggy with sweat when we woke up.

Needless to say, dozens of meagerly clothed, viral young men blissfully conked out in mid-afternoon gave rise, so to speak, to many an opportunity for devilment.

Men asleep in the bottom bunks were the inevitable victims, easy prey to the ignominy of having their tumescent private member, tied, often by one of their own shoelaces, to the springs of the top bunk – after which, a leather-lunged fellow airman waiting furtively by an exit would bellow, "Barracks, attention!" a command announcing that an officer had entered the building. Then the airman with the Klaxon enhanced vocal cords would run like hell.

A big red-headed kid from Oklahoma, the second time he was victimized, caught up with the perpetrator, who had foolishly ducked into the barracks' latrine, and gave him a decidedly unpleasant shampoo, which brought to a sobering end, at least while I was a resident of that barracks, any more rascality of that nature.

During our training – specifically while marching to school for classes – our squadron competed with the other dozen or so squadrons for alignment honors by passing before a jury of base commanders. We never won the prize, was never excused from our next turn at KP (or some such blue-ribbon award along those lines) mainly because the lad I enlisted with – the year before a fullback on the Meadville High School football team – was congenitally unable to walk without bobbing up and down like a cork in unsettled waters.

"Ted" couldn't walk two steps without appearing to be setting off across a newly ploughed field. He tried mightily to walk without loping, even practiced by shuffling around the perimeter of our barracks on flexed knees. In fact, the image of Ted, looking the entire world like an oversize orangutan struggling to walk both erect and smoothly at the same time is my funniest memory of duty at Keesler AFB.

Marching past the reviewing stand, we were an integral body of six hundred, fatigue-garbed men, harmoniously in step with the music, our bodies swaying rhythmically in unison – except for Ted's statue-like noggin bobbing up and down asynchronously in a middle row of some seventy rows of smartly stepping airmen.

Stationed at Soule City AFB – at K-16, its service designation – the Korean War ended mid-way through my rotation to that country. Soule, South Korea's capital is situated some ten miles south of the 38th Parallel, the geographic latitude marker that theoretically divided the front lines opposing forces engaged in never-ending skirmishes of that "police action," as over-educated, politically correct weenies of the press and academe inevitably characterized the Korean War.

My tour in Korea wasn't the best of times, but compared to the situation faced by the Army dogfaces dug in at the front, it was a ride on a merry-go-round.

And, speaking of "riding" . . .

Someone, before I arrived to begin the duty of maintaining the GCA radar unit used to land planes in bad weather at the Soule airport, invented what we came to call "Jeep Riding," a name apparently shanghaied from the sport of rodeo bull-bronco-ing.

In Jeep Riding, the broncobusters clung prostrate and spread eagle to the top of the jeep that was entrusted to our radar maintenance crew – the papa-san assigned to our crew had scrounged plywood somewhere and made our highly aerated jeep into a sturdy, air-tight coupe – while the driver executed all kinds of sharp turns, quick stops, and gear-gnashing reverses.

The arena was the stretch of land lying between our maintenance shack and the berm of the main runway of the airport serviced by our radar unit. Much of the time the area was a boggy quagmire of brown mud, a condition favorable to surviving uninjured the ignominy of being thrown from the top of the jeep.

We'd be sitting around BS-ing and getting a little tight on beer– those of us who were off duty – when someone, a fellow tin-shack, bunk-mate, out of the blue, would yell, "Post time!" and the fun would begin.

No one, miracle of miracles, was ever seriously hurt Jeep Riding, as, truthfully, being thrown off didn't happen often since tire traction was practically zilch in the two-inch-deep layer of mud.

In one instance, our maintenance chief may have suffered a broken wrist falling from his place behind the driver's wheel: for some freak reason, the tires actually grabbed when he made a sharp right turn. In spite of swelling and discoloration, he wisely refused to report to the base dispensary, so no one ever knew if he actually broke his wrist. (Had he reported his injury, and the truth of his accident found out, he might have been court-martialed.)

Another memory I brought home with me from Korea was finding out, during my first five-day R and R, "Rest and Re-hab" visit to Tokyo, that the Japanese, our mortal enemy of World War II, which had ended in their surrender barely a half-dozen years earlier, were not the buck-toothed, slit-eyed, simian-like creatures most Hollywood movies and some Service films had us young greenhorns of world travel believing: they were physically ordinary, if short, but punctual, hard working, honest, and consummately polite.

Which brings me to this observation (abruptly, and I apologize, but I'm out of space): had Dickens written, "It was the best of times, it was the worst of times, it was a time of learning, his opening line in A Tale of Two Cities would have precisely characterized my four years in the U.S. Air Force.

THE DAWNING OF THE AGE OF INVENTION

Introduction

The Prehistoric Society, based at University College London, the United Kingdom, is a community of prodigiously smart, men and women who study the human past as it existed before the symbolic cave scratchings of pre-history. Their many learned essays are not only convincing but also exquisitely written. Too often, however – especially regarding early post-ice-age inventions – they are just plain wrong. In this section, "The Dawning of the Age of Invention," I set the record straight.

I clarify two particularly egregious misrepresentations by the Society in "And President Washington thought wooden teeth were a bummer," which disclosed the real truth about dentistry as practiced before recorded history, and in "The first hand-propelled wheelbarrow," which not only chronicled the implementation of a wheelbarrow but also touched on the discovery of the wheel itself. Regrettably, the acclaim I anticipated for correcting those issues of false history never materialized, and I believe there are two reasons for this obvious miscarriage of academic justice. First, I presented my counter arguments in a humorous manner, which no doubt under-weighed the real significance of my insights. And, second, as my arguments were published in newspaper columns instead of academic monthlies, a proper reception never materialized.

My hope is that by including those two columns in this book, and by adding other allied, essay-like articles – equally persuasive but fully somber in tone – I will finally accomplish my objective of setting the record straight in the matter of important inventions that we Homo sapiens have freebooted as the stuff of our own doing.

Perhaps you are wondering, "How does he know about these things?" To put it simply, I'm marginally psychic. However, because the gift to see what others cannot even imagine is innate and controversial, I decided to write my two original pieces as if the happenings occurred in my dreams. It was a miscalculation on my part that lamentably undersold my arguments.

In any event, I herewith include, unedited, my two original columns covering the prehistoric practice of dentistry and the circumstances hinting at the invention of the wheel.

And President Washington thought wooden teeth were a bummer

Anymore, some of my dreams are set in the Stone Age. I'm not sure why. When I was a kid I read the comic strip "Alley Oop," which was named for the dinosaur-riding, stone-ax wielding character created by cartoonist Vincent T. Hamlin. I liked that strip, but I also enjoyed Alex Raymond's "Flash Gordon," and I never dream about zipping around the heavens in a rocket ship.

Our family physician, Doctor Ka-ching, says it's not unusual for seniors to dream about really old stuff. Or, as he deftly explained, "You have aging spots on your hands, don't you?" He didn't elaborate, which was just as well because he would have charged me more for my visit.

I still have most of my own teeth. One molar, however, has a cavity large enough to hold a Bing cherry – according to my tongue – and the filling has tumbled out twice in the last year.

During my last dental appointment Dr. Diesel (not his real name but apropos of his manner) said he'd have to yank the tooth if the filling came out again. It did, naturally, and the night before my scheduled visit for the extraction I had another of my Stone Age dreams.

As usual, I materialized on the scene unobtrusively and invisible. The surroundings were either of a dental office or of a rock quarry: the background of a dream is like that you know.

Hugi, my stone-age alter ego, it turned out, is lying supine on top of a pile of rocks that have been fashioned into a high-backed chair with a pinkish granite foot-rest. Besides a long sloping forehead, strong jaw line, and heavy brow ridges, the left side of Hugi's jaw bulges as if he's crammed a billiard ball into his mouth.

Dr. Kary, a mate taller but similar in appearance to Hugi is standing over him. "It's too early," he says. "The sun is not high enough."

"O what?" Hugi says crossly, interrupting his own moaning.

Dr. Carry looks at Nano, his assistant. Full-breasted and shorter than either man but no less husky, she is kneeling nearby arranging a set of sharpened animal bones on a flat rock. "He said, `So what, Doctor,'" Nano explains, rising to her feet.

Dr. Carry leans into Hugi's face. "You want to know, 'So what, eh?' Well, Hugi, so what if I can't see and pull the wrong tooth? Eh? That's 'So what, 'Pal!'"

"It happened to Klem," Nano says indifferently.

Dr. Carry gives her a dirty look. "He was my first patient. Ever."

"You mean," Nano mumbles, "first victim ever."

Dr. Carry apparently doesn't hear her. "Give Hugi a sip of wine," he orders.

Nano hands Hugi a wine-filled birch-wood vessel that is lined with the stomach of a young beaver. "Take a good slug," she orders.

Hugi takes a hefty pull from the vessel and lets out a whoop that would turn a wooly mammoth in mid-charge. Bolting upright, he spews out the wine. "I'm out a here," he blurts, pushing forcefully away from the make-do chair of rocks.

Dr. Carry and Nano together press Hugi back into the rock chair. Hugi settles down and resumes groaning, his voice now enriched with the harmonics of a man who can't stop whimpering.

"I assumed as much," Dr. Carry says to Nano. He cuts his eyes toward a thicket of broad-leaved herbs and low shrubs that have taken root a few yards away.

Nano nods, disappears behind the bushes, and returns with a long-handled wood mallet. Its head, roughly cylindrical, is wrapped in a pelt with the fur turned out.

Dr. Carry says to Hugi, "Show me again. Where it hurts."

Hugi glares. "'Oron!" He points to his swollen jaw.

"Open wider!" Dr. Carry orders, pretending he needs to scrutinize the inside of Hugi's misshapen jaw.

Hugi's jaw quivers, his mouth opens slowly, and his eyes close. Dr. Carry signals Nano. She whacks Hugi solidly on the head with the mallet causing his head to fall to one side. His eyes roll up, and his mouth falls open.

Nano steadies Hugi's head, turns to Dr. Carry, and nods.

Dr. Carry props Hugi's mouth open with a short twig of wood and matter-of-factly asks Nano, "Which mallet was that?"

"Number-two," Nano answers. "I was afraid the number-one would wear off too quickly. The number-three and he'd–"

"Record it," Dr. Carry interrupts crisply. He leans back and scratches marks on the partially de-barked trunk of a big tree close at hand.

"The number three," Nano continues, standing again at Hugi's side, "and he'd be conked-out the rest of the day. Remember how Vurn couldn't find his way home until the next morning?"

"Vurn would get lost behind the outhouse pit," Dr. Carry snaps.

Dr. Carry looks over Nano's arrangement of animal bones and points to one with a barbed hook carved into one end. Taking the carved bone from Nano, he maneuvers it into Hugi's mouth, props his knee against Hugi's chest, and begins pulling.

Hugi's loud moaning doesn't quite drown out Dr. Carry's grunting.

Huge birds begin circling observantly in the sky. Several land in a nearby tree, their heads bobbing impatiently.

Hugi's eyes twitch and his legs jerk convulsively. Nano whacks him hard on the head again, and he settles limply back into the chair.

That's how my dream ended, with Hugi suffering a blow to his noggin that would ring the brass bell atop a twenty-foot pole at a carnival game

Nano earlier had mentioned that Vurn, one of Carry's patients, was anesthetized so heavily he couldn't find his way home. I suppose that's what set me to wondering how long it would be until Hugi could manage three steps in succession before pitching forward onto his face. Would his bison-horns war helmet still fit? Would he be known thereafter as "Knobs"? Or, perhaps as "Lumpy"?

Partly awake and partly asleep, that's the kind of a dumb question that takes hold of my mind when I'm coming out of a dream. Fully sober finally, I realized that I had just witness the beginning of the age of dentistry.

The next day, Dr. Diesel, solemnly listened and several times nodded understandingly while I described my dream as if I were still Hugi.

"Missy!" he yelled as soon as I finished. "I'm ready for Hugh. Bring the red croquet mallet. But, just in case, bring the green one, too."

The first hand-propelled wheelbarrow

Our TV, the audio set low, was tuned to a channel displaying the tape of a 1970s game show. My wife was working a crossword puzzle and glancing at the TV screen between pondering possible one-word answers. I was reading the Forward to *A Brief History of Time*, renowned physicist Stephen Hawking's popular science book.

A teaser on the back cover of the book implied that nonscientists could easily understand his watered-down technical exposition, so I shelled out twelve bucks for a copy. Nothing if not sensible about money, I was determined I'd finish his book, resolved to correct my worm's-eye view of wormholes, weigh in on super gravity, and once and for all nail down an understanding of Heisenberg's Uncertainty Principle.

"Hard to believe," I said, "how the faster you move the slower time passes."

Nellie, if anything, concentrated more fiercely on her crossword puzzle.

"That's a scientific fact," I went on. "Dr. Einstein figured it out."

"Umm," Nellie answered thoughtfully.

"It stops altogether at the speed of light if you . . . time does, I mean, stops flowing on. As your measuring system moves faster and faster."

Nellie nodded. "I was watching you wheel-barrow that top soil this afternoon" – she penciled in a word – "I wouldn't be too concerned if I were you."

Used to Nellie's sarcasm, I pretended not hear her snide remark. "You know that could be the basis for a Time Machine – a way to travel back in time. Think about it. You could visit the cave where your ancestors once lived." *"And not that long ago, either, Dear."*

"Uh-huh."

"I bet NASA could juice up one of its human centrifuges so it'd spin a person fast enough."

"Fast enough for what?" Nelly said. "What are you fussing about, Hugh?"

"Fast enough," I answered gently, as always, "that the passenger's wristwatch would run slower."

Shaking her head, she finished printing another word.

"Sure," I continued, "running the centrifuge clockwise would transport a person into the future, counterclockwise into the past. Eyeballs in, eyeballs out."

"Eyeballs what!"

"That's how the astronauts describe their rides in the centrifuge," I explained.

"Uh-huh."

"I'd sign up for a trip in a New York minute. I'd take along my Camcorder. Hmm."

"A Neanderthal!" I say excitedly, finding myself standing next to a woman wearing a sleeveless, two-strap frock of muskrat pelts that falls to an inch or so below her knees.

Although her features are almost cartoonish, her face is clearly feminine. She obviously didn't hear my exclamation, and apparently she can't see me.

Glancing about, I see that I'm leaving footprints. I can't make out what clothes I'm wearing, if any, but I'm unmistakably bare-footed.

Shortly we're joined by a scraggily bearded male of the same aboriginal build as the woman; he is also wearing a simple garment of pelts sewen together. His outfit, however, has only a single shoulder strap. Apparently, he can't see me either.

"Fern," the man says, "where's your mate? The other hunters have already left!"

Fern points toward a thicket of bulrushes and cups her hand to her mouth. "Toom! Yo, Toom! Gumy is here."

No answer. She calls again, but still no answer. Lifting her head and aiming her jaw at a round, flat rock lying a few yards away, she says to Gumy, "Have you seen his wheel?"

"His what?"

"His wheel . . . he calls it."

Gumy snorts. "Wheel? What's that?"

"You're looking at one."

"Yeah, what's it for? Rolling down hills? Ha ha."

"No-o-o"– Fern draws the word out –"for his wheelbarrow."

"Wheelbarrow?" Gumy says. His eyes dart about rapidly before settling again on Toom's rounded stone. He walks to where it is leaning against the trunk of a rowan tree. "There's a hole in the middle."

Fern shrugs. "There's supposed to be."

"Right," Gumy says suspiciously. "Hey Toom! Get your fat (short, unclear word) over here!"

"He's coming," Fern says. "You can't hear him?"

Toom, fussing distractedly with his shoulder strap, pushes through the stand of bulrushes.

Shaking his head, Gumy picks up the round stone. "This'll never work," he says to Toom.

"Say what?" Toom replies, stopping alongside Fern.

Goom stands the stone disk upright on the ground. It falls over. He stands it back up, and it topples over again. He turns victoriously to Fern.

"You'll have to show him," Fern says to Toom.

Toom sighs and walks importantly to where Gumy had found his round stone leaning against the rowan tree. Nearby, lying on the ground is a short stick that has been stripped of its bark. He waggles the stick under Gumy's nose and then slips it through the hole in the wheel.

Toom gives the stone wheel a spin. It comes to a stop, and he looks at his mate. Fern nods and disappears in their cave. She returns with a beaver-pelt rucksack affixed to her back. Toom sets about stuffing the rucksack until it is lumpy with dried chips of short-faced baby bear dung.

Kneeling, Fern looks up expectantly at her mate. Toom bends down and sets the wheel upright in front of her. Leaning forward, her arms astraddle the wheel, Fern seizes the wooden axle near each end.

After satisfying himself that Fern has gripped the axle tightly, Toom grabs her ankles and proudly wheels her past Gumy.

Fern, when Toom finally pulls to a halt, slips off the rucksack, scrambles to her feet, and yells to me, "Impressive, huh Hugh?"

I'm wondering how in the deuce she knows my name, when she loudly repeats it, adding, "The news is on!"

"The what is on?" I hear myself say crossly.

"The news," my wife answers. "You fell asleep."

I find the TV controller in my lap and switch on the ABC station transmitting from nearby Erie, Pennsylvania.

I glance at my watch. It is two minutes after eleven. "How long was I asleep?"

"I don't know," my wife answers. "How fast were you spinning?"

Homer was a good poet, but he was not the first ever

Toom, sitting cross-legged in front of the fire that is bristling warmly at the mouth of his cave, is cutting a notch in the shaft of his hunting spear, a whittled-down rowan limb.

"I'm running out of room," he says, admiring the shaft's many scoring notches. He means for Fern, his mate, who is standing nearby, to hear his boast of hunting prowess. Her mind, however, is elsewhere.

He repeats his boast.

Fern nods absentmindedly. Her lips articulate an unvoiced thought; she shakes her head. After few seconds her lips again move rapidly, and her head bobs decisively.

"What the heck are you thinking," Toom says.

"I'm composing," Fern answers.

"Composing?"

Fern nods. "Yes, working up a poem."

"Right," Toom says. "What's a poem?"

Fern turns the question over in her mind. "A . . . poem," she begins hesitantly, "is a . . . group of sentences that go good together."

Toom stops notching his spear. "Yeah," he says. "Go good where together? To the tribal poop hole? Ha, ha."

Fern shakes her head. "No, Beaver Brain. They're sentences that sound good when you say them."

"You mean," Toom says, "sound good like when I'm strumming my mammoth-rib lute and Riff's keeping time on the tribal rain drum?"

Fern cuts her eyes toward the nearby rowan tree from which Toom had hacked off a branch for his spear. "Uh, not exactly."

"So?" Toom says.

The thought of hearing one of Riff's and her mate's musical duets inspires Fern: "Listen," she says, "to how sweetly these two lines go together." Modulating her voice, she says, "Here lie the bones of a bad musician. Stoned to death at the first intermission."

Toom shrugs. "Why?"

"Why what?" Fern replies confusedly.

"Why'd they kill him?"

Fern takes a deep breath and expels the air in a long sigh. "That's not . . . it doesn't matter. Didn't you catch how the words 'musician' and 'intermission' sounded sweet together?"

"What in heck 's sweet about getting stoned to death?" Toom says.

"You're missing the . . . ." Fern says. After a long second she continues: "I made that up, about a musician getting killed. So I could rhyme musician with intermission."

"Rhyme?" Toom says. "C'mon Fern, speak Neander!"

"Rhyme *is* a Neander word," Fern snaps. "It means . . . oh, never mind."

"Yeah," Toom says. "I can understand killing a bad cook. But killing a musician, whether he's good or bad, just ain't civilized."

Fern stares at the fire for a long moment and then turns and walks briskly into their cave. When she returns, Toom is admiring his newly updated spear.

"Now listen carefully, Dear," she says. She waits for his undivided attention. "Trees are green. Right? The sky is blue. Right? Trees are green, the sky is blue. I love kids, and so do you."

Toom grins, rises, and takes a step toward the mouth of their cave.

Fern's eyes roll skyward, and she shakes her head disgustedly. "No. I don't mean . . . ." She stomps back into the cave.

"What in heck 's the matter with you today!" Toom yells after her.

"You!" Fern answers.

Toom pretends to throw his spear at an animal and then takes a step into the cave. "Me?" he says, "What'd I do?"

"Nothing," Fern says, exhaustion sapping her usually husky voice.

Toom fetches his spear and returns. Fern joins him near the fire. "Now, Dear," she says, "don't pay any attention to what the words mean, just to how they sound."

Toom nods. "Go ahead."

Fern strikes a pose and gestures toward a trail used by migrating animals. She tells Toom to listen closely. "Graze not with the reeking herd (she waves toward the big rowan tree) nor roost with the sullied flock (her head tilts back and her gaze finds the sky) but soar like that stoic bird, the eagle atop the rock." She points at the distant mountains.

Toom is touched. "Just beautiful, Fern. Just . . . amazing. Only, what did you mean about sentences sounding good together? Maybe, if I played along with my lute?"

Yeah. Maybe if you could tell a round rock from a Terror Bird's egg. "No, that's not it. I'll run it by Riff's mate. Maybe she--"

Toom snorts. "Run it by Narg? She wouldn't know an eagle if one pecked her on the butt."

Note: An eighteenth-century poet, whose name I haven't been able to run down, cribbed Fern's lines about the stoning of the bad musician. Poet Elinor Wylie also stole Fern's lines about soaring like a stoic eagle. So much for honor among poets

Fishing for cardinal numbers

Toom and Gumy have just returned from Big Lake and are admiring their catch of fish, which they have proudly arranged on the ground in front of Toom's and Fern's cave.

As if reflecting on the obvious, Toom mentions casually that they both caught the same number of fish.

"Oh no," Gumy says. "I caught the most. That's plain enough."

"'Oh no' yourself," Toom says. "We caught the same number." He yells into the cave. "Fern, dear, can you come here for a moment?"

"No way," Fern says after hearing Toom out. "I'm not getting in the middle of this one."

Gumy smiles pleasantly at Fern. "Please. Just count Toom's catch and then count mine."

Fern walks hesitantly to a place between the two groups of neatly arrayed fish. "One . . . two . . . many," she counts. After a few seconds of studying one group, she turns and looks at the other group. Pointing consecutively at each fish, she says, "Same number. One . . . two . . . many."

Toom glances smugly at Gumy. "I told you," he says.

"Something ain't right here," Gumy says. Shaking his head, he strings his fish together, hoists them over his shoulder, and heads for his cave.

The next day Gumy visits Toom to tell him that he's figured it out. It's early in the morning when he arrives. He is unable to hide his excitement.

Toom, resting on his haunches and only half awake, is staring dumbly at the embers he had just stoked fire from. "Got what figured out," he says grumpily.

"I'll show you," Gumy says.

Kneeling in front of Toom, Gumy unhooks a leather ditty bag from the braided waistband of his loincloth and empties a handful of smooth, round pebbles on the ground. He separates one pebble from the others.

"How many?" he asks Toom.

Toom looks suspiciously at the pebble and then back at Gumy.

"Just count," Gumy orders.

Toom folds his arms across his chest. "One."

"Now how many?" Gumy says, placing a second pebble beside the first one.

Toom shrugs. "One . . . two."

Gumy adds a third pebble. "And now?"

Toom yawns noisily. "Many."

"Good," Gumy says, adding a fourth pebble. "Now?"

For a few seconds Toom finds the distant woods vastly interesting. "Many," he says finally.

"How can that be?" Gumy says. "There's more than before."

Toom uncrosses his arms. He cups his chin in his hand. Deep frown lines pull his thick eyebrows closer together. "Well . . . many's many," he says finally.

Gumy looks at Fern who is watching from behind Toom. She returns a noncommittal glance. He adds a fifth pebble to the four already on the ground.

"What is this," Toom asks wearily, "some kind of dumb kid's game? The answer's still 'many.'"

"I see what you mean," Fern says quietly to Gumy. "We need more counting numbers."

"Exactly!" Gumy exclaims. "Otherwise, Toom caught the same number of fish as me, and you know that ain't right."

"Oh blisht!" Toom snaps, glaring hard at Gumy.

"Depends," Fern says. She wanders back into the cave.

"The heck it does," Toom yells after her.

"We'll see," Gumy says to Toom. He gathers his pebbles, favors Toom with a haughty look, and leaves.

Of course we don't know exactly when humans first learned to count objects past two in quantity, but my psychic reading of two prehistoric males arguing over bragging rights after a fishing trip is far more plausible than the whorly version of counting higher than two promoted by England's Prehistoric Society.

The first bisexual tunic

"Close your eyes," Fern says to Toom, who is lying prostate on a ledge of shale that is protruding from a wall of their cave. "Why?" he says, staring dully at the ceiling.

Toom props himself up on one elbow. Seeing that Fern is hiding something behind her back, he sits up, and rests his feet on the floor of the cave.

"Hold out your hands," Fern orders. "And don't open your eyes."

Toom does as he is told, and Fern lays a neatly folded garment on his outstretched hands.

"Wow!" he exclaims. "What's the occasion?"

Fern smiles. "Try it on."

Toom rises to his feet and unfolds his present, a pinafore-like outfit made of weasel pelts. He holds it up. "Wow!" he exclaims.

"It's for winter," Fern says. "And it's reversible."

"Wow," Toom exclaims. "And it's what?"

"Re-vers-a-ble," Fern says, separately enunciating each syllable. "You can wear it with either the fur out or the skin out."

Toom says, "Well, I'll be hog-tied, face-down."

Fern's face clouds up. "You don't like it, do you?"

"Of course, I like it," Toom says. "Only . . . it has two shoulder straps. Instead of one. Is that how you . . . intended?"

"Slip it on," Fern says.

Toom steps out of his skimpy summer loincloth and pulls Fern's handiwork on over his head. The straps catch on his shoulders; the hem falls to a few inches above his knees.

"The length is perfect," he says. "Only–"

"Only," Fern says, "you don't like it having two shoulder straps?"

"Uh . . . not on a man, Dear."

"They draw attention to your shoulders," Fern says, backing away to fully appreciate her mate's new look. "Ever notice how you have just about the broadest shoulders in the tribe?"

"I do?" Toom says, clearly pleased by the compliment.

Thickest head, too. "Yes, indeed, Hon. I heard Estr say that she wished Gumy had half your shoulders." *And I wish you had half Gumy's brain.*

Toom nods. "Gumy's jealous of me. Remember the time–"

"Turn around," Fern orders.

Toom obediently shows her his back. He rolls his shoulders.

"Um, massive," Fern says. "Irresistible."

Hoping to find Gumy, whom he figures will be fishing the main tributary of Big Lake, Toom sets out wearing his new threads. On the way, he passes a wide place in the stream where a bunch of tribal women are cleaning dinnerware. Two are scrubbing food residue off thin platters of stone.

He slows down. "Ahem," he utters loudly.

One woman looks up. "It's only Toom," she whispers, without moving her lips. She resumes scrubbing the left-over vittles from a platter, one of a dozen stacked on a nearby rock. The other woman nods slightly.

Toom, contrary to tribe protocol, initiates a conversation. "Nice day," he says.

Both women nod.

Toom retraces his path a few steps and waits. The women don't know he's still around. He turns his back and flexes his shoulders. "What do you think?" he says.

The women look up; they exchange glances of uncertainty. "Yes," one woman says to Toom. "The weather is really nice."

The other woman nods agreeably.

Gumy is knee deep in midstream, both hands cupped powerfully around a big fish he's just caught. He doesn't see Toom arrive.

"Hang in there!" Toom yells.

Gumy starts. The fish slips from his hands and briskly swims away. He glares at Toom.

Slowly his glare softens. He begins to giggle and soon doubles over in laughter.

"What?" Toom snaps.

Gumy sobers and makes his way to shore. Toom eyes him warily.

"Why," Gumy asks, "are you wearing one of Fern's outfits?" He starts laughing again.

Toom vigorously shakes his head. "It's my new winter duds, fish brains. Fern just made it."

Gumy, feigning admiration, circles Toom. Suddenly he hoists the hem of Toom's outfit and bends down for a close look. "They're still attached," he says. "It's not what I expected." He can't keep from giggling.

Toom tears his garment from Gumy's grip and stalks away. Over his shoulder, he tells Gumy that he is a pile of woolly-mammoth dung.

"What happened," Fern says to Toom.

"Gumy happened," Toom grumbles. "He liked my new winter frock and tried to wrest it from me. I kicked his ham good."

Fern is sympathetic. "I'll sew on a new strap, Hon."

"Better not," Toom says thoughtfully. "I'd have to fight Gumy again. Likely, his brother too."

Fern stares at her mate. His brow is furrowed in thought; it is obvious his mind is on another matter.

"Whatever you want, Dear" Fern says. "Only, one strap doesn't do your shoulders justice."

"It's just as well," Toom says. "I'm not a showoff like that damn Gumy."

A dining room for nobles

Toom, bent forward at the waist and lurching from side to side, is lugging a large flat stone on his back. Gasping for air, he says to Fern, "How about . . . this . . . one?"

Fern leisurely inspects his offering.

"For sky's sake," Toom blurts out, "make up your mind! This thing's as heavy as a short-faced bear."

"The marbling is good," Fern says pensively.

"Fern!"

"We'll try it," she says.

Toom, each step an adventure, shuffles to a corner of their cave where Fern has set up two-foot-long, rough-hewed logs at the four corners of a rectangle. Together they form a table by easing the rock off Toom's back and onto the upright logs.

Fern backs a few steps away and after a second shakes her head. "Nope. The moss is too close to Eemerald green – not right for my birch wood chairs. I need moss that is closer to Hunter Green."

Toom, kneeling and resting his head on his arms, which he has folded on the top of the makeshift table, looks up. "Well," he says firmly, "I sure ain't lugging another table top up here."

Fern shrugs. "Well, I sure hope you enjoyed last night, because it'll be many moons before–"

"Okay," Toom snaps. He rises, piecemeal, each of his unfolding angles accompanied by a groan, and sets off slowly for the pit that serves as the tribe's slapdash stone quarry.

"Same place?" Toom asks. Staggering worse than before; he has fetched another flat rock.

Fern nods. *"No. Under the legs this time."* "Yes, Hon. Please."

They gingerly set the rock on the legs. Fern walks a few steps away and then abruptly turns on her heel. "I like it," she says after a long second.

"I'm . . . going . . . fishing," Toom says, each word separated by a gulp of air.

"Not yet, you're not," Fern says.

"The frak I'm not," Toom says.

Toom, kneeling, leans back. He tosses aside the long stick he just used to a coax a wisp of flame from the handful of twigs smoldering in the pit in front of their cave. "I'm going fishing," he says, rising to his feet.

"Stoke the fire again," Fern says. "And put logs on it."

Toom protests, but Fern cuts him off. "I'm cooking all day," she says, her tone suggesting that he should not have forgotten that fact.

Fern, later, studying her new table, hears Toom softly say, "I'm out of here."

She saunters to the cave's entrance. The fire is burning nicely. After a moment, she groans and yells at Toom who is trotting down a far slope. He seems not to hear. She screams his name. He slowly comes to a stop. His shoulders heave. He turns and heads back to their cave.

Fern, hands on her hips, meets him at the fire. "You used lizard poop!" she says, glaring and holding her nose. "What'd I tell you?"

"The frakking fire wouldn't burn," Toom grumbles.

Fern continues glaring. "Get Gumy," she says. "He can build a fire without using lizard poop."

Toom quickly begins snatching the smoldering lumps of dried lizard dung from the fire.

"All of them," Fern commands. "Besides, we'll need chairs."

Toom says, "We'll need what?"

"Chairs," Fern says. "To sit on. They're all the rage."

"Frak," Toom says. "We'll sit on logs, like always."

"Grab that chair at the end of the table," Toom says to his mate, gesturing expansively in the direction of one of Fern's four new backless, tree-stump chairs.

Gumy, who has followed Toom into the cave stops alongside Gumy. his pal. "How's the boss?" Toom says to him, genially.

"Fine," Gumy answers. "Grab that what?"

Toom gestures again. "I made 'em," he says. "That's a table . . . and chairs."

Gumy's eyes narrow dubiously.

"Ta–ble. And chairs," Toom says slowly. "They're all the rage. Wait 'til Estr sees 'em. She'll want four of her own."

When rain drops are grapes, Gumy says, Aloud, he says, "What are they for?"

"To eat off of, Moose Brains. What else?"

"Oh," Gumy says. He backs onto an edge of Fern's new rock table and rests his feet on the seat of one of the four stump-high seats that Toom has fitted with braided woolly mammoth covers. "Not bad," he says. "Not bad at all. Comfy."

Toom nods smugly.

"Hey! Gumy says, "What's for dinner?" He smacks his lips. "I hope its Fern's specialty, long-horn bison ham?"

Toom shakes his head. "Not tonight. We're having baby-back aardvark ribs. You don't see Tuk around do you?"

Gumy glances about and shakes his head.

"Like I said when we found the little beggar, if we couldn't cave-break him he'd make a tasty pot roast."

You think of everything, Toom," Gumy says.

The perilous pastime of bowling

"The goal," Toom tells his pal, Gumy, "is to knock all the sticks down."

Gumy screws up his eyes. "Why?"

"Because that how you score points."

"Score points?" Gunny says querulously.

"Points."

"Why?" Gumy says, still squinting.

"Because," Toom answers irritably, "the more sticks you knock –"

"No," Gumy says, sharpley "I mean, why knock the frakking sticks down at all? What's the purpose."

"It's fun," Toom says. "You'll see."

Gumy, shaking his head, walks rapidly some thirty steps to where Toom has set twenty sticks upright and arranged them into a four-foot by five-foot rectangle. He looks back at Toom, who has been joined by his mate, Fern. "Like this?" he yells, kicking over the sticks one at a time.

"*He's a frakking moron,*" Toom says to Fern. "Not that way, Moose Brains!" he yells. "You don't kick them over."

Toom orders Fern to set the sticks back up.

"I've got hides to chew," she says, turning and walking into their cave.

Toom glowers and shakes his fist at her back. "Stand them up again," he yells to Gumy.

"Why?" Gumy yells back.

"Oh frak," Toom says. He trots to where Gumy is disdainfully eyeing the scattered sticks and neatly resets each one. Returning to where he introduced his new game to Gumy, he scratches a line in the ground with his toe.

"Watch this," he says, picking up a hefty, nearby stone that is reasonably spherical. After a long moment of intently staring, he steps up to the line and rolls the stone toward the sticks. It cleaves the array near the middle and bounces off a tree standing some ten feet beyond. Half the pins are toppled.

Gumy snorts derisively. "Let me try it," he says.

"No," Toom says, quickly moving to recover his stone. "I roll again."

"Why?" Gumy says.

"That's a rule," Toom says. "This time, you hunker down behind the sticks and stop my rock. Then I'll do it for you."

Toom's second roll barrels cleanly through the swath left by his first delivery, easily breaches the barricade Gumy has formed with his hands, and smacks Gumy in a shin. Gumy lets out a yelp, keels over, and seizes his right leg below the knee with both hands. He glares at Toom, his hostile look undercut by his non-stop moaning.

Fern, rushing from the cave, kneels beside Gumy. She looks sympathetically at Toom. "What happened?"

"You know old Gumy," Toom says matter-of-factly, "He can't stand a little pain."

"I said," Fern snaps, "what happened?"

"The rock hit him!" Toom blurts out. "He'll be all right."

I'll rub your shin with quickberry leaves, Fern tells Gumy.

"I'm okay," Gumy says, rising and hopping around on his left foot.

He hobbles back to where Toom is waiting. "My turn," he blurts at Gumy. "This time you stop the frakking rock."

"Frak you," Toom says. "Think I'm a stupid moose?"

"Why not set the sticks closer to the tree?" Fern says.

Toom gives Fern a nasty look, and she saunters back into their cave.

"Fern has a point," Gumy says, once he's certain Fern is out of earshot.

"Yeah," Toom says. "Her head. Besides, I'd already thought of that."

Gumy helps Toom set the sticks up in front of the tree. He picks up Toom's rock, heads to where Toom has scratched the line in the dirt, takes three steps forward, and scratches a new line.

"Okay," Toom says. "Only," he admonishes, "you have to use your own rock."

Gumy thinks over Toom's remark. "Why?"

"It's a rule," Toom says.

Gumy drops Toom's rock and disappears into the woods. Five minutes later he returns carrying a roundish stone twice the size of Toom's.

"Oh no," Toom says. "Not legal. Your rock can't be bigger than mine. That's a rule."

"You know what you can do with your frakking rules!" Gumy snaps. Toeing the new line, he cups his rock in both hands, hunches over, and chucks it toward the sticks. His aim is true, and most of the sticks are knocked down.

"Doesn't mean a thing," Toom says, who is standing a good fifteen feet to the side of the pins. "You cheated."

"Says you," Gumy says.

"You used too big a rock," Toom tells him. "Besides, you weren't behind the line."

"I was so!"

"You were not."

"Was too."

"Was not."

"Frak you."

"Frak you, too."

"Okay then," Toom says, gathering the sticks. "If that's the way you want to be. It's my game." Carrying all twenty sticks under one arm, he marches into his cave.

Toom called his new game "Rock and Sticks." Fern called it "Rolling a Stone." She eventually persuaded Toom to arrange the sticks in a triangle with a base line of sticks at the back. Also, on the day Toom missed a lone back-corner stick five times running, she convinced him that a player's chances should be limited to two rolls. Toom, when Fern began regularly felling more sticks than he did, declared that "Rock and Sticks" was a woman's game unworthy of real men, and he never tried it again.

Standing up to the challenge of ensuring fertility

Fern and Toom are sitting alone eating supper in front of their perpetual fire. Fern is toying with her food, a dispirited look on her face. Toom is gnawing mightily on the thigh of a barbecued vulture leg.

"We ought to have had kids by now," Fern says. "Two, anyway. Estr's belly is big again, and I'm many moons older than she is. Your mother keeps asking."

"You're doing something wrong," Toom says.

Of course, it's me. "Like what?" Fern says

"Well," Toom says. "It sure ain't my fault. You said yourself that compared to Gumy I'm way big–"

"It's not that," Fern snaps, "something's wrong."

"Yeah. Well what else could it be then . . . if it's not you?"

"Lots of things," Fern says. "Why don't you talk to Gumy."

"Gumy!" Toom bellows. "He's never speared a woolly rhinoceros in his whole life!"

"Well, he's doing something right," Fern says.

"Why don't you talk to Estr," Toom says.

"I did. She said that the moon has to be gone when we–"

"Estr's batty."

"I don't know," Fern replies, her voice soft and uncertain. "Maybe I'll talk to Narg. She and Riff have Wak and Blam. And, Narg's working on skunk-pelt swaddling."

Toom grunts disgustedly. "They're vegetarians."

"I wonder if that's it," Fern says, perking up. "Neither Gumy or Estr eat a lot of meat."

"That's only because Gumy's no hunter," Toom says. He sighs loudly, as if suddenly burdened of a heavy weight. "Never mind, I'll talk to him."

Toom finds Gumy squatting in front of his cave honing the cutting-edge of a clam-shell hide scraper. "I see you're keeping busy," he sings out from a few strides away.

Suspicious as ever of one of Toom's robust greetings, Gumy's reply is terse. "Always," he answers.

"Thought I'd swing by for a little flap-jawing" Toom says. "Then maybe we'll go fishing."

"Uh-huh," Gumy says. "Flap-jawing about what?"

Estr steps from the cave and welcomes Toom. Her belly is noticeably swollen. Gumy jumps up and avuncularly pats it several times. Toom pretends not to notice.

"How's Fern," Estr says. "Is she—"

"No signs yet," Toom says, moodily.

Estr finishes her question: ". . . going to rehearsal tomorrow?"

"I guess so," Toom mumbles.

"Tell Fern I'll see her there," Estr says.

Toom agrees to forward Estr's message. She thanks him, says she has quickberries to stem, and walks back into the cave.

"I have a question," Toom begins heartily. "Estr is always pregnant. And Fern wants to know what it is that she's doing wrong, why she can't get her own little Toom started."

Gumy, back to sharpening the hide scraper, glances over his shoulder at the opening to their cave. Satisfied that Estr has disappeared inside, he says to Toom, "You know of course that it has to be raining."

"Oh, frak yes," Toom says. "I've always known that. What else."

Gumy checks again to make sure they're still alone. "You do stand on your head, don't you?"

Toom's brow furrows; he squints. "Well," he says, "not, uh, always . . . not every time."

Gumy clicks his tongue. "Water doesn't run uphill, you know."

"Right," Toom says, nodding thoughtfully.

His mind taken up with that thought, Toom turns and slowly walks away.

"Wait," Gumy says. "There's more."

Toom hurries back.

"Something else," Gumy says, "I always eat a good hod of cauliflower heads two hours before."

"Now, that's one thing I haven't been doing," Toom replies submissively. "I didn't know it mattered."

"Oh my yes," Gumy says. "Prepares the old lady, too. If you know what I mean?"

Toom nods. "Besides, I love cauliflower,"

"There you go," Gumy says encouragingly.

Toom again turns to leave. "How many times do you do it?" Gumy says.

"Per session?" Toom answers. "Oh, never less than twice."

"What!" Gumy exclaims. "You're kidding! Three times is the absolute minimum. No wonder . . . . In your case, I wouldn't stop short of four. You know, one for the pot."

Toom is troubled. "Four times, huh? Right straight through? No stopping?"

"Stop in the middle," Gumy admonishes, "and . . . well . . . the word dwarf comes to mind."

Estr suddenly steps from the entrance of their cave. "Gumy, that's enough," she says. Her voice is low but authoritative.

"I was just trying to help," Gumy says, winking at his mate. "It embarrasses Fern to talk about sex. So, I was helping Toom with her questions."

Toom nods at Estr and trots off. Gumy yells after him to keep doing pushups. Toom's head bobs once determinedly, and he picks up the pace.

What'd Gumy have to say," Fern says to Toom.

Struggling to breath after his long jog from Gumy's, Toom doesn't answer right away. "Nothing I didn't already know," he says, finally. "Only . . . .

Fern waits patiently for Toom to settle down.

"Only," Toom resumes, "he said you have to eat a pot of cauliflower heads an hour before."

"I hate cauliflower," Fern says. "The smell alone gags me."

"Me too," Toom says. "Still, if it helps, we better eat some."

"What else?" Fern says.

"That was about it," Toom says.

Fern walks slowly away. She is about to leave their cave when she hears Toom grunting. This goes on for several seconds. She returns to where she had left him recovering from visiting Gumy. He is standing on his head close to the cave's back wall, which the heels of his feet are resting against for balance.

"What in the world are you doing?" Fern asks.

Toom, struggling to remain vertical, is nettled by her question, "Water," he snaps, "doesn't run up hill, you know."

Fern, after a few seconds, says abruptly, "No way, Jose."

Premier democracy

"I've made up my mind," Toom says, nudging his mate who has just fallen asleep. "I'm running."

Fern sleepily rises up on one elbow. Her reply crackles. "You're what!"

"Yep," Toom says. "I'm tossing my war helmet in the ring. I'll become a candidate for tribe elder."

"You're dreaming," Fern says. She falls back on her side. "Go poke the fire."

"Gumy's running, and he—"

"Yeah," Fern says. "And if Gumy was eating yellow snow you'd want dibs."

"And he doesn't have the brains of a tree stump."

And you do? "Whatever. We'll discuss it in the morning. Go back to sleep."

"I'm older than he is, too," Toom says. "Many moons older. Besides–"

"Toom!"

Fern, emerging from their cave, shields her eyes from the morning sun. After a long yawn, she says to

Toom, "Why are you wearing your new moose-horn helmet?"

Toom, squatting atop the boulder they roll in front of the cave's entrance at night, is staring fiercely at a distant stretch of mountains. He doesn't answer.

Fern yawns again and rubs the sleep from her eyes. "Why are you—"

"I heard you," Toom snaps. "I'm thinking."

My worst fear. "About what, Darling?"

"I'm thinking about what to say in my acceptance speech – for when I'm voted a tribe elder."

Fern says, just audibly, "Guess I wasn't dreaming." She raises her voice: "Suppose you lose."

"Say what!" Toom exclaims indignantly. "I'll win . . . easily."

"Uh-huh. But just suppose–"

"All I got to do," Toom says, "is toss my helmet in the ring." His visage softens. "It's what Gumy told me. I can sure as frak do that." After several moments, he adds, "Where's the ring at?"

Fern sighs. "No, Toom. Throwing your hat in the ring is a figure of speech."

"Yeah," Toom says, "but where at?"

"It's a metaphor, Hon!"

For a few seconds Toom doesn't answer. Finally, he says, "So? I know that. But where's it at?"

Fern silently implores the heavens for guidance. She looks back at her mate. "It surrounds the communal poop hole," she says.

Toom nods slowly. He rises and marches into their cave, on the way doffing his helmet.

What are you doing?" Fern asks.

"I ain't about to wear my new helmet," he says. "Where'd you put my old one?"

A titanic raft

"You're going where?" Estr says to Gumy, who has set off determinedly in the direction of Big Water lake.

Gumy answers without slowing. "Toom wants me to help him build a raft."

"Another one?" says Estr.

"Yes. His old one sunk, and he–"

"It sank! Toom made a raft that sank. How in the world . . . that has to be a first, even for Toom. Rafts don't sink."

Gumy shakes his head disdainfully. "Women."

"What'd he make it out of?" Estr asks, "long rocks?"

"Of course not. He made it out of rowan logs"

"Then," Estr says, "it didn't sink."

Gumy says, "It sure as frak didn't fly away."

"About as likely," Estr mumbles.

"What kept you?" Toom asks, looking up from where he is sorting lengths of twine that have been woven together from strands of bison gut and the hair of a woolly mammoth. "The sun's already above the trees."

"Estr," Gumy answers. "You know how wives are. I had to answer a lot of dumb questions. What's with the rock?"

Toom has dragged a dozen rowan logs, all freshly cut, to a sandy stretch on the shore of Big Water lake. A small boulder is sitting nearby. Roll marks stretch into the woods behind it.

"It goes on the raft," Toom answers. "Something to sit on while we're fishing."

Toom stands and walks to the end of the biggest log. "This one," he says, pointing, "will go in the middle. Give me a hand, here."

They drag the log to where one end is resting at the edge of the water.

"Remember," Gumy says giggling, "the time you built a tree-stand inside your cave and couldn't get it out because the opening was too small? Busted my (unmentionables) on that one."

"You going to help?" Toom says crossly. "Or, just stand around yakking?"

By mid-afternoon they have lashed ten logs together side-by-side. Gumy spots Estr and Fern watching from a bank some seventy yards away. He says softly to Toom, "We have company."

Toom, busy visually estimating the weight of the boulder, turns and locates the women. "Go back home," he yells, pumping his fist. "You know wives are bad luck at a launching."

Shaking their heads, the women slowly trudge back into the woods. "Like it's our fault their every new boat sinks like a cave-door rock," Estr says to Fern.

Together, Toom and Gumy finish lashing on the raft's cross braces. Toom walks slowly around the raft kicking the ends of the outside logs. He orders Gumy to fetch the boulder.

Gumy looks at the big rock and then back at Toom. "Right," he says sarcastically.

Toom says, "Roll it. Same as I did."

Gumy protests but eventually works the boulder to a place beside the raft. "When you're ready," he says, breathing hard.

Toom nods. "I'm ready."

They push the raft halfway into the lake, wrestle the boulder onto the raft, and then skid it to a place near the middle of the large keel log. The front of the raft dips more and more as the big rock is slid forward. It finally comes to rest on the lake's muddy bottom.

Gumy looks uncertainly at Toom. We need to get the whole raft into the water, Toom tells him.

Cursing and grunting, they slide the raft all the way into the lake – only instead of floating it cleaves to the lake's floor.

"The water's not deep enough," Toom explains. "C'mon."

Sustained by more grunting and cursing, they slide the raft farther into the lake, to where the water is waist deep. The top of the big rock doesn't much more than break the water's surface.

"Still not deep enough," Toom says.

"That's not it," Gumy says.

"You don't understand water," Toom snaps.

"Me!" Gumy exclaims. "No, *you* don't understand water."

While they're arguing, a woman's voice rings out. "Is it okay to come by now?"

"That's Fern," Toom says, careful not to look in the direction of her voice. Shortly, however, he looks her way. "Yeah, yeah, okay now." Grab your fishing pole, he says to Gumy.

When Fern and Estr reach the edge of the shore, their mates are sitting back to back on the rock fishing.

"Aren't your feet cold," Estr says to Gumy.

"Oh, damn!" Toom says loudly. "You scared the fish away."

Plucking for rain

"Listen to this," Toom says to Fern, his mate. She has just returned from gathering a hod of firewood.

"In a minute," Fern says.

Toom is sitting cross-legged on the ground between the entrance to their cave and their perpetual fire. Pressed edgewise to his chest is a harp-like contraption made of the opposing bottom ribs of a baby mammoth chest that are fastened to what's left of the dead beast's sternum. A length of caribou gut is tautly strung across the tips of the ribs.

Fern adds her freight of dead limbs to the woodpile. "I'm listening," she says, straightening the pile with her foot.

Toom plucks the string of gut several times and looks up at Fern. "Ever hear anything like that?" he says.

Fern shakes her head. *Not since the last time you pigged-out on cauliflower heads.* "No – not, really," she says.

Toom again vigorously plucks the string. "That ought to bring the rain, eh?"

Fern nods. "We need more firewood."

Fern retraces her path into the woods. Toom, while she's away, entertains himself with a snappy pluck pluck pluck (pause) pluck pluck pluck. He repeats the double tri-part sequence, adding a crescendo of five plucks in the middle.

Fern returns with more wood.

"Now listen," Toom orders. He plucks away for a good half minute, his gaze steady on the score of his new composition, which he has recorded as a string of eleven identical marks in the dirt. "Well?" he asks, setting aside his mammoth-rib harp.

"Cool," Fern says.

"I'm going to show, Riff," Toom says.

"Not Gumy?"

"You ever see Gumy dance? If anything, he scares the rain away."

Fern, busy painting her toenails with violet-colored berry nectar, hears grunting coming from outside the cave. She investigates and finds Riff helping Toom set the tribe's rain-making drum, a big hollow log peeled of all bark, across two smaller logs.

Riff sees her. "We're going to make rain!" he yells.

Fern looks at the sky, which is cloudless in all directions. *Sure you are.* "We need it!" she yells back.

"Ready?" Toom says to Riff.

Riff nods enthusiastically.

Toom begins strumming his one-string harp. Midway into his well-practiced tune he abruptly stops and stares angrily at Riff, who, a two-inch diameter stick clutched firmly in each hand, is obliviously whacking away at the big hollow log.

"It ain't working," he says irritably when Riff finally glances his way.

Riff's steady, two-fisted blows slow to a stop. Scowling, he looks to Toom for an explanation.

"Follow my lead," Toom orders.

Riff looks at Fern who is sitting quietly on the wood she has fetched and arranged neatly into a rick. "Don't ask me," she says, shrugging.

"The only time you drum is when I nod," Toom says to Riff.

Riff, after a while, gets the hang of it, their duet producing this cadence:

Pluck (nod) bonk

Pluck pluck (nod nod) bonk bonk

Pluck pluck pluck (nod non nod) bonk bonk bonk

Etc.

They pause after every three renderings and search the sky for rain clouds. An hour passes; the sky is still clear.

Riff stops drumming. "It ain't working," he says. "How about if I bonk and then you pluck?"

Toom, his visage stern, shakes his head. "That ain't it. We need dancers. Fern you–"

"I'll find Gumy," Fern says.

"Not Gumy!" Toom shouts after her.

Thirty minutes pass, Fern hasn't returned, and Toom and Riff are still plucking and bonking.

"It's no use," Toom says, stopping. He wipes his brow with his forearm. "We need dancers."

"I wonder what happened to Fern," Riff says.

Toom shrugs. "Who cares? We'll get dancers and pick it up again at high-sun tomorrow."

Riff says, "I'll copy your arrangement on the wall of my cave. So I won't forget it."

"Good," Toom says. "It's damn complicated."

In 1991, near the city of Bern Switzerland, a gathering of anthropologists and archeologists took sides over the question of whether Riff's crude scratches replicating Toom's score was primitive evidence of chamber music or of rap. Blows followed.

The making of a visionary

Walking from their family cave, Fern spots Toom, her mate, standing motionlessly on a knoll facing the blinding early morning sun. His left hand is shielding his eyes; his right hand is clutching a walking stick. He obviously hasn't poked the fire, so Fern, with his walking stick, stirs it until flames break out.

"The fire was almost out," she yells. "What are you doing?"

Toom, without turning, gestures dismissively with his stick.

Fern walks toward where Toom is imitating the statue of an explorer who is trying to make out the course ahead. "I don't see anything," she says shaking her head slightly. "You'll go blind."

Toom ignores her.

"You hear me!" Fern yells crossly.

Toom spins on his heel. "I'm having a vision!"

"That's not how you have a vision," Fern snaps. "You don't even know what a vision is."

Toom turns back toward the sun. "Oh no? I'm in the middle of one."

"What's it about?"

After a few seconds, Toom says, "You wouldn't understand. Warrior stuff."

Fern says, "You can have a vision without leaving our cave. Even at night. With our beaver-pelt blanket pulled over your head. Might improve our sex life."

"That's the dumbest thing I've ever heard," Toom says.

Fern sighs loudly and walks back into their cave. She begins sharpening a flint spear head. Ordinarily a man's job, the knack of forming a point by striking off thin slivers of flint is beyond Toom's dexterity.

Before long, Fern hears strange noises coming from just outside the cave. She grabs her hyena thighbone club, edges to a point just short of the cave's entrance, and cautiously peers out. Toom is poking the side of the hill that envelops their home with his spear. "Toom," she says. "What on earth are you doing?"

Toom winces. "I can't see."

"I told you!" Fern exclaims. "Over here!"

Toom sidles toward the sound of Fern's voice. She leads him into their cave and maneuvers him to a place in front of a rock ledge protruding from a wall. "Sit down," she orders, pushing lightly on his chest.

Toom cautiously backs onto the ledge. His head drops heavily. "How long," he asks plaintively, "am I going to have this vision?"

"I don't know," Fern says. "A while. What are you seeing now?"

"Nothing!" Toom answers sharply. "I just told you. I can't see a frakking thing."

"In your mind's eye, Toom. Can you see me?"

"I just said—"

"I mean, imagine its nighttime and we're in bed. What do you see?"

Toom giggles. His head comes up and he grins slyly. "We're–"

Fern interrupts him. "Can you see me racing for the horizon?"

"Kind of," Toom says.

"Look hard," Fern says. "Because that is a real vision."

The postman always rings once

"Who in the frak is that," Toom says to Fern, suspicion tempering his voice. Fern has joined him at the entrance to their cave.

Shielding her eyes from the glare of the bright western sun, her gaze steady on the approaching figure, she says, "He's not from around here. And would you look at his helmet! Horns as long as my arms."

"Frak!" Toom barks. "No bull elk ever grew horns that long."

"Maybe they're not elk horns," Fern says.

"Whatever," Toom says. "You better fetch my war whacker."

"He's not armed," Fern says.

"No matter," Toom says. "I can't chance it."

The stranger, who has been jogging at a good clip, slows to a walk. He stops several strides short of where Toom and Fern are standing and shows them two empty palms. "How-dee," he says.

His eyes narrowed suspiciously, Toom looks hard at Fern.

Fern nods. "He's greeting us."

"How-dee," the visitor says again.

Toom slightly raises his chin. He pokes himself hard in the chest several times with his index finger. "Toom."

"Torr," the visitor says, pounding his chest with a balled hand.

The two men take each other's measure.

Toom is the first to speak. "Travel far?" he says, gesturing with a sweep of his hand toward the place where Torr emerged from the woods.

Torr nods vigorously. "Many valleys, many streams, many woods."

Toom utters a snort of disgust and says to Fern, "Frak, that ain't so far."

Fern giggles. "I'm Fern," she says to Torr.

Torr shifts his gaze to Fern and nods slowly.

Toom orders Fern back into their cave. "Finish chewing that chuckwood pelt," he adds gruffly.

"My you have big horns," Fern says to Torr.

"Y'all are too kind, ma'am," Torr says, running his hands out each horn as far as he can reach.

"Hear that," Fern says. "He's a southerner." Her gaze remains fast on Torr.

Toom sniggers. "Tell me," he says sarcastically to Torr, "how do you hunt wearing that . . . frakking thing on your head?"

"Do what, now?" Torr says.

"See," Fern says. "I told you he's from the South." She runs in place and pretends to shoot an arrow. She points at his helmet. "My mate wants to know how you chase coelodontas with your helmet on."

"Ah," Torr says, nodding. He turns his helmet sideways so that one horn points forward and the other backward. Smiling at Toom, he jogs a few steps and launches an imaginary spear.

"Just as I thought," Toom says. He turns his head slightly and cuts his eyes toward Fern. "Ever in your life see anything sillier?"

"We're forgetting our manners," Fern says. She points to a cut of moose ham hanging from a sapling that is bent low over their fire pit. "You're welcome to stay for dinner – spend the night, if you like."

Torr's visage becomes wistful. "I can't stay, ma'am. I have an important message for Chief Garciak." From a pouch tied to his loincloth, he pulls a thin slate with pictures etched on both sides. He shows it to Toom.

Toom studies the pictures for a while and hands the slate to Fern. After turning it over several times, she says to Toom, "It's to a Chief Garciak." She shrugs. "He's holding out in the big hills. It's from . . . someone named Offa. That's all I can–"

"Exactly my reading," Toom says. He turns to Torr. "The big hills, that's cyclops country."

Torr looks at Fern. She hunches up, sets a fierce look to her face, and takes a few steps.

"They won't catch me," Torr says shaking his head. He looks at Fern, points his finger at his ear and waggles it in a circle. "Too dumb."

"He better hope they don't," Toom says to Fern.

Fern smiles. "Maybe," she says to Torr, "you can swing by here on your way back."

"I'll sure try, Ma'am" Torr says.

"What'd he say?" Toom says to Fern.

"He said he'll be returning home by a different route."

Skirting the fire pit, Torr breaks into a trot. "Y'all take care," he yells over his shoulder.

Fern waves and Torr slightly nods.

Toom and Fern watch Torr until he vanishes into the woods.

Fern pokes the fire, and Toom strides purposefully into their cave. Seconds later, banging noises ring-out from inside the cave.

Fern gives the fire a vigorous stir and trots back into the cave. Toom is smacking his helmet viciously against the cave's back wall. One horn of his helmet, badly marred, is lying on the floor. The other is stubbornly refusing to break away from the head piece.

Toom finally dislodges the second horn. Out of breath, he backs onto a log that he and Fern have dragged into the cave and made into a crude sofa. Fern sits down beside him and tenderly rubs his thigh.

Toom finally catches his breath. "It's my shoulders," he says tautly. "Not my legs."

Fern, shaking her head, returns to tending the fire.

www.ingramcontent.com/pod-product-compliance
Lightning Source LLC
Chambersburg PA
CBHW071643090426
42738CB00009B/1415